ROAD SUBGRADE AND PAVEMENT ENGINEERING

路基路面工程

刘 玉 主编

人民交通出版社股份有限公司
北京

图书在版编目(CIP)数据

路基路面工程 = Road Subgrade and Pavement Engineering：英文 / 刘玉主编. — 北京：人民交通出版社股份有限公司，2020.11
ISBN 978-7-114-14526-1

Ⅰ.①路… Ⅱ.①刘… Ⅲ.①路面—道路施工—英文 Ⅳ.①U416.204

中国版本图书馆 CIP 数据核字(2019)第 193191 号

书　　名：ROAD SUBGRADE AND PAVEMENT ENGINEERING
　　　　　路基路面工程
著 作 者：刘　玉
责任编辑：李　瑞
责任校对：刘　芹
责任印制：刘高彤
出版发行：人民交通出版社股份有限公司
地　　址：(100011)北京市朝阳区安定门外外馆斜街 3 号
网　　址：http://www.ccpcl.com.cn
销售电话：(010)59757973
总 经 销：人民交通出版社股份有限公司发行部
经　　销：各地新华书店
印　　刷：北京印匠彩色印刷有限公司
开　　本：787×1092　1/16
印　　张：16
字　　数：419 千
版　　次：2020 年 11 月　第 1 版
印　　次：2020 年 11 月　第 1 次印刷
书　　号：ISBN 978-7-114-14526-1
定　　价：60.00 元

(有印刷、装订质量问题的图书由本公司负责调换)

Preface of the Book Series

With the rapid development of China's globalization, improving English communication skills has become increasingly important nowadays. The first step to enhance English skills is through implementations of English courses of college students, which is usually given in the first two years of the four-year undergraduate program. However, for students whose majors are engineering, the college English courses play limited roles in their future careers, even though those courses are necessary for improving their common-life communication skills. The second step is through professional English courses, which provide students with the opportunities of learning engineering-related courses in English, but the credit hours of those courses are very limited. The third step is through the bilingual teaching or full-English teaching, which gives students the opportunities of not only learning career-related knowledge but also improving the proficiency in professional English communication skills.

In the past 20 years, the bilingual teaching has received attentions increasingly. And, it will become one of the major teaching modes in the coming future due to the following reasons. First of all, bilingual teaching can be easily accepted by the new-generation college students, since most of them learn English from their childhood. Secondly, more and more college teachers who attain their doctoral degrees in English-speaking countries have the abilities to implement the bilingual teaching. Thirdly, the bilingual teaching has become one of the most critical tasks of universities in China.

Under the above background, Highway School of Chang'an University has established the bilingual program in *Road, Bridge, and Cross-River Engineering* since 2009 as well as in *Transportation Engineering* since 2014. Over 40 courses are now being taught in bilingual modes. Since Engineering standards/codes of China are different from those of the foreign countries, it is inappropriate to teach Chinese students with the original English-written textbooks whose contents are engineering practices of foreign countries. Therefore, the textbook series in Civil and Transportation Engineering was proposed in July 2014. Herewith, there are some major features of this textbook series:

1. The main contents of the textbooks in this series are written according to the course syllabuses of the two bilingual programs. Standards and engineering

practices of China are included in the engineering-related textbooks.

2. The authors of the textbooks are experienced professors or associate professors who are teaching the bilingual courses.

3. Professors in English-speaking countries are employed to proof-read the textbooks.

4. With regards to the textbooks documenting Civil and Transportation Engineering of China, it could be used as reference by practitioners who are engaged in the internal projects.

It is hoped that the textbook series will not only contribute to the efficient bilingual teaching, but also serve as the English-written media advertising the Chinese specifications in Civil and Transportation Engineering.

Innovative Education Center
Highway School, Chang'an University
August 9, 2018

Preface of This Textbook

In the past nine years, I have been teaching the bilingual course of *Road Subgrade and Pavement Engineering* to undergraduate students at Chang'an University. My students are from the two bilingual programs (Guo-Ji-Gong-Cheng-Ban in Chinese) of Highway School in Chang'an University. One of them is the bilingual program in Road, Bridge, and Cross-river Engineering, and another in Transportation Engineering. The premary teaching target of those two bilingual programs is to educate students with the integration of Chinese Engineering expertise and English communication skills. However, it has been difficult to find a suitable textbook due to the following reasons: First of all, the bilingual programs are still young, and few references are available; Secondly, the textbook authors should have expertise in both Chinese engineering knowledge and English writing skills; Thirdly, the authors must have enough time and bilingual teaching experience. Due to the above reasons, I have compiled my teaching materials from the past years and put together this textbook as an alternative to facilitate my bilingual teaching and hope it will be also helpful to teachers or engineers in highway engineering field.

According to the teaching target, I have limited the content to Subgrade and Pavement Engineering of China. The primary references while preparing this book are the Chinese textbooks, the national design, construction, or testing specifications of China. This textbook is divided into 11 chapters. Chapter One introduces the historical development of highway engineering and its basic concepts. The subsequent five chapters, from two to six, present the basics of Subgrade and Pavement Engineering, which include traffic loading, environmental conditions, subgrade and paving materials, highway drainage, subgrade service ability and stress analysis and pavement service ability and stress analysis. Chapters from seven to nine discuss the design of subgrade, asphalt pavement, and concrete pavement, respectively. Chapter 10 introduces the construction aspects of subgrade, asphalt pavement, and concrete pavements. Chapter 11 makes a brief introduction to the maintenance of subgrade and pavements. In this edition, the last two chapters are not included and will be included in the next edition. In addition to the above chapters, engineering examples or case studies are presented in appendices at the end of the textbook.

I would like to express my sincerest appreciations to all those who encouraged me or contributed to the completion of this complex work. I sincerely thank Professor. Yu Chen from the Highway School of Chang'an University, who made a great contribution to the completion of this textbook. He worked on the organization of this textbook and participated in the writing of Chapters five and seven. I sincerely thank Professor Chichun Hu from South China University of Technology and Professor Xiaoping Ji from the Highway School of Chang'an University, who provided information of Chapters eight and nine. I sincerely thank Professor Hongliang Qi who presented information of Chapter 4. I also would like to thank Dr. Mohd Rosli Mohd Hasan, from the School of Civil Engineering, University Sains Malaysia (USM), Ph. D. students Xiaodong Zhou and Dongzhao Jin from Michigan Technological University for proofreading and revising the whole textbook. I sincerely thank my graduate students who made considerable contributions to amend the figures, tables, and examples. I sincerely thank Zhexin Lv, Jiubo Sun, and Guohang Deng from Chang'an University who contributed to the appendices. I also sincerely thank Tianjiao Song, Shaojie Xu, Jiaji Ma and Weicheng Zheng from Chang'an University, who have assisted me for the final revision. Although most portions presented in this textbook were edited or written by myself, much information was obtained from the published pieces of literature or specifications. I would like to gratefully acknowledge any individuals or institutes whose information is used in this textbook.

Liu, Yu
Innovative Education Center
Highway School, Chang'an University
August, 2019

Contents

1. Introduction 1
    1.1 Historical Development of Roads in China 1
    1.2 Highway Subgrade and Pavement Structures 3
    1.3 Design Factors 6
    1.4 Road Subgrade and Pavement Engineering 9
    1.5 Summary & Key Points in Chapter 1 10
    Problems and Questions 11

2. Traffic Loads and Environmental Conditions 12
    2.1 Traffic Loads and their Impacts 12
    2.2 Traffic Data and Collection Methods 15
    2.3 Traffic Data Analysis 22
    2.4 Determination of Accumulative ESAL 27
    2.5 Pavement Environment and Effects 28
    2.6 Climatic Zoning for Highway in China 36
    2.7 Climate Zones for Asphalt Pavement Performance 38
    2.8 Temperature Gradient for Rigid Pavement Design 39
    2.9 Summary and Key Points in Chapter 2 40
    Problems 41

3. Subgrade Soils and Pavement Materials 44
    3.1 Subgrade Soil Classification 44
    3.2 Subgrade Moisture Conditions and Evaluation 48
    3.3 Subgrade Bearing Capability 53
    3.4 Materials Used in Pavement Engineering 55
    3.5 Material Structural Characterization 58
    3.6 Material Mechanical Characterization 60
    3.7 Summary 69
    Problems 69

4. Highway Drainage System 71
    4.1 Introduction 71

4.2　Surface Drainage 72
4.3　Subsurface Drainage 81
4.4　Summary of Chapter 4 83
　　Problems and Questions 83

5. Subgrade Serviceability and Stress Analysis 84
5.1　Subgrade Serviceability and Distresses 84
5.2　Subgrade Stress Analysis and Working Area 87
5.3　Side Slope Stability Analysis 89
5.4　Stress Analysis for Retaining Wall Design 101
5.5　Summary of Chapter 5 106
　　Problems and Questions 106

6. Pavement Serviceability and Stress Analysis 108
6.1　Asphalt Pavement Serviceability and Distresses 108
6.2　Concrete Pavement Serviceability 116
6.3　Stresses and Strains in Flexible Pavements 119
6.4　Concrete Pavement Stress Analysis 126
6.5　Summary of Chapter 6 137
　　Problems 138

7. Highway Subgrade Design 141
7.1　Design Methodology 141
7.2　Design Principles or Basic Requirements 143
7.3　Roadbed Design 144
7.4　Subgrade Cross-section Design 149
7.5　Subgrade Drainage Requirements 159
7.6　Subgrade Slope Protection and Retaining Structures 159
7.7　Subsidiary Facility Design 165
7.8　Summary of Chapter 7 166
　　Problems and Questions 166

8. Asphalt Pavement Design 170
8.1　Design Methodology 170
8.2　Design Theory, Criterion, and Parameters 172
8.3　Design Data Collection and Analysis 175
8.4　Pavement Combination Design 179
8.5　Mix Proportion Design and Material Parameters 187

8.6	Verification of Layer Thickness	197
8.7	Drawings of Pavement Design	208
8.8	Summary of Chapter 8	208
	Problems and Questions	208

9. Concrete Pavement Design 210

9.1	Design Methodology	210
9.2	Design Theory, Criteria, and Parameters	212
9.3	Design Preparation and Data Analysis	216
9.4	Concrete Pavement Combination Design	219
9.5	Mix Proportion and Pavement Thickness Verification	228
9.6	Concrete Pavement Design Examples	231
9.7	Summary of Chapter 9	241
	Problems and Questions	241

References 243

1. Introduction

1.1 Historical Development of Roads in China

The historical development of Chinese roads can be divided into four stages, namely the ancient post roads (1066BC—1912), simply built public highways (1912—1949), lower classes of highways (1949—1980s), medium and high classes of highways (1980s—present). *Each stage of the development is pertinent to the development of society and the road serviceability requirements.*

The earliest roads of China were called the 'post roads' or the 'ancient post roads'. A post road was a road mainly designated for transportation of military supplies, orders, or postal mails. In ancient China, the post roads were equivalent to main roads or highways, but only major towns were connected. The most frequent users of the post roads were the post riders who usually carry important mails with special military orders. According to the textbook authored by Deng[1], the earliest development of the post roads can be traced to the Shang Dynasty (from 1600BC to 1046BC). Then in the Western Zhou Dynasty (from 1046BC to 771BC), the post road system was built and the corresponding road management system was also developed. In the Qin Dynasty (from 221BC to 206BC), 12000 kilometers of post roads were constructed to form an extensive large post road network. In the Western Han Dynasty (from 206BC to 25AD), 3000 post houses were built and the post roads were further developed. The most famous post road system at that time was called 'the Silk Road' which was a well-known road around the world. After 3500 years of development from the Shang Dynasty to the early twentieth century, most major towns of ancient China were connected with the post roads which made a great contribution to the ancient society and economy development. Those post roads were simply built with granular materials or block stones and few considerations were taken on the road surface smoothness. At that time, those roads were good enough for horses, carriages and pedestrians.

In 1901, the first motor car was imported to China from America. Then, more and more motor vehicles were introduced to China: the car ownership of China was 5000 in 1949. In order to meet the minimum requirements of running motor vehicles, 130000 kilometers of the simply-built public roads or highways were constructed from 1912 to 1949. Evidently, compared with the modern traffic flow, the traffic volume was very small, and the vehicle speeds were very low, and the axle loading was also not too heavy. Under those service conditions, the simply-built public roads were constructed with thin layers of granular materials (such as graded sands or stones) and relatively rough surfaces. Therefore, most of the traffic loads were taken by the pavement subgrade or foundation, and most of the pavement designs were conducted based on simple empirical methods.

At the time when the People's Republic of China was born in 1949, the mileage of public roads decreased from 130000km to 80000km due to destruction and damage in war. With the rapid development of China's economy after 1949, traffic volume, vehicle speeds, and axle loads were increasing from year to year. The simply-built public roads became insufficient to meet economy development, and it became significantly important to develop new roads which should have better serviceability than the existing simply-built public roads. In the 1960s and 1970s, the Daqing and Shengli oilfields were discovered and exploited, respectively. Those two oilfields made a great contribution to the development of asphalt pavements through providing paving asphalt materials. Till the 1980s, the total mileage of paved roads had reached 942100km. Most of them were lower classes of highways (Class III and IV) and only a few of them were Class-II highways. Most of the paved roads used simple structures, for example a 2~8cm thin asphalt surface layer over a lime-stabilized base layer upon the subgrade.

As a result of reform and opening-up policy, China's social economy had been rapidly developed and traffic volume was kept increasing from year to year since the 1980s. In addition to cars and light-loaded trucks, more and more heavy-loaded and overloaded trucks joined in the traffic flow. In order to meet the emerging service conditions, pavements should be built with the thicker asphalt layers. Unfortunately, the fact was that the production of asphalt was very limited and insufficiently met the needs of asphalt pavement construction. A new pavement structure, as the solution to this situation, was proposed by prof. Qinglin Sha, which is known as the semi-rigid pavement structure. The details about this special pavement structure will be introduced in the subsequent chapters of this textbook. From the 1980s to present, more than three million kilometers roads were constructed and most of which were medium and high classes of highways (Class I or Class II). By the end of 2019, the total mileage of roads had reached 4.84 million kilometers.

In summary, from the ancient post roads to the modern high classes highways, plenty of experience in road subgrade and pavement engineering were gained. In the future, more and more new technologies will be developed to meet the emerging situations. In this textbook, however, the emphasis is not on the subgrade or pavements of street roads in the cities, but focused on the subgrade and pavements of highways connecting cities.

1.2 Highway Subgrade and Pavement Structures

1.2.1 Concepts of Highway Subgrade and Pavement

The word 'Subgrade' has different definitions in different situations: In the U.S. dictionary, it is defined as 'the prepared earth surface on which a pavement or the ballast of a railway track is placed or upon which the foundation of a structure is built'; while in the British dictionary, it is defined as 'the ground beneath a roadway or apavement. 'In this textbook, the highway subgrade is referred to a geotechnical structure on which a pavement is placed as illustrated in Fig. 1-1.

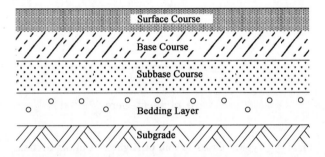

Fig. 1-1 Composition of Subgrade and Pavement Structure

In the British dictionary, 'pavement' is a hard-layered structure that forms a road carriageway, airfield, vehicle park, or other paved areas. In this textbook, a pavement is defined as a layered structure paved on a subgrade. In case of China's engineering practice, a pavement structure consists of surface course, base course, subbase course, and bedding layer as illustrated in Fig. 1-1.

1.2.2 Highway Subgrade Types

Highway subgrade geometries are dependent on their locations in the road alignment: when the subgrade surface is higher than the natural ground elevation, additional materials should be borrowed to form the subgrade. This type of subgrade is named with 'embankment' or 'fill'. When the subgrade surface is lower than the natural ground elevation, excavation is needed to form the subgrade. In this situation, the subgrade is named with 'cut' or 'cutting'. Sometimes, both filling and cutting appear in a single subgrade cross-section. This type of subgrade is called 'cut and fill'.

In summary, highway subgrade can be categorized into three types, namely embankment or fill as shown in Fig. 1-2, cut as shown in Fig. 1-3, and cut-fill as shown in Fig. 1-4. When landforms, surrounding environments, and underlying soil properties are considered, these three categories of subgrade may be further divided into different sub-types.

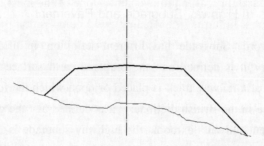

Fig. 1-2 Typical Cross-section of Highway Embankments

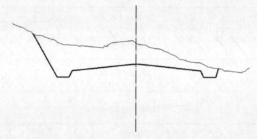

Fig. 1-3 Typical Cross-section of Highway Cutting Sections

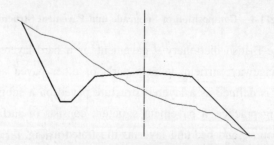

Fig. 1-4 Typical Cross-section of Highway Cut-fill Sections

1.2.3 Highway Pavement Types

In the United Kingdom, pavements are categorized into four types: flexible, flexible composite, rigid, and rigid composite. In France, pavements are categorized into full-depth asphalt pavements, hydraulically bound material (HBM) base pavements, composite pavements, rigid base pavements, and rigid pavements. In America, pavements are categorized into three major types: flexible or asphalt pavements, rigid or concrete pavements, and composite pavements. It is evident that there are various methods for categorizing pavements. The major focus of this textbook is on highway pavements in Chinese practice and those in other countries are not presented in details.

In China, two major pavement types are asphalt pavements and concrete pavements of which surface courses are asphalt and cement concrete, respectively. Due to the advantages of high stiffness value, low air voids, earlier open to traffic, and better durability, asphalt pavement is one of the most popularly-used pavement types in China. In terms of asphalt mixture composition or design methods, asphalt pavement may be further divided into asphalt concrete pavement, asphalt macadam pavement, asphalt penetration pavement, stone-mastic asphalt pavement, asphalt-treated pavement, and other asphalt pavements. Based on the stiffness of base courses, asphalt pavements may be further categorized into flexible pavements and semi-rigid pavements. When the base courses are paved with granular materials and/or asphalt materials, pavements are categorized as flexible pavements. When the base courses are hydraulically bound materials (cement, lime, or fly ash stabilized mixtures), pavements are called the semi-rigid asphalt pavements. In Chinese engineering practice, the majority of highways have been constructed with the semi-rigid asphalt pavements. Fig.1-5 shows typical structures of asphalt pavements.

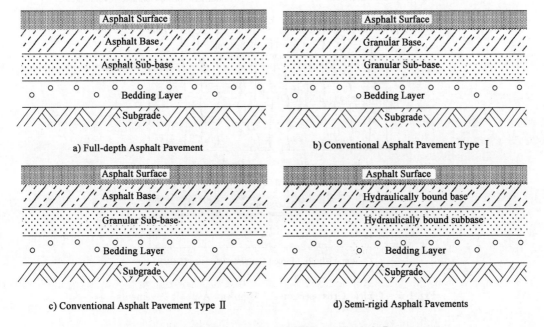

Fig. 1-5 Typical Cross-sections of Highway Asphalt Pavements

Concrete pavement is another popularly-used pavement type which can be further categorized as jointed plain concrete pavement (JPCP), jointed reinforced concrete pavement (JRCP), and continuously reinforced concrete pavement (CRCP) as shown in Fig. 1-6. Evidently, for a JPCP, the transverse joint spacing is much shorter and no cracks are allowed within the concrete slab. When reinforcements are applied, the joint spacing can be up to 15m for JRCP and the transverse joints are not needed for CRCP. However, the crack spacing may decrease as the joint spacing increases.

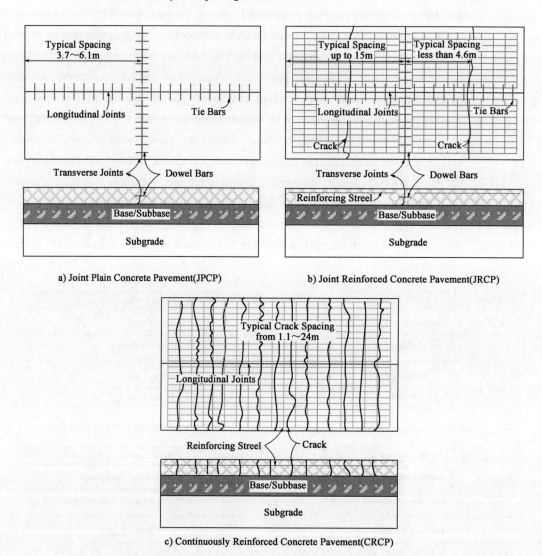

Fig. 1-6 Typical Cross-sections of Highway Asphalt Pavements

1.3 Design Factors

As discussed above, subgrade and pavements have different types of structures that may be selected or used in different conditions. For engineering design purposes, the following factors should be considered:

1.3.1　Traffic Loads

When a vehicle is running on a pavement surface, vehicle weight and its cargo may induce forces which are distributed to each axle of the vehicle. The axle loads are further transferred onto tires and finally applied to the pavement surface. Therefore, the traffic loads are referred to the tire-pavement interaction forces which may include the vertical pressure and the horizontal frictional forces.

In pavement engineering, traffic loading is one of the most important factors and usually characterized by the axle loads, the number of load repetitions, tire-contact areas, and vehicle speeds. Details will be provided in Chapter 2 of this textbook.

1.3.2　Environmental Conditions

Environmental factors which may impact subgrade and/or pavements include temperature and water which are various from hour to hour through a day and from month to month through a year.

First of all, environmental conditions may influence the construction of subgrade or pavement structures. For instance, it is hard to pave asphalt mixtures at low temperatures and construction must stop in a rainy day.

Secondly, environmental conditions may significantly influence properties of subgrade soils or pavement materials. For instance, asphalt mixture stiffness values may dramatically decrease with service temperatures increasing and soil shear strengths may be significantly reduced with the water content increasing.

Thirdly, environmental conditions may induce additional stresses which may accelerate the failure of subgrade or pavement structures. For instance, with water content decreasing, tensile stresses may be induced in the cement-stabilized base and cracks may be induced due to the tensile stresses. When temperatures differ significantly, the curling stresses may be induced within the concrete slab and cracks may be created due to the curling stresses. There are many other examples which illustrate the effects of environmental conditions.

Fourthly, different environmental conditions may be coupled: during winter time, frost-heave may occur as a result of coupled effects of low temperature and water.

Evidently, environmental conditions are significantly crucial in highway subgrade and pavement engineering. Methods or specifications should be provided to quantify the environmental conditions for meeting requirements of subgrade and/or pavement engineering. More detailed discussion will be provided in Chapter 2.

1.3.3 Materials

In the Mechanistic-Empirical design method, material properties must be specified, so that the designers can determine the subgrade and/or pavement responses, such as stresses, strains, and displacements in the critical components. Then, these responses are used with failure criteria to predict whether failures will occur or the probability that failures occur. Details of material characterization are presented in Chapter 3.

1.3.4 Highway Drainage System

During the highway service period, the surface water may enter pavement and subgrade through cracks, joints, and air voids while the underground water rises up due to effects of capillary action. As a result, subgrade and pavement distresses gradually occur due to effects of the undesirable water. Therefore, it is significantly important to consider the highway drainage design in the process of subgrade and pavement design. In fact, in Chinese practice, drainage design is a part of subgrade and pavement design. Details about highway drainage design are included in Chapter 4.

1.3.5 Failure Criteria

The life cycle of a pavement life starts when it is newly-built and ends when it is insufficient to serve traffic. Due to the traffic and environmental effects, the pavement general conditions are deteriorating and the corresponding distresses may occur. At a certain point, the distresses become so severe that the pavement is considered insufficient. The failure criteria are indicators to represent or evaluate the general pavement conditions and different failure criteria are used for various design methods. Followed are failure criteria for the national asphalt and cement concrete pavement design methods:

(1) Asphalt Pavements: It is generally agreed that both permanent deformation and cracking are primary types of distresses to be considered in asphalt pavement design. The failure criteria are fully discussed in Chapter 8.

(2) Cement Concrete Pavements: Different from asphalt pavement, cement concrete has very high stiffness and permanent deformation is not considered in most design methods. Fatigue cracking has long been considered the major criterion. Recently, pumping, erosion, faulting, and joint deterioration are also considered in cement concrete pavement design. Details are fully discussed in Chapter 9.

1.4 Road Subgrade and Pavement Engineering

Subgrade and pavement engineering is the process of creating and maintaining paved structure surfaces to meet the needs of traffic and the environmental conditions. As shown in Fig. 1-7, three key elements in pavement engineering are service conditions, service abilities, and activities of professionals, respectively. The service conditions are referred to traffic and environment conditions which are the two most important design factors as mentioned above. The service abilities are referred to performance or properties of a pavement structure to meet the service conditions, which may include stiffness, strength, stability, durability, smoothness, and skidding resistance.

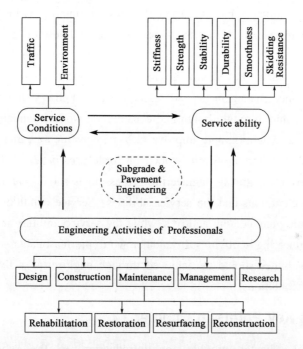

Fig. 1-7 Three Key Elements of Pavement Engineering

- **Stiffness** or modulus is an instinct of a road structure which tells how deformable a road structure will be under traffic loads. The higher stiffness value provides the stronger supporting to vehicles, but it may result in uncomfortable vibrations and noises. The lower stiffness value provides the weaker supporting to vehicles, but it may provide less vibration, less noise, and larger frictional coefficient. Elastic stiffness reflects a road structure behaves elastically, while viscoelastic stiffness tells a structure behaves viscoelastically.
- **Strength** is the bearing capability, a limit, or a maximum value, which tells how strong a road structure will be under traffic loads. Two road

structures with the identical stiffness features may have the identical mechanical behaviors under the lighter traffic loads, but their abilities may be different in resisting heavier traffic loads.
- **Stability** is another bearing capability which tells how stable a road structure will be under traffic and environmental conditions.
- **Durability** is a long-term capability which tells how long a road structure can resist effects of traffic and environmental conditions.
- **Smoothness** is one of the important index of evaluating pavement quality, which tells how comfortable vehicles are running on the road structure.
- **Skidding resistance** is a service ability which tells how a road structure resists the horizontal force effects. The larger skidding resistance a road structure has, the safer vehicles are running on the pavement surface.

More details of the above six service abilities are provided in the Chinese textbook[1]. The engineering activities of professionals are the major job positions in Subgrade and Pavement Engineering, which include design, construction, maintenance, management, and research. As a highway engineer, one can create a road structure through design and construction works, maintain the structure through maintenance works, and improve design, construction, and maintenance through management and research works. In order to better fulfill those engineering activities, the highway engineering professionals should carefully consider both the service conditions and the service abilities: Service conditions are prerequisites for performing engineering actitives, while the service abilities are anticipated results of the engineering actitivities. In another word, the reasonable subgrade and pavement service abilites should be achieved through engineering activities with considering service conditions.

1.5 Summary & Key Points in Chapter 1

This chapter provides an introduction: to the subgrade and pavement engineering. It covers four major sections: historical development of Chinese roads, subgrade and pavement structures, design factors, and the definition of road subgrade and pavement engineering. If readers have difficulties in understanding some concepts of this chapter, further details will be provided in the subsequent chapter. Followed are key points of Chapter 1:

(1) The four stages of the historical development of Chinese roads: the ancient post roads, simply-built public roads, lower classes of highways, and higher classes of highways.

(2) A highway subgrade can be defined as geotechnical structure on which a pavement is placed. There are three typical subgrade types, namely embankment or

fill, cut, and cut-fill.

(3) A pavement is a layered structure seated on the subgrade. In terms of types of pavements, there are various classification methods. Pavements may be categorized into asphalt, concrete, unbound granular, and composite pavements according to different paving materials while they may be categorized into flexible, rigid, and semi-rigid pavements based on the stiffness values of their base layers.

(4) In pavement design, factors which should be paid special attentions are traffic loads, environmental conditions, materials, drainage, and failure criteria.

(5) Road subgrade and pavement engineering is the process of creating and maintaining a paved structure to meet traffic and environmental conditions. This definition tells us three key contents of subgrade and pavement engineering, namely the service abilities, service conditions, and engineering activities.

Problems and Questions

1. Why are these pavements generally built in layers?
2. Why are not all pavements very thick or very thin?
3. While designing a road pavement, are both weight and number of vehicles important?
4. What are the different types of rigid pavements?
5. What are the different types of asphalt pavements?
6. Why is research on pavements important?
7. What are the general areas of research on pavements?
8. Conduct an Internet search and list the primary pavement-related research being carried out in different parts of the world.
9. Do you know the possible job possitions in pavement engineering? Please list and briefly explain them.
10. Pavement service ability is the capability of a pavement structure to serve traffic and environmental conditions. Could you list the key service abilities of a highway pavement?
11. In order to create a high-quality pavement, there are five key design factors. Could you list and explain them?

2. Traffic Loads and Environmental Conditions

Roads are constructed to serve vehicles under given environmental conditions. Both traffic and environmental conditions are key factors causing pavement deterioration. It should be noted that vehicles have various weight and motion features, and the traffic loads are different from one vehicle to another. Additionally, the environmental is various from hour to hour and day to day throughout a year. One of the important tasks of pavement engineering is to reasonably quantify traffic loads and environmental conditions. This chapter introduces effects of traffic loads and environmental conditions and presents the corresponding analysis approaches which are commonly used in Chinese practice.

2.1 Traffic Loads and their Impacts

As shown in Fig. 2-1, the weight of a vehicle (W) is transferred to the suspension system which distributes a load of W to the vehicle axles and then to the wheels of each axle. As a result, the sum of axle loads (P) is equal to the vehicle weight (W) and the sum of wheel loads is equal to a total load of each axle. The wheel loads are further distributed to the pavement surface through tires to induce the pavement-tire interaction pressure which consists of the vertical pressure and horizontal frictions. The vertical pressure may be static or dynamic, while the friction may be the rolling friction or the sliding friction. As detailed below, the

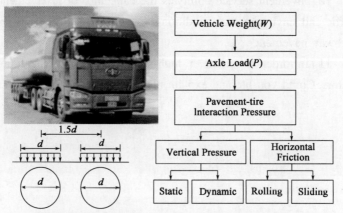

Fig. 2-1 Mechanical Analysis on Vehicular Loading

static vertical pressure is the main input for characterizing traffic loads, but the effects of vehicle motion (acceleration, deceleration, steadily moving, and parking) are considerable and should be taken into account. Followed is a discussion on static and dynamic pavement-tire interactions:

Static Contact Pressure and Loading Area: A vehicular load is applied on the pavement through axles, wheels, and tires. When a truck is stopping at the parking lot, its vertical contact pressure is mainly from the tire inflation pressure if tires are treadless or the tire walls do not carry loading. In fact, the contact area or tire imprint shape is irregular and the contact stress is un-uniformly distributed. However, the irregular imprint is commonly modeled with a circular shape which carries a uniformly distributed vertical stress as shown in Fig. 2-2.

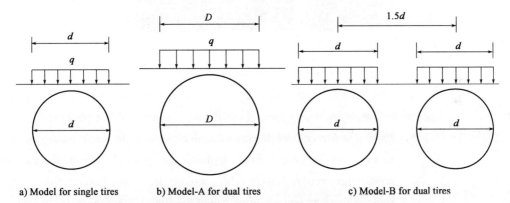

a) Model for single tires   b) Model-A for dual tires   c) Model-B for dual tires

Fig. 2-2 Models for calculating tire-pavement interaction forces

As mentioned above, the contact pressure (q) is estimated from the tire inflation pressure which can be considered as a constant. It is evident that heavier loading results in larger contact area. Assuming the load applied on the wheel is P, the diameter of the contact area can be determined by Equation 2-1 for the model for single tires and the Model-B for dual tires, while the diameter is determined by Equation 2-2 for the Model-A for dual tires.

$$d = \sqrt{\frac{4p}{\pi q}} = 2\delta \tag{2-1}$$

$$D = \sqrt{\frac{8p}{\pi q}} = \sqrt{2}\,d \tag{2-2}$$

Example 2-1:

The total axle load of tridem axles as shown in Fig. 2-3 is equal to 180kN and the tire inflation pressure is 0.7MPa. Assuming that tires are treadles or the tire walls do not carry loading, determine diameters of the equivalent circular loading area.

Solution:

A total of six dual tires take the triple-axles load of 180kN. Therefore, each dual tire takes $180/12 = 15$kN or $P = 15$kN. Since the tire walls carry no loads, the contact pressure $p = 0.7$MPa. For dual tires, there are two models: 1) With the Model-B, two tires are considered separately, the diameter d of each circular area can be calculated with Equation 2-1 and equal to $\sqrt{4 \times 15/(\pi \times 0.7)} = 0.1652$m; 2) With the Model-A, two tires are equivalent to a single circular area. The diameter D can be calculated with Equation 2-2 and equal to 0.2336m.

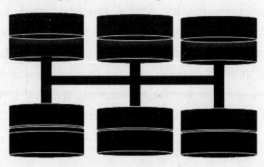

Fig. 2-3   Example 2-1

Dynamic Pavement-tire Pressure: When vehicles are running on the pavement, the contact pressure may be considerably different from the static pressure. Followed are a few facts about dynamic pavement-tire pressure:

- *Pavement-tire contact pressure fluctuates around its static value*: as shown in Fig. 2-4, the fluctuation amplitude is about 130kN while the static contact pressure is 100kN. The ratio of the fluctuation amplitude to the static contact pressure is often called the impact coefficient. In this case, the impact coefficient is about 1.3. In fact, the impact coefficient is less than 1.3 when a vehicle travels on a well-paved pavement at a speed of less than 50km/h. It should be noted that the impact coefficient may increase with vehicle speeds and pavement surface roughness. Therefore, the impact coefficient should be considered in pavement design even though it has not been used in most of the existing pavement design methods.

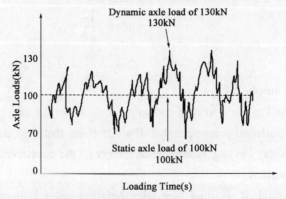

Fig. 2-4   Pavement-tire Contact Pressure Fluctuates When a Vehicle Running on the Pavement

- *Pavement-tire contact pressure is an instant load*: The loading time of a vehicular load is from 0.01 second to 0.1 second. According to AASHTO road testing results, vehicle speed may considerably affect deflection at pavement surface as shown in Fig. 2-5. It is evident that the increasing vehicle speed from 10km/h to 80km/h results in about 40% reduction of deformation for asphalt pavements or 23% reduction of deformation for rigid pavements.

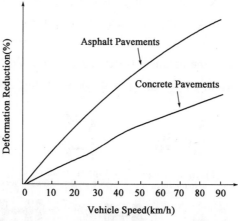

Fig. 2-5 Effects of vehicle speed on pavement vertical deformation

- *Pavement-tire contact pressure is a repeated load*: for a given road cross-section, one vehicle goes and another comes. As a result, at a specific point in this cross-section the vehicular load is a repeated load. Due to the viscoelastic behaviors of asphalt materials and aggregate particle re-arrangement or redistribution of subgrade and base materials, the pavement deformation may be accumulated under each load application. In addition to the accumulative deformation, fatigue damage is another concern pertinent to the repeated load.
- *Horizontal force is also an important feature of the dynamic pavement-tire contact pressure*: When a vehicle is accelerated, its driving wheels have frictional forces in the traffic direction and its driven wheels have frictional forces in the opposite direction. Similarly, when a vehicle is decelerated, its driving wheels have frictional forces opposite to the traffic direction, while its driven wheels have the frictional forces in the traffic direction. When a vehicle is steadily moving at a constant speed, the frictional force at the pavement-tire interface can be ignored.

2.2 Traffic Data and Collection Methods

As mentioned above, traffic loading is from the pavement-tire interaction which is dependent on the vehicle types, axle types, traffic volume, and axle load magnitude. In this section, concepts of axle types, vehicle types, traffic volume, and axle load magnitude are introduced followed by corresponding traffic data collection methods.

2.2.1 Vehicle Axles and Classification

Vehicular loading is transferred to axles, then to tires, and then to the pavement surface. Therefore, axle loading is usually used as the key parameter for characterizing traffic loading in pavement engineering. The focus of this section is on the discussion about vehicle axle configuration and classification.

According to the national asphalt pavement design specification[2], truck axles can be categorized into seven types as shown in Fig. 2-6.

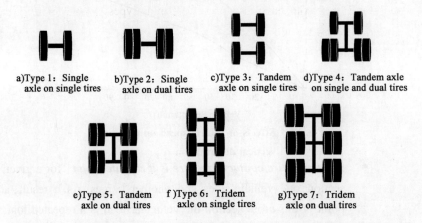

a) Type 1: Single axle on single tires b) Type 2: Single axle on dual tires c) Type 3: Tandem axle on single tires d) Type 4: Tandem axle on single and dual tires

e) Type 5: Tandem axle on dual tires f) Type 6: Tridem axle on single tires g) Type 7: Tridem axle on dual tires

Fig. 2-6 Axle types based on the national asphalt pavement design specification

- Axle Type 1 is a single axle on single tires that is popularly used as the front axles of trucks. This type of axle consists of one axle with one tire at each side as shown in Fig. 2-6a).
- Axle Type 2 is a single axle on dual tires that is commonly used as the rear axles of trucks. This type of axle consists of one axle with two tires at each side as shown in Fig. 2-6b).
- Axle Type 3 is a tandem axle on single tires which is not popularly used. This type of axle is composed of two axles spacing less than 3.0 meters and each of the two axles has one tires at each side as shown in Fig. 2-6c).
- Axle Type 4 is a tandem axle on single and dual tires which is not popularly used. This type of axle has two axles spacing of fewer than 3.0 meters. One of the two axles has two tires at each side and the other has one tire at each side as shown in Fig. 2-6d).

- Axle Type 5 is a tandem axle on dual tires that is one of the most popular axle types used as the truck rear axle. This type of axle has two axles spacing less than 3.0 meters and each axle has two tires at each side as shown in Fig. 2-6e).
- Axle Type 6 is a tridem axle on single tires which is not popularly used. This type of axle has three axles spacing less than 3.0 meters and each axle has one tire at each side as shown in Fig. 2-6f).
- Axle Type 7 is a tridem axle on dual tires which is a popular axle type. This type of axle has three axles spacing less than 3.0 meters and each axle has two tires at each side as shown in Fig. 2-6g).

Example 2-2:

As shown in Fig. 2-7, a truck has four axles: the front axle has two tires, while the other three axles have four tires. Determine types of axles: a) $b = c < 3m$; b) $b > 3m, c < 3m$.

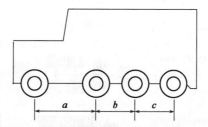

Fig. 2-7 Diagram Used in Example 2-1

Solution:

①the front axle is the single axle on single tires while the remaining three axles can be considered as a tridem axle on dual tires according to China's national pavement design specification[2]; ②the front axle is the single axle on single tires while the remaining three axles are single axles on dual tires.

It should be noted that tridem axles and tandem axles are only employed in asphalt pavement design. In rigid pavement design, all types of axles are considered as single axles according to the national design specification[2].

2.2.2 Vehicle Types

According to the textbook edited by Prof. Deng[1], vehicles traveling on pavements can be categorized into two basic classes, namely passenger vehicles and trucks. The passenger vehicles can be further classified into three basic types, namely small, medium, and large passenger vehicles based on how many passengers they can take. The small vehicles have less than 6 seats and they are light and high-speed. The medium passenger vehicles have 6-20 seats while the large passenger vehicles have more than 20 seats. Trucks can be further classified into integral trucks, trailer trucks, and semitrailer trucks.

In the national design specification of asphalt pavements[2], vehicles are categorized into 11 types as shown in Table 2-1. It should be noted that the schematic diagram in the third column shows the typical representatives instead of all potential representatives.

Table 2-1 Vehicle types based on the national design specification[2]

Types	Main features	Schematic Diagram	Representatives
Type 1	Vehicle with two axles and four wheels		Model 11 (both front and rear axles are Type I)
Type 2	Passenger vehicle with two axles and no less than 6 wheels		Model 12 (Front axles is Type I and rear axle is Type 2) Model 15 (Front axles is Type I and rear axle is Type 5)
Type 3	Integral trucks with two axles and no less than 6 wheels		Model 12 (Front axles is Type I and rear axle is Type 2)
Type 4	Integral trucks with three axles (Front axle is a single axle)		Model 15 (Front axles is Type I and rear axle is Type 5)
Type 5	Integral trucks with four axles (Front axle is a single axle)		Model 17 (Front axles is Type I and rear axle is Type 7)
Type 6	Integral trucks with four axles (Two front axles)		Model 112 (Front axles are Type I and rear axle is Type 2) Model 115 (Front axles are Type I and rear axle is Type 5) Model 117 (Front axles are Type I and rear axle is Type 7)
Type 7	Semitrailer trucks with no more than four axles (single front axle)		Model 125 (Front axle is Type I and rear axle is Type 2, and semitrailer axle is Type 5)
Type 8	Semitrailer trucks with five axles (single front axle)		Model 127 (Front axle is Type I and rear axle is Type 2, and semitrailer axle is Type 7) Model 155 (Front axle is Type I and rear axle is Type 5, and semitrailer axle is Type 5)

Types	Main features	Schematic Diagram	Representatives
Type 9	Semitrailer trucks with no less than 6 axles (single front axle)		Model 157 (Front axle is Type I and rear axle is Type 5, and semitrailer axle is Type 7)
Type 10	Semitrailer trucks with two front axles		Model 1127 (Front axles are Type I and rear axle is Type 2, and semitrailer axle is Type 7)
Type 11	Trailer trucks		Model 1522 (Front axles is Type I and rear axle is Type 5, and trailer axle are Type 2) Model 1222 (Front axles is Type I and rear axle is Type 2, and trailer axle are Type 2)

2.2.3 Traffic Volume

Traffic volume can be defined as a measure of vehicles passing a specific road cross-section in a given period. Based on the length of time, traffic volume can be hourly traffic (HT), daily traffic (DT), weekly traffic (WT), monthly traffic (MT), annual average daily traffic (AADT), accumulative traffic. For the purpose of traffic collection, hourly traffic and daily traffic are commonly used. In pavement engineering, AADT is one of the key parameters and can be determined through daily traffic (DT) as expressed in Equation 2-3.

$$\text{AADT} = \frac{\sum_{n=1}^{365} \text{DT}_n}{365} \qquad (2\text{-}3)$$

It should be noted that traffic flow may be composed of different types of vehicles. In other words, among the AADT of Equation 2-3, there are various types of vehicles included. Since different type's vehicles impact pavement performance in different ways, it is necessary to distinguish them. In the national asphalt pavement design specification[2], the vehicle class distribution factor (VCDF) is used to quantitatively capture the effects of vehicle types as shown in Equation 2-4.

$$\text{VCDF}_m = \frac{\text{AADT}_m}{\text{AADT}} \qquad (2\text{-}4)$$

Where:

AADT_m is the annual average daily traffic for vehicle type m;

VCDF_m is the vehicle class distribution factor for vehicle type m;

AADT is the total annual average daily traffic.

2.2.4 Axle Load Magnitude

Through the traffic volume data, the number of vehicles can be determined and the total number of axles can also be computed if the number of axles for each vehicle is given. The focus of pavement engineering, however, is on the axle load which is the key factor for determining the pavement-tire interaction pressure. Therefore, it is necessary to collect the traffic data of axle load magnitude.

For the concrete pavement design, the axle configurations are not distinguished and the multiple axles should be considered in separate single axles. For instance, a tandem axle should be considered as two single axles in collecting the axle load data in the concrete pavement design.

For the asphalt pavement design, the axle configuration must be distinguished and the multiple axles should be considered in one integrated axle. For instance, a tandem axle should be considered as one axle even though it consists of two axles.

Example 2-3:

With the traffic data as listed in Table 2-2, determine the axle load magnitude data for the asphalt pavement design and concrete pavement design, respectively.

Table 2-2 Traffic data for example

Vehicle Types	Axle Load Magnitude (kN)		AADT
Type 3	Front	40	600
	Rear	60.5	
	Trailer	0	
Type 4	Front	55	500
	Rear	2×66	
	Trailer	0	
Type 9	Front	54.6	100
	Rear	2×91	
	Trailer	3×110	
Type 3	Front	30.5	400
	Rear	90.8	
	Trailer	0	
Type 4	Front	45	300
	Rear	2×55	
	Trailer	0	
Type 9	Front	50	220
	Rear	2×86	
	Trailer	3×120	

Solution:

The solutions are shown in Table 2-3 and Table 2-4.

Table 2-3 Solution to the axle load magnitude data for asphalt pavement design

Vehicle Type	Single axle on single tire		Single axle on dual tires		Tandem axle on dual tires		Tridem axle on dual tires	
	Axle load (kN)	Number of axles	Axle load (kN)	Number of axles	Axle load (kN)	Number of axles	Axle load (kN)	Number of axles
Type 3	40	600	60.5	600				
Type 4	55	500			132	500		
Type 9	54.6	100			182	100	330	100
Type 3	30.5	400	90.8	400				
Type 4	45	300			110	300		
Type 9	50	220			172	220	360	220

Table 2-4 Solution to the axle load magnitude data for concrete pavement design

Vehicle Type	Axle load (kN)	Number of axles
Type 3	40	600
Type 3	60.5	600
Type 4	55	500
Type 4	66	500 × 2 = 1000
Type 9	54.6	100
Type 9	91	100 × 2 = 200
Type 9	110	100 × 3 = 300
Type 3	30.5	400
Type 3	90.8	400
Type 4	60	300
Type 4	75	300 × 2 = 600
Type 9	64	220
Type 9	96	220 × 2 = 440
Type 9	120	220 × 3 = 660

2.2.5 Traffic-monitoring Technology

Three basic traffic-monitoring technologies are available to collect traffic data, namely the automatic traffic recorders (ATR), automated vehicle classifiers (AVC), and weight-in-motion (WIM). These three systems are typically installed in the driving lanes and the traffic data are recorded at normal driving speed.

ATRs are the cheapest traffic monitoring systems that consist of various sensors and a data acquisition system. Evidently, with ATR technologies, only a subset of traffic data elements can be collected for pavement analysis or design. However, their low cost allows installation of a considerable number of these systems installed throughout a network of roads. These data, supplemented by AVC and WIM data, provides estimates of the axle loads experienced in multitude of locations throughout a road network.

AVCs record vehicle volume by vehicle classification which is defined in terms of the number of axles by axle configuration. AVC data contains more information than ATR data, it still lacks a data element crucial to pavement analysis or design process, namely the load of the axles.

WIM technology expands on the information collected by AVCs by providing the load of each axle passing over the system. It is obvious that the WIM technology may provide a complete set of traffic data elements needed for pavement analysis or design.

2.3 Traffic Data Analysis

2.3.1 Axle Load Spectrum

Different vehicles have different axles and the axle load magnitudes may be different even though the axle types are identical. Thus, it is evident that the axle load composition in traffic flow may play a significant role in determining pavement deterioration. In order to quantify the axle load composition feature, the axle load spectrum is defined as a histogram of the axle loads vs the corresponding frequencies (percentage of a specific axle load). The x-coordinate is the axle load at the interval of 2.5kN for single axle on single tires, 4.5kN for single axle on dual tires, 9.0kN for tandem axles, and 13.5kN for the tandem axles in the asphalt pavement design specification[2], while the x-coordinate is the axle load at the interval of 5.0kN in the concrete pavement design specification[3]. The interval values may be different for different projects as long as they are convenient and accurate.

With the data in Table 2-3 and Table 2-4, the axle load spectrum of the single axle on single tires for asphalt pavement design, and that of single axles for concrete pavement design are plotted in Fig. 2-8 and Fig. 2-9.

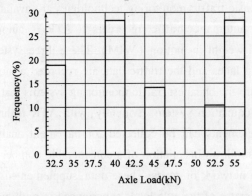

Fig. 2-8 Axle load spectrum for the single axle on single tires in Table 2-3

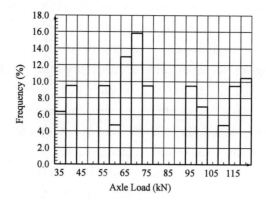

Fig. 2-9 Axle load spectrum for the single axles in Table 2-4

2.3.2 Transverse Distribution of Wheel Track

As shown in Fig. 2-10, the wheel passes are various at different locations of a given pavement cross-section due to tire thickness much narrower than the cross-section. The ratio of the wheel passes of the unit width to the total width of the cross-section is defined as the transverse distribution frequency of wheel tracks. The sum of the frequencies within the certain width (50cm in general) is called the transverse distribution coefficient of wheel tracks. In the concrete pavement design, the transverse distribution coefficient is commonly used to evaluate effects of wheel tracks at the critical loading position.

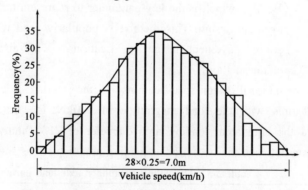

Fig. 2-10 The transverse distribution frequency of wheel tracks (mixed two-directional lanes)

2.3.3 Vehicle Load Equivalency

As discussed above, vehicles and axles are various from one to another and may result in various effects on pavement deterioration. The accumulative deterioration may be quantified in three different ways, namely the variable traffic and vehicle, the fixed traffic, and the fixed vehicle[25]:

- In the variable traffic and vehicle method, both traffic and vehicle are individually considered. In other words, traffic loads can be divided into various groups and pavement stresses, strains, and deflections under each group of loads will be determined separately and used for design purposes. Obviously, it is much more complex compared with the two methods below. However, when this method is used in computer-aided pavement design the efficiency is not a problem.
- In the fixed traffic method, pavement thickness is governed by an equivalent single-wheel load (ESWL) and effects from the number of load repetitions can be converted to that from ESWL. As a result, the pavement design can be conducted based on a single wheel load. For design projects of airport pavements design or highway pavements design with the heavy wheel loads, but light traffic volume, this method is frequently used. Details are not provided in this textbook.
- In the fixed vehicle method, pavement thickness is governed by the number of repetitions of a standard vehicle or axle load. If the axle loads are not the standard axles, they must be converted into the standard vehicle or axles in pavement design by an equivalent axle load factor (EALF). The effect of a non-standard axle may be equivalent through multiplying its EALF. The sum of the equivalent effects of all axle loads in the entire design period results in an equivalent single axle load (ESAL) which is the key parameter to represent traffic loading effects in pavement design. This method is popularly used worldwide[4-6] and the national pavement design specifications[2,3] are also based on the fixed vehicle method.

In the national design specifications[2,3], the standard axle load is a single axle on dual tires with the load magnitude of 100kN, the tire imprint pressure of 0.7MPa, the equivalent loading area diameter of 213.0mm, and the distance of 319.5mm between the two circular loading area centers as shown in Table 2-5.

Table 2-5 The national standard axle load parameters

Design axle load	Tire imprint pressure	Load area diameter	Distance between the two circular loading area centers
100kN	0.7MPa	213.0mm	319.5mm

An EALF defines the damage per pass to a pavement by the axle in question relative to the damage per pass of the standard load (100kN). Equation 2-5 shows the definition of the EALF:

$$\text{EALF}_x = \frac{N_s}{N_x} \tag{2-5}$$

Where N_s is the number of passes of the standard axle and N_x is the number of passes of the axle load x.

The design of a pavement structure is based on the total number of passes of the standard axle load during the design period, which is defined as the equivalent single axle load (ESAL) and computed by Equation 2-6.

$$\text{ESAL} = \sum_i^m n_i \times \text{EALF}_i \qquad (2\text{-}6)$$

Where n_i is the number of passes of the ith axle load during the design period.

Since it is not feasible to measure N_s and N_x in Equation 2-5, the empirical or theoretical equations are developed to compute the EALF. The EALF depends on the type of pavements, structural capacity or thickness, the type of axles, and terminal conditions in which the pavement is considered failed. In the national design specifications[2,3], the EALF is computed with the Equation 2-7.

$$\text{EALF}_x = \alpha \left(\frac{P_x}{P_n} \right)^n \qquad (2\text{-}7)$$

Where P_x, P_n are the magnitude of the axle load x and the standard axle load; α and n are the coefficients related to the type of vehicle axles, pavement type, and design criteria.

The coefficient is determined through multiplying the axle-related coefficient of c_1 by the tire-related coefficient of c_2 for the asphalt pavement design, while it is equal to 1 for concrete pavement design.

Since traffic volume is commonly collected and recorded in terms of vehicle passes instead of axle passes. Therefore, the EALF or ESAL factor of each vehicle may facilitate the determination of the accumulative ESAL of the pavement design life. The ESAL of a vehicle is defined as the truck factor (TF) and computed by

$$\text{TF} = \sum_{k=0}^m \text{ESLF}_k \qquad (2\text{-}8)$$

in which m is the number of axles of this vehicle, ESLF_k is the EALF for each axle.

Once the truck factors (TF_i) of vehicles are determined, the equivalent single axle load (ESAL) can be determined in the Equation 2-9.

$$\text{ESAL} = \sum_i^m \text{AADT}_i \times \text{TF}_i \qquad (2\text{-}9)$$

Example 2-4:

Fig. 2-11 shows two types of vehicles. The daily traffic for vehicle Type 3 and 2 are 1000 and 1500, respectively. The coefficients of α and n are 4.5 and 4.0 for the single axle on single tires and they are 1.0 and 4.0 for the single axle on dual tires. Determine the truck factors for each type of vehicles and the total ESALs.

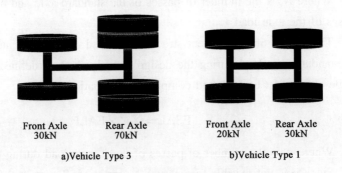

Fig. 2-11 Two types of vehicles

Solution:

Step 1: Calculate EALF for the single axle on single tire: $EALF_{30kN} = 4.5 \times \left(\dfrac{30}{100}\right)^4 = 0.0365$; $EALF_{30kN} = 4.5 \times \left(\dfrac{20}{100}\right)^4 = 0.0072$;

Step 2: Calculate EALF for the single axle on dual tires: $EALF_{70kN} = \left(\dfrac{70}{100}\right)^4 = 0.2401$;

Step 3: Calculate truck factors: $TF_{VT3} = EALF_{30kN} + EALFF_{70kN} = 0.0365 + 0.2401 = 0.2766$; $TF_{VT2} = EALF_{30kN} + EALF_{20kN} = 0.0365 + 0.0072 = 0.0437$;

Step 4: Calculate the total ESAL: $ESAL_{total} = 1000 \times TF_{VT3} + 1500 \times TF_{VT2} = 276.6 + 65.6 = 342.2$.

2.3.4 Traffic Growth Factor

For the purposes of pavement structure design, it is necessary to estimate the cumulative number of 100kN equivalent single axle load for the design period. The above sections have demonstrated the computation of the daily and annual traffic, while this section deals with the prediction of future traffic which is often based on the past traffic history. The traffic may remain constant or increase in an arithmetic growth rate or a geometric growth rate. In most cases, the predicted traffic increases in a geometric growth rate (g) and the growth factor (G) can be determined for the analysis period of n with the Equation 2-10.

$$G = \dfrac{(1+g)^n - 1}{g} \tag{2-10}$$

With the Equation 2-10, the growth factors for different analysis periods and the annual growth rate are computed and listed in Table 2-6. In this way, users may easily find the growth factor without the Equation 2-10.

Table 2-6 Traffic Growth Factors

Analysis Period (n)	Annual growth rate, g (%)								
	1	3	5	7	9	11	13	15	17
1	1.00	1.00	1.00	1.00	1.00	1.00	1.00	1.00	1.00
2	2.01	2.03	2.05	2.07	2.09	2.11	2.13	2.15	2.17
3	3.03	3.09	3.15	3.21	3.28	3.34	3.41	3.47	3.54
4	4.06	4.18	4.31	4.44	4.57	4.71	4.85	4.99	5.14
5	5.10	5.31	5.53	5.75	5.98	6.23	6.48	6.74	7.01
6	6.15	6.47	6.80	7.15	7.52	7.91	8.32	8.75	9.21
7	7.21	7.66	8.14	8.65	9.20	9.78	10.40	11.07	11.77
8	8.29	8.89	9.55	10.26	11.03	11.86	12.76	13.73	14.77
9	9.37	10.16	11.03	11.98	13.02	14.16	15.42	16.79	18.28
10	10.46	11.46	12.58	13.82	15.19	16.72	18.42	20.30	22.39
11	11.57	12.81	14.21	15.78	17.56	19.56	21.81	24.35	27.20
12	12.68	14.19	15.92	17.89	20.14	22.71	25.65	29.00	32.82
13	13.81	15.62	17.71	20.14	22.95	26.21	29.98	34.35	39.40
14	14.95	17.09	19.60	22.55	26.02	30.09	34.88	40.50	47.10
15	16.10	18.60	21.58	25.13	29.36	34.41	40.42	47.58	56.11

2.4 Determination of Accumulative ESAL

In most design specifications[2-6], the accumulative ESAL in a given design period should be determined as the key design parameter to represent effects of traffic loading. In this section, the following two procedures will be introduced for determining the accumulative ESAL, namely the "TF_i" method and the "ATF" method.

2.4.1 "TF_i" Method for Determining Accumulative ESAL

As shown in Fig. 2-12, the key of the "TF_i" method is to determine the truck factor of each type of vehicles. Once the TF_i is determined, the accumulative ESAL of the vehicle type i can be easily determined based on the flowchart shown in Fig. 2-12. Then the total ESAL is a sum of T_i.

2.4.2 "ATF" Method for Determining Accumulative ESAL

As shown in Fig. 2-13, the key of the "ATF" method is to determine the average truck factor. Once the ATF is determined, the accumulative ESAL can be easily determined based on the flowchart shown in Fig. 2-13.

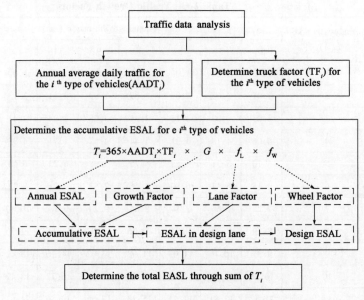

Fig. 2-12 Flowchart of determining the accumulative ESAL with the "TF_i" method

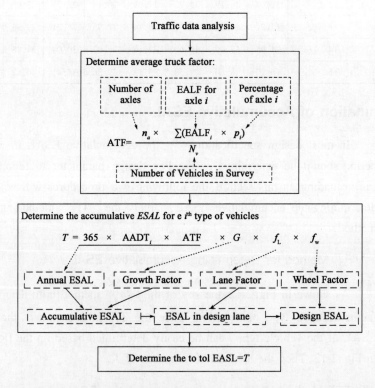

Fig. 2-13 Flowchart of determining the accumulative EASL with the "ATF" method

2.5 Pavement Environment and Effects

Different from the other civil engineering structures, pavement is a long, narrow, and layered structure that is exposed to various and complex environmental conditions. Therefore, environmental conditions are the major design considerations of both flexible and rigid pavements. Temperature and water are two important environmental parameters which will be detailed in the subsequent contents.

2.5.1 Temperatures in Pavement Structure

Impacted by various levels of solar radiation, winds, ambient temperatures, geographic locations, etc., pavement temperatures are various from hour to hour, month to month, and year to year, from regions to regions, one location to another, and surface to top as demonstrated below.

Pavement temperatures are various from hour to hour and one location to another: As shown in Fig. 2-14 a), asphalt pavement temperature of 2cm beneath the surface is 23℃ at mid-night and it increases to 50.5℃ at 2:00pm in the afternoon. The temperature difference is 27.5℃. As shown in Fig. 2-14 b), concrete pavement temperature of 1.5cm beneath the surface is 22.9℃ at mid-night, 21.5℃ at 6:00am in the morning, and then increasing to 31.5℃ at 3:00pm. As shown in Fig. 2-14, pavement temperatures in different depths are various from hour to hour: temperatures in different depths within concrete pavements are various in a synchronous way, while temperatures in different depths within the asphalt pavement are also various, but they are not as synchronous as those in the concrete pavement.

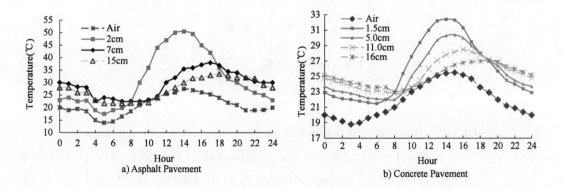

Fig. 2-14 Pavement temperatures various during the day of May 27th 1980

Fig. 2-15 shows asphalt pavement and concrete pavement temperature variations with depth. The following findings can be observed that: a) 8:00am and 5:00pm are the two turning time points for asphalt pavements. From 8:00am to 5:00pm, the pavement temperatures are decreasing from top to bottom (the top surface has the highest temperature), while from 5:00pm to 8:00am of the next day, the pavement temperatures are increasing and then decreasing from top to bottom (the middle depth of the asphalt course has the highest temperature). b) 8:00am and 8:00pm are two turning points for the rigid pavement temperature variation. At 8:00am, the temperatures are decreasing and then increasing with depth (the highest temperature is at 7cm). From 9:00am to 8:00pm the pavement temperatures are decreasing from top to bottom (the maximum temperature is at the top surface) while from 8:00pm to 8:00am of the next day, the pavement temperatures are increasing from top to bottom (the maximum temperature is at the bottom).

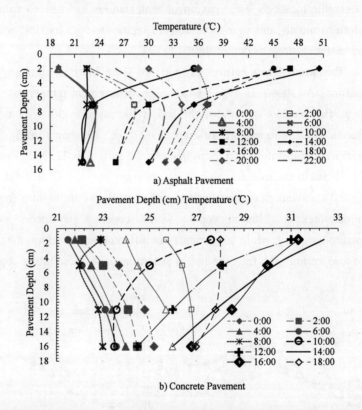

Fig. 2-15 Temperature vs pavement depth from mid-night to 7:00 at morning

It should be noted herein, the original data of Fig. 2-14 ~ Fig. 2-17 from the Chinese textbook[1,9] and it was collected in an unknown region of China in May 27th 1980.

Temperatures are various from month to month and from one location to another; as shown in Fig. 2-16, the three cities in the United States of America are significantly different. The monthly temperatures of Honolulu from January to December are similar to each other; the monthly temperatures are ranging from 25 ℃ to 30 ℃. However, the temperatures of the other two cities are significantly different from month to month; the monthly temperature differences between January and July are over 20 ℃.

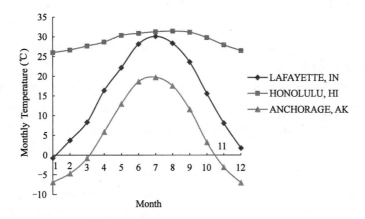

Fig. 2-16 Temperatures of three cities in the United States of America

Temperatures are various from year to year. As shown in Fig. 2-17, in the same location, the monthly average temperatures may be significantly different from year to year; the monthly temperature in December can be as large as 9.1.

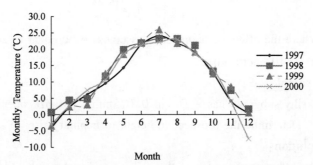

Fig. 2-17 Average monthly temperatures of Lafayette from 1997 to 2000

In summary, pavement temperatures are always changing and dependent on pavement types, seasons, regions, pavement depths, winds, rainfall, etc. Therefore, efforts should be made to understand the fundamentals about pavement temperatures.

2.5.2 Water in Pavement Structure

In addition to temperature, water is another important factor which should be paid special attentions to. However, the effects of water and the need for drainage are often overlooked in pavement design and construction. Three sources of water should be taken into consideration in pavement design and construction, namely groundwater seepage, capillary action, and precipitation which will be discussed in this section.

Ground Water: Groundwater becomes an issue when the water table rises to intersect the pavement layers. If that is the case, the drainage system should be improved by lowering the water table below pavement layers. Details are out of the scope of this chapter and will be provided in the later chapter or references of road drainage design.

Capillary action: Capillary action is important for moving water around. It is defined as the movement of water within the space of a porous material due to the forces of adhesion, cohesion and surface tension. The forces of cohesion occurs because water molecules like to stay close together, while the force of adhesion occurs because water molecules are attracted and stick to other substances. Adhesion of water will cause an upward force on the liquid at the edges and result in a meniscus which turns upward. The surface tension acts to hold the surface intact. Capillary action occurs when the adhesion is stronger than the cohesive forces between the liquid molecules. In geotechnical engineering, the capillary rise above the water table, h_c (meters), can be computed as inversely proportional to the effective diameter of the soil pores, d (mm):

$$h_c = \frac{0.03}{d} \quad (2\text{-}11)$$

Where the effective diameter is assumed to be equal to 20% of the D_{10} grain size (i.e., 10th percentile).

Example 2-5:

A silty subgrade has a D_{10} of 0.075mm (the size opening of the No. 2000 sieve). Determine the prospective height of capillary rise.

Solution:

The effective diameter of the soil pores for this subgrade $d = 0.2 \times 0.075 = 0.015$. Submit d into Equation 2-11, the capillary rise $h_c = 0.03/0.015 = 2$ (meters).

Precipitation: The main source of water in the pavement layers is from precipitation or rainfall. However, designers often pay less attention to this water resource since they believe that the subgrade is permeable or pavement surface is impermeable. The fact is that pavement surfaces are permeable and waters can enter into pavement structure through cracks, voids, or joints, while subgrade is permeable, but its drainability is still limited. This point is well expressed in Cedergren stating: "most of the world's pavements are so leaky that far more water soaks in than can drain away into the subsoil." There are two considerations in handling precipitation and drainage in pavement design:

- In order to prevent pavement layer saturation, drainage rates need to be larger than infiltration rates.
- If pavement layers become saturated, they need to be drained within a

prescribed period to prevent traffic-associated or frost-associated damage. Details on drainage, infiltration rates, frost-associated or traffic associated damage of saturated pavements are out of the scope of this chapter.

2.5.3 Impacts of Environmental Conditions on Pavements

As mentioned above, the two primary environmental factors, which should be considered in the pavement design, are temperature and water. Both factors are not constants and changing during the pavement life. This section herein discusses on mechanism and examples of those factors impacting pavement performance:

Mechanisms of environment impacting pavement performance can be categorized into the following types: first of all, environment may directly affect pavement material properties. For example, increasing temperatures result in decreasing of asphalt material stiffness. Increasing water contents result in reduced shear strength of unbound granular materials. Secondly, changing of environmental conditions may result in additional internal stresses within the pavement structure. For instance, changing of temperature or water contents may result in changing of pavement material volume. When the volume changing is restricted by material boundaries, stresses may be created within the pavement materials and the boundaries.

Impacts of temperature on asphalt concrete stiffness are illustrated in Fig. 2-18: with temperature increasing, both dynamic modulus and creep stiffness of asphalt concrete materials are significantly decreasing. As shown in Figure 2-18a), dynamic modulus values of -5℃ at different loading frequencies are more than 12GPa, while they are reduced to less than 3GPa when the temperature is increasing to 21℃. As shown in Fig. 2-18b), the creep stiffness of 1second at -20℃ is more than 11GPa, while the stiffness at 0℃ is reduced to less than 3GPa,

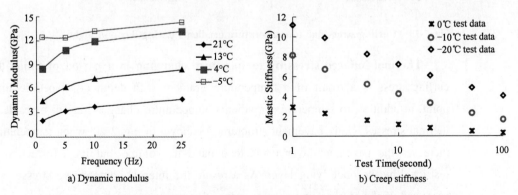

Fig. 2-18 Effects of temperature on asphalt concrete stiffness

Thermal-induced stress by temperature gradients with depth: as illustrated in Fig. 2-15, temperatures are always different from top to bottom of both asphalt and concrete pavements. In other words, temperature gradients exist in pavement structures and inevitable. As shown in Fig. 2-19, during the daytime, a pavement layer has higher temperature on the surface and lower temperature at the bottom. As a result, it tends to curve upward, while in the night time, the pavement layer has lower temperature on the surface and higher temperature at the bottom, it tends to curve downward. Therefore, the pavement surface has compression during the daytime and tension in the nighttime, while the bottom of the pavement layer has tension in the daytime and compression in the nighttime. The higher values of the temperature gradient are, the larger damage on the pavement layer is. Theoretically, the curling stresses exist in both asphalt and concrete pavements. In fact, the curling stresses in concrete pavements are much more significant than those in asphalt pavements which behave visco-elastically and have a better capability of relaxation. Therefore, curling stress is considered as an important factor in the rigid pavement design and paid less attentions in the asphalt pavement design. It should be noted, however, that the curling stress should be considered for asphalt pavements under the following two situations: ① the extremely large temperature gradients; ② the extremely low temperatures.

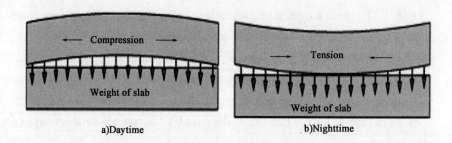

Fig. 2-19 Curling stress due to temperature gradients during day and night

Thermal-induced stress by temperature changing in a period of time: the curling stress is a result of a temperature gradient with depth at a specific time point. In addition to temperature gradients, temperature changes may also result in thermal stresses within pavement structure. As shown in Fig. 2-20, when temperature increases, the pavement layer tends to expand its volume, but its deformation is restricted by the underlying layer. As a result, the internal compressive stresses are produced. If the temperature is decreasing, the tensile stresses are produced due to the pavement layer contraction.

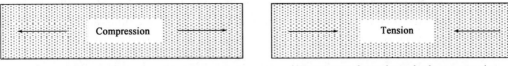

a) Temperature increasing and volume expansion   b) Temperature decreasing and volume contraction

Fig. 2-20 Compressive & tensile stresses due to temperature changing

Effects of water contents on subgrade or soil-like material modulus: subgrade strength is from the effective stress of soils which are negatively impacted by the water content. When the subgrade reaches the saturated state, the subgrade will lose all of its shear strength. Fig. 2-21 shows the effects of water content on subgrade soil resilient modulus (MR). It can be observed that the resilient modulus decreases from 100MPa to 20MPa with water contents increasing from 18% to 30%.

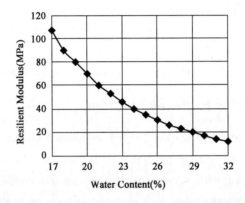

Fig. 2-21 Resilient modulus vs water contents of subgrade soils

Frost-thaw effects under heavy traffic: in the winter time, the freezing of pore water in frost-susceptible subgrade may result in heaving and higher resilient modulus, while during the spring-thaw conditions, the base or subgrade layers can be sufficiently weakened by the presence of pore water to fail under the action of heavy axles. If that is the case, considerations should be provided during pavement design and construction. For instance, measures should be taken to prevent or minimize frost-thaw effects by utilizing carefully-designed materials or pavement structures.

Pumping and faulting in jointed Portland concrete pavement: the presence of water and rapid movement of truck axles may result in rapid movement of base or subgrade pore water which brings small particles or fillers out through concrete slab joints. This may cause the safety of driving as well as erosion and settlement of downstream slab edge, called *faulting*.

Freezing and thawing of the roadbed soil: freezing and thawing effects on roadbed soils have traditionally been a major concern in pavement engineering. During the freezing phase, the occurrence of frost heaving may cause a reduction in the serviceability of the pavement; while during the thaw-weakening phase, the pavement subgrade may be weakened in terms of modulus and shear strength. Fig. 2-22 shows modulus changes of a pavement.

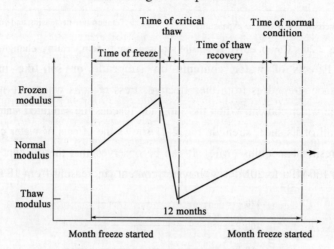

Fig. 2-22 Subgrade modulus variations throughout a year[4]

2.6 Climatic Zoning for Highway in China

As mentioned in section 2.1, environmental conditions are the key factors that may significantly impact pavement performance. Additionally, China covers a vast geographic area with various natural or climatic conditions. In order to facilitate highway pavement design, it is essential to develop methods for characterizing the environmental and natural conditions of different regions. Based on this background, the *standard of Climatic Zoning for Highway*[30] was developed and took effect on January 1st 1987. Followed is a brief introduction to this standard and readers may refer to the original standard for more details.

2.6.1 Three Principles for the Climatic Zoning

With the purpose of facilitating highway infrastructure development, three principles were used in developing climatic zoning standards as follows:

The 1st principle is the *similarity*: factors of concerns in pavement constructions should be similar or identical in the same natural zone. For pavement construction in the northern regions of China, the main concern is pumping effects, while the primary concern becomes rainfalls and erosion for construction in the southern regions of China.

The 2nd principle is the *differential*: different zones should have different temperatures, precipitation, and elevations.

The 3rd principle is the *dominance*: there are various factors which are composed of a natural zone. Among those factors, some are leading factors that govern the primary climatic conditions, while others are minor factors that give fewer effects on pavement construction and in-service performance. For instance, in the southern part of China, interaction effects of water and temperature are not main concerns since it is less possible to have frost-heave and thaw-weakening effects. In this case, water is the major concern in dividing climatic zones. In the northern part of China, the northwesten and the northeast regions have similar low temperatures, but the northwest regions have less water than the northeasten regions. As a result, the former has less frost-thaw effects than the latter. Therefore, the leading factor is water instead of temperatures in the northen part of China.

2.6.2 Climatic Zoning for Highway Engineering

Based on the three principles above, the climatic zoning was divided into three levels, namely level 1, level 2, and level 3. A total of seven level-1 natural zones are divided and denoted by I, II, III ······ VII, 33 level-2 zones are developed under level 1 zones and denoted by I_1, I_2, II_1, II_2 ······ and 19 deputy zones under the level-2 zones denoted by II_{2a}, II_{4a} ······ The level 3 natural zones are developed by each province and no national specification are provided in the climatic zoning standard[30].

(1) **The level-1 natural zones**: the seven level-1 natural zones are created mainly based on annual average temperature, the monthly average temperature in January, and elevation. The annual average temperature of −2 ℃ is the division line between permafrost and seasonally frozen regions, while the January monthly average temperature of 0 ℃ is the division line between the seasonally frozen regions and the never-frozen regions. In terms of elevations, contour lines of 3000m and 1000m are the two division lines used for dividing natural zones. In addition to the three primary indicators, the humidity coefficient is also referred for dividing level-1 natural zones, but it is the key indicator for dividing the level 2 zones as demonstrated below. The climatic zoning specification[30] presents details of the seven level-1 zones and their corresponding features which include zone number, zone names, annual average temperature, the monthly average temperature of January, the max frozen depth, the humidity coefficient, the elevation, and soil types. The seven level-1 natural zones are numbered as I, II, III, IV, V, VI, and VII.

(2) **The level-2 natural zones** are divided mainly based on the humidity coefficient. The humidity coefficient K is defined as the ratio of the annual rainfall R(mm) to the annual evaporation loss Z (mm):

$$K = \frac{R}{Z} \qquad (2\text{-}12)$$

(3) **The level-3 natural zones** are divided under the 52 level-2 zones by each province based on the following conditions: ① hydrothermal, geographical, and geomorphic conditions; ②geomorphic, hydrological, and soil conditions or properties.

2.7 Climate Zones for Asphalt Pavement Performance

Compared with other civil engineering materials, asphalt materials have viscoelastic or visco-plastic properties and their performance is significantly dependent on temperature and moisture conditions. In order to do better design and construct asphalt pavements, the climate zoning method was developed through the *National Scientific Key Project of the Eighth Five-Year Plan* in the 1990s. The climate zoning method was developed based on the climate data of 30 years from 615 weather stations. Three key factors or indices were considered in the development of the climate zoning methods, namely high temperatures, low temperatures, and annual rainfall. Based on the three key factors or indices, the entire China was divided into various climate zones as described below:

(1) **High-temperature index**: the high temperature is defined as the highest average temperature of the hottest month in the past 30 years. Based on the high-temperature index, climate zones are divided into three levels as shown in Table 2-7: the climate zone 1 is the burning hot summer zone, the zone 2 is the hot summer zone, and the zone 3 is the cool summer zone.

Table 2-7 Climate zones based on the highest temperature

High-temperature Zones	1	2	3
Zone Names	Extremely hot in summer	Hot in summer	Cool in summer
Highest monthly temperature in the past 30 years (℃)	>30	20~30	<20

(2) **Low-temperature index**: the low temperature is defined as the extreme low temperature of the past 30 years. Based on the low-temperature index, climate zones are divided into four levels as shown in Table 2-8: zone 1 is the zone of extremely cold winter, zone 2 is the zone of severe cold winter, zone 3 is the zone of cold winter, and zone 4 is the zone of warm winter.

Table 2-8 Climate zones based on the lowest temperature

Low-temperature zones	1	2	3	4
Zone names	Extremely cold winter	Very cold winter	Cold winter	Warm winter
The extreme low temperature (℃) of the past 30 years	<-37.0	[-37.0, -21.5]	[-21.5, -9]	>-9

(3) **Annual Rainfall Index**: Based on the annual rainfall index, climate zones are divided into four levels as shown in Table 2-9: zone 1 is the over-wet zone, zone 2 is the wet zone, zone 3 is the dry zone, and the zone 4 is the over-dry zone.

Table 2-9 Climate zones based on the annual rainfall

Annual zones	1	2	3	4
Zone names	Over-wet	Wet	Dry	Over-dry
Annual rainfall (mm)	>1000	[1000,500]	[500,250]	<250

Combining the three indices, a specific zone can be denoted as f-s-t where f is 1, 2, or 3 and s or t can be 1, 2, 3, or 4. Readers may find details in the national specification of asphalt pavement construction[7,8].

Example 2-6:

Given a climate zone is 1-2-3, determine its high-temperature, the lowest temperature, and annual rainfall of this zone.

Solution:

From Table 2-7, the high temperature is higher than 30 ℃. From Table 2-8, the low temperature is between -37℃ and -21℃. From Table 2-9, the annual rainfall is about 250 ~ 500mm.

2.8 Temperature Gradient for Rigid Pavement Design

2.8.1 Heat in Pavements

Since the solar radiation and ambient temperatures are changing from time to time, the pavement surface temperature is various and temperature gradients with depth are produced. These temperature gradients may give significant effects on both flexible and rigid pavement behaviors: for flexible pavements, temperatures affect asphalt modulus and in turn affects pavement fatigue and plastic deformation, while for rigid pavements, temperature gradients result in thermal stresses as discussed below:

(1) **Direct tensile or compressive thermal stress due to uniform temperature changing**: when temperatures are slowly changing from T1 to T2, thermal stresses produced in concrete slabs are direct tensile or compressive. This type of thermal stresses may result in concrete slab broken. More details will be given in Chapter 9.

(2) **Thermal curling stress due to temperature gradients with depth**: curling stresses are very common in concrete pavements. As shown in Fig. 2-19, during the daytime, a concrete slab has higher temperature on the surface and lower temperature at the bottom, as a result, it tends to curve upward; while in the night

time, the concrete slab has lower temperature on the surface and higher temperature in the bottom, it tends to curve downward. Therefore, the concrete slab surface has compression during the daytime and tension in the nighttime, while the bottom of the slab has tension in the daytime and compression in the nighttime. The higher values of the temperature gradient are, the larger damage in the concrete slab is.

2.8.2 Temperature Gradients in Rigid Pavement Design

Compared with asphalt materials, cement concrete materials have less temperature-dependent properties, but they are significantly impacted by temperature differences. Therefore, the max temperature gradient (T_g) is taken as an important design input for cement concrete design. Table 2-10 shows the empirical values of T_g in different natural zones. It should be noted that the values in the table are not the best or most accurate values. If there are data from field tests, the authors would suggest to utilize the field-measured T_g as pavement design inputs.

Table 2-10 Maximum temperature gradient (T_g) for rigid pavement design

Highway natural zones	II & V	III	IV & VI	VII
Maximum temperature gradient (°C/m)	83 ~ 88	90 ~ 95	86 ~ 92	93 ~ 98

Note: 1. the higher elevation the larger value of the maximum temperature gradient;
2. the higher humidity the smaller value of the maximum temperature gradient.

2.9 Summary and Key Points in Chapter 2

This chapter has discussed on environmental concerns in pavement design, which covers environmental factors and their effects, the national climatic zoning methods, climate zoning methods for asphalt materials, and temperature gradient for cement concrete pavement design. Of course, there are many other aspects pertinent to the pavement environment, but they are out of the scope of this book.

As mentioned in reference[24], the importance of environmental factors in pavement design cannot be overemphasized and adequate design provisions should be given to control the effects of various environmental conditions. Even though efforts have been made in the past decades and considerations should be made on climatic zoning for highways and climate zoning for asphalt pavements, there is still a lack of fundamental understanding of various environment-related pavement distresses and efficient methods for characterizing environmental effects in pavement design. Therefore, additional efforts should be made in this area especially on integrating the currently developed new technologies into pavement design as demonstrated in the mechanistic pavement design guide (MEPDG).

Problems

1. Could you tell the reasons why vehicles and axles are categorized into different types?

2. For asphalt pavements, in the climatic zone 1-2-4 the number '1' represents the highest temperature, the number of '2' represents (   ), and the number of '4' represents (   ).

3. A truck has three axles whose EALF of the front wheel is 0.05 and the two rear axles are 0.5 and 0.45. The truck factor is (   ).

4. In order to characterize daily traffic, AADT is commonly used to calculate the accumulative traffic volume. Full name of AADT is (   ).

5. Could you explain the concepts of truck factor, average truck factor, equivalent axle load factor (EALF), and equivalent single axle loads (ESAL)?

6. With the WIM method, the weight of an empty truck is 145kN where the front axle load is 45kN and the two rear axle loads are 50kN. After it is fully loaded with 210kN of the cargo, its front axle load becomes 55kN and each of the two rear axle loads become 150kN. (1) Compute the total ESAL caused by one pass of this truck (empty and full). (2) Determine the pavement-related efficiency of this vehicle in terms of the kN of cargo carried per ESAL. (3) If the half-full cargo is carried by this truck, the front axle load is 50kN and each of the two rear axle loads is 100kN, compute the pavement-related efficiency of this truck. Given the pavement type is rigid pavement and EALF is shown in the Figure. P2-1.

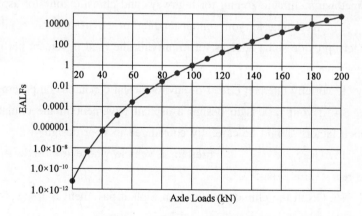

Fig. P2-1 EALFs vs Axle Loads

7. There are two types of pavement-tire interactions, namely static and dynamic. Could you explain the features of those two types of interactions?

8. Given the monthly average daily traffic volume of January in 2017 and the monthly increasing rate is 5%. Determine the AADT.

9. Given the AADT of type 3, type 7, type 8, and type 9 are 1500, 1800, 500, and 900, determine the vehicle class distribution factors (VCDFs) of those four types of vehicles.

10. Fig. P2-2 shows a vehicle of type 5. The axle loads of the front axle and the rear tridem axle are 50 kN and 210kN. (1) Determine the truck factor for the asphalt pavement design; (2) Determine the truck factor for the concrete pavement design.

Fig. P2-2 Axle configuration of the type 5 vehicle

Notes: The EALF can be determined through the Fig. P2-1 for the concrete pavement design while it can be determined in Equation below for the asphalt pavement design.

$$\text{EALF} = 3.2 \times \left(\frac{p_i}{p_s}\right)^4 \qquad (\text{P2-1})$$

11. Based on what you have learned from this chapter, tell and describe your hometown's climatic zoning for highways and climatic zone for asphalt pavements.

12. According to your understanding of environmental conditions and their effects, provide some advices for improving the road pavement performance in your hometown.

13. Briefly interpret effects of environmental conditions on pavement performance.

14. If your task is to design a asphalt pavement in the climatic zone 1-1-4, which factors should be carefully considered in your design?

15. There are _____ tires for a vehicle whose front axle is type-1 axle and the rear axle is type-5.

16. Given the climatic zone of an asphalt pavement is 1-4-1, could you tell the possible natural zones?

17. Pavement traffic loading is a kind of repeated load. In other words, pavement deterioration is a result of traffic loading repetitions. But sometimes, overloading may also result in pavement damage in one time of load application. How do you think this statement?

18. For the concrete pavement with a slab of 25cm, the temperature gradient is

_____ ℃/m if the temperatures for the top surface and bottom surface of the slab are 35℃ and 15℃, respectively.

19. Traffic loading is not only the pavement service condition, but also one of the most important design factors. AADT, AADTT, ESAL, EALF, TF, ATF, and VCDF are some of the key concepts for characterizing traffic loading. Could you illustrate their relations with examples?

20. According to the Chinese standard, vehicle axles are classified into seven types, the type-1 and type-2 axles are the single axles, type-3, type-4, and type-5 are the _____ axles, while type-6 and type-7 are the _____ axles.

21. The axle load spectrum is defined as a histogram of the axle loads vs the corresponding frequencies (percentage of a specific axle load). The x-coordinate is the axle load at the interval of 2.5kN for single axle on single tires, _____ kN for single axle on dual tires, 9.0 for tandem axles, and 13.5kN for the triple axles in the asphalt pavement design specification, while the x-coordinate is the axle load at the interval of _____ kN in the concrete pavement design specification. The interval values may be different for different projects as long as they are convenient and accurate.

22. There are three types of vehicles running on a road. The traffic data of those three types of trucks are: AADTTs = 1000, 500, and 100; TFs = 1.3, 2.0 and 2.5. Compute the daily ESAL _____.

3. Subgrade Soils and Pavement Materials

3.1 Subgrade Soil Classification

The target of soil classification is to identify suitable subgrade materials and predict the probable behaviors through systematically categorizing soils according to their engineering characteristics. It should be noted that the detailed investigation of the soil properties is still essential even though the engineering properties of given soils can be predicted reliably from its classification. There are two commonly used methods for soil classification, namely the *American Association of the State Highway and Transportation Officials (AASHTO), Classification System* and the *Unified Soil Classification System (USCS)*. In Chinese textbook, the AASHTO classification system is not introduced while a modified version of the USCS method is included. In this textbook, both the modified USCS and the AASTHO classification system are briefly stated in this section.

3.1.1 Modified Unified Soil Classification System

As demonstrated in Chinese textbook edited by Prof. Xiaoming Huang, based on the sieve size distribution, plasticity index, organic materials soils are classified into four major groups, namely the over coarse-grained soils, the coarse-grained soils, the fine-grained soils, and special soils. As shown in Fig. 3-1, the four groups of soils are sub-divided into 12 different types.

(1) **Over Coarse-grained Soils** are referred to those soils with more than 15% of particle larger than 60mm. For soils with more than 75% by weight having particle size larger than 60mm, it can be classified as boulder (cobble); for soils with 50% ~ 75% by weight having particle size larger than 60mm, it can be classified as boulder (grait) with soil; for soils with 15% ~ 50% by weight having particle size larger than 60mm, it can be classified as soil with boulder (graits).

(2) **Coarse-grained Soils**: For soils with less than 15% by weight having particles size larger than 60mm and more than 50% by weight having particles size larger than 0.075mm, it can be classified as coarse-grained soils. For coarse-grained soil, it can be identified as gravel type soil if there are more gravel particles than sand particles, otherwise it can be identified as sand type soil.

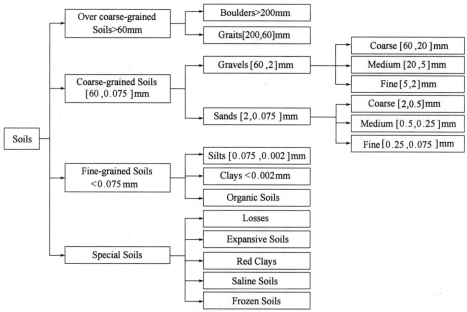

Fig. 3-1 The Soil Classification System for Highway Engineering in China

(3) **Fine-grained Soils are** referred to those with more than 50% particles smaller than 0.075mm. Its classification system can be referred to Fig. 3-6. For fine-grained soil with less 25% coarse-grained particles by weight of total soil samples, it can be identified as either silty-soil or clayey soil; For fine-grained soil with 25% ~ 50% coarse-grained particles by weight of total soil samples, it can be identified as either silty-soil or clayey soil with coarse-grained soils; For soils with 5% ~ 10% organic materials, it can be classified as soil with organic materials (You Ji Zhi Tu in Chinese); For soils more than 10% organic materials, it can be classified as organic soil (You Ji Tu in Chinese).

(4) **Special Soils** are referred to loess, expansive soil, red clay, salty soils, and frozen soils. Loess is clay with low liquid limit (CLY); expansive soil is clay with high liquid limit (CHE); and red clay is silt with high liquid limit (MHR). The salty soils are with higher percentage of salty materials while the frozen soils are referred to the subgrade soils under the freezing conditions.

More details about this soil classification system can be found in the Chinese textbooks[1,9,10] and the specification of laboratory testing of soils[11].

3.1.2 AASHTO Soil Classification System

In highway engineering, the most popularly used method for classifying soils is the AASHTO soil classification system[12]. Soils are classified into seven groups, A-1 through A-7, with several subgroups based on its particle size distribution, liquid limit, and plastic index as shown in Table 3-1. Within each group, soils are

Table 3-1 AASHTO Classification of Soils and Soil Aggregate Mixtures

General Classification	Granular Materials (35% or Less Passing No. 200)							Silt-Clay Materials (More than 35% Passing No. 200)			
	A-1		A-3	A-2				A-4	A-5	A-6	A-7
Group Classification	A-1-a	A-1-b		A-2-4	A-2-5	A-2-6	A-2-7				A-7-5, A-7-6
Sieve analysis											
Percent passing											
No. 10	50 max.	—	—	—	—	—	—	—	—	—	—
No. 40	30 max.	50 max.	51 min.	—	—	—	—	—	—	—	—
No. 200	15 max.	25 max.	10 max.	35 max.	35 max	35 max.	35 max.	36 min.	36 min.	36 min.	36 min.
Characteristics of fraction passing No. 40:											
Liquid limit	—	—	—	40 max.	41 min.	40 max.	41 min.	40 max.	41 min.	40 max.	41 min.
Plasticity index	6 max.		N.P.	10 max.	10 max.	11 min.	11 min.	10 max.	10 max.	11 min.	11 min.
Usual types of significant constituent materials	Stone fragments, gravel and sand		Fine sand	Silty or clayey gravel and sand				Silty soils		Clayey soils	
General rating as subgrade	Excellent to good							Fair to poor			

* Plasticity index of A-7-5 subgroup $\leq$ LL − 30. Plasticity index of A-7-6 subgroup > LL − 30.

SOURCE: Adapted from standard Specifications for Transportation Materials and Methods of Sampling and Testing, 27th ed., Washingtom, D. C., The American Association of State Highway and Transportationg Officials, copyright 2007. Used with permission.

3. Subgrade Soils and Pavement Materials

evaluated through using an empirical equation to determine the group index (GI). Fig. 3-2 shows the empirical equation and the meanings of each parameter in the equation.

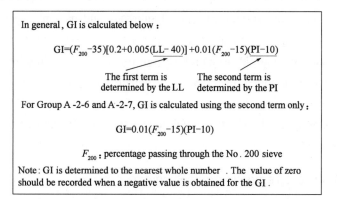

Fig. 3-2 The Soil Classification System for Highway

Example 3-1:

From testing of a soil sample, data is listed in the table below: determine the classification of the soil.

Sieve No	Percent Finer	Plasticity Tests
4	97	LL = 48%
10	93	PL = 26%
40	88	
100	78	
200	70	

Solution:

Since more than 35% of the materials passes the No. 200 sieve, the soil is either A-4, A-5, A-6, or A-7. LL > 40%, therefore the soil cannot be in group A-4 or A-6. Thus, it belongs to either A-5 or A-7. The PI = 48% - 26% = 22% > 10%, thus eliminating group A-5 is eliminated. The soil is A-7-5 or A-7-6. LL-30 = 18 < PI = 22%, therefore the soil is A-7-6. Through Fig. 3-2, GI = 15. Therefore, the soil is A-7-6(15).

3.1.3 Engineering Properties

Soils classified as A-1-a, A-1-b, A-2-4, A-2-5, and A-3 can be used satisfactorily as subgrade or subbase material if properly drained. In addition, such soils must be properly compacted and covered with an adequate thickness of pavement (base and/or surface cover) for the surface load to be carried.

When soils are properly drained and compacted, their value as subgrade material decreases as the GI increases. For example, a soil with a GI of zero (an indication of a good subgrade material) will be better as a soil with GI > 0.

3.2 Subgrade Moisture Conditions and Evaluation

As mentioned in Chapter 2, the key environmental factors are temperature and water which can significantly affect subgrade and pavement performance in several ways: ①Temperature and water contents are various from time to time throughout the year and can have an effect on the strength, durability, and load-carrying capacity of roadbed materials; ② Another major impact is the direct effect on roadbed swelling, pavement blowups, frost heave, etc. In this section herein discusses subgrade moisture conditions which are determined by water contents and temperatures.

3.2.1 Water and Temperature in Subgrade

As demonstrated in the reference[1], temperature and water must be presented simultaneously for the frost-thaw effects on the pavement subgrade. The sources of water may be from the underlying ground water table, infiltration or gravitational flow, and the water held within the voids of fine-grained soils:

(1) **Underlying ground water** may enter the pavement roadbed region due to water table increasing, capillarity action, and temperature variation. Effects of this type of water sources are dependent on roadbed soil types and climatic conditions. The capillarity action becomes severer for fine-grained soils and the water moves from the locations of high temperatures to those of low temperatures.

(2) **Infiltration or gravitational flow** may enter the roadbed region through cracks, joints, shoulders, and the medium strip. The original water sources may be from rainfall, melted snow, and etc. Effects of this type of water sources are dependent on climatic conditions and the pavement drainage system. For a relative dry region or a well-designed drainage system, only very limited water may be retained in the roadbed and therefore the roadbed may receive very limited effects of this type of water sources.

(3) **The water held within the voids of fine-grained soils** may directly impact the roadbed performance. This type of water sources may be retained in the newly-built roadbed or in the in-service roadbed.

Temperatures are various from day to day throughout the year and usually indirectly impact roadbed soils through coupling the effects of water retained in the subgrade. Followed are two major concerns of subgrade temperatures:

(1) Temperatures may result in water moving from the higher temperature regions to the lower temperature regions. As a result, water may move from the bottom to up during the winter time while it may move from up to bottom during

the summer time.

(2) Temperatures may make water frozen in the winter time and melted in the spring time for highway engineering in a seasonal frost area. As a result, the subgrade performance may be various from one season to another as demonstrated in Fig. 3-3: In the winter time frost-heave effects may occur while in the spring time thaw-weakening may occur. Both frost-heave and thaw-weakening are detrimental to subgrade and pavement structures.

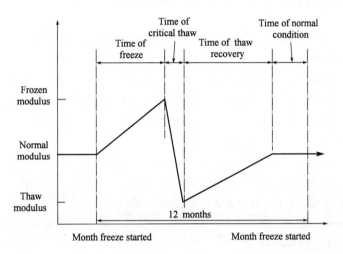

Fig. 3-3 **Representation of roadbed modulus variations through a year**

3.2.2 Subgrade Moisture Conditions

Water retained in subgrade may result in different moisture conditions which significantly impact roadbed soil engineering properties. Therefore, in most design specifications[3,13,14], subgrade moisture conditions should be classified:

In the *National Subgrade Design Specification* (2015)[13] subgrade is classified into three moisture conditions of wet, moist, and dry based on the equilibrium moisture contents.

In the *National Asphalt Pavement Design Specification* (2006)[14] subgrade is classified into four moisture conditions of over-wet, wet, moist, and dry based on the average consistency of the roadbed and the subgrade critical height.

The fact, however, is that the moisture conditions are various from one season to another for a specific roadbed. For a seasonal frost area, a roadbed may experience over-wet, wet, moist, and dry conditions from spring to winter. It is hard to represent a subgrade moisture condition with a fixed parameter. In the AASHTO pavement design guide[4], one year is separated into different component time intervals where different moisture conditions are defined. For instance, one year may be divided into four time intervals namely the frozen season (from mid-January to mid-February), the wet periods (March through May and mid-September through mid-November), and the dry periods (June through mid-September and mid-November through mid-January). After separating the time intervals and determining the moisture conditions, the design parameters (resilient modulus for instance) may be determined according to the moisture conditions.

3.2.3 Subgrade Moisture Evaluation Methods

According to the national pavement design specifications[2,3], the subgrade should be in dry or moist conditions in order to guarantee road pavement's stability and deformation performance. If subgrade is in wet conditions, special treatments should be given before constructing the pavement structure. Therefore, it is necessary to measure or estimate subgrade wet condition. There are different methods for this purpose. Followed is a brief introduction to those methods:

The first method is equilibrium moisture prediction method.

During the service life, subgrade moisture values are various from time to time due to effects of the water table and surface water. However, the variation rate may become stable after 2~3 years. The moisture at the stable variation rate is called the equilibrium moisture.

As shown in Fig. 3-4a), when capillary wetting surface is below the subgrade work zone, the subgrade moisture is mainly impacted by climatic conditions. Therefore, this condition is defined as the dry condition. As shown in Fig. 3-4b), when capillary wetting surface is above the roadbed surface, the entire subgrade is under effects of capillary water. This condition is considered as the wet condition. As shown in Fig. 3-4c), When the capillary wetting surface is within the subgrade work zone, the subgrade moisture may be impacted by both the climatic conditions and the capillary water. This condition is called the moist condition, 'dry', 'wet', 'moist' are the three basic moisture conditions.

The key considerations of the equilibrium moisture prediction method are 'saturability' and 'Thornthwaite Moisture Index (TMI)'. Under the wet condition, Table 3-2 may be used for determining the saturability when soil types and water table are given. Under the dry condition, users may first determine the TMI through looking up Table 3-3 and then determine saturability through looking up Table 3-4. Under the moist condition, subgrade soil saturability can be determined by dividing the roadbed into two parts whose moisture conditions are dry and wet, respectively. The weighted average value of the two saturabilities are used to evaluate the subgrade moisture condition.

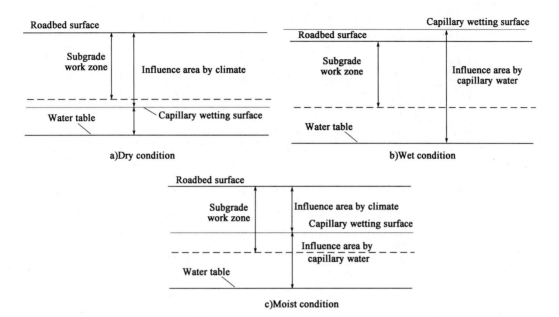

Fig. 3-4 Demonstration of equilibrium moisture

Table 3-2 Saturability of subgrade soils under the wet condition(%)

Soil Types	Distance between the water table and a specific position (m)						
	0.3	1.0	1.5	2.0	2.5	3.0	4.0
Silty gravels(GM)	69~84	55~69	50~65	49~62	45~59	43~57	—
Clayey graves (GC)	79~96	64~83	60~79	56~75	54~73	52~71	—
Sands(S)	95~80	70~50	—	—	—	—	—
Silty sands(SM)	79~93	64~77	60~72	56~68	54~66	52~64	—
Clayey sands(SC)	90~99	77~87	72~83	68~80	66~78	64~76	—
Silty soils with low liquid limit(ML)	94~100	80~90	76~86	83-73	71~81	69~80	—
Clayey soils with low liquid limit (CL)	93~100	80~93	76~90	73~-88	70~86	68~85	66~83
Silty soils with high liquid limit (MH)	100	90~95	86~92	83~-90	81~89	80~87	—
Clayey soils with high liquid limit (CH)	100	93~97	90~93	88~91	86~90	85~89	83~87

Notes: 1. For sands(SW、SP), the equilibrium moisture is inversely proportional to D60;
2. For the other fine-grained soils, the equilibrium moisture is proportional to the passing percentage of particles less than 0.075mm.

Table 3-3 TMI values under various natural zones

Natural Zone			TMI	Natural Zone		TMI
I		I1	−5.0 ~ −8.1	IV	IV1	21.8 ~ −25.1
		I2	0.5 ~ −9.7		IV1a	23.2
II	II1	Heilongjiang	−0.1 ~ −8.1		IV2	−6.0 ~ 34.8
		Liaoning, Jilin	8.7 ~ 35.1		IV3	34.3 ~ 40.4
		II3a	−3.6 ~ −10.8		IV4	32.0 ~ 67.9
		II2	−7.2 ~ −12.1		IV5	45.2 ~ −89.3
		II2a	−1.2 ~ −10.6		IV6	27.0 ~ 64.7
		II3	−9.3 ~ −26.9		IV6a	41.2 ~ 97.4
		II4	−10.7 ~ −22.6		IV7	16.0 ~ 69.3
		II4a	−15.5 ~ 17.3		IV7b	−5.4 ~ 23.0
		II4b	−7.9 ~ 9.9	VI	VI_1	−15.3 ~ −46.3
		II5	−1.7 ~ −15.6		VI_{1a}	−40.5 ~ −47.2
		II5a	−1.0 ~ −15.6		VI_2	−39.5 ~ −59.2
III		III1	−21.2 ~ −25.7		VI_3	−41.6
		III1a	−12.6 ~ −29.1		VI_4	−19.3 ~ −57.2
		III2	−9.7 ~ −17.5		VI_{4a}	−34.5 ~ −37.1
		III2a	−19.6		VI_{4b}	−2.6 ~ −37.2
		III3	−19.1 ~ 26.1		—	—
		III4	−10.8 ~ −24.1		—	—
V		V1	−25.1 − 6.9	VII	VII_1	−3.1 ~ −56.3
		V2	0.9 ~ 30.1		VII_2	−49.4 ~ −58.1
		V2a	39.6 ~ 43.7		VII_3	−22.5 ~ −82.8
		V3	12.0 ~ 88.3		VII_4	−5.1 ~ −5.7
		V3a	−7.6 ~ 47.2		VII_5	−20.3 ~ −91.4
		V4	−2.6 ~ 50.9		VII_{6a}	−10.6 ~ −25.8
		V5	39.8 ~ 100.6		—	—
		V5a	24.4 ~ 39.2		—	—

Table 3-4 Saturability of subgrade soils of various TMI values(%)

Soil Types	TMI					
	−50	−30	−10	10	30	50
Silty gravels(GM)	20 ~ 50	25 ~ 55	27 ~ 60	30 ~ 65	32 ~ 67	35 ~ 70
Clayey graves (GC)	45 ~ 48	62 ~ 68	73 ~ 80	80 ~ 86	84 ~ 89	87 ~ 90
Sands(S)						
Silty sands(SM)	41 ~ 46	59 ~ 64	75 ~ 77	84 ~ 86	91 ~ 92	92 ~ 93
Clayey sands(SC)	39 ~ 41	57 ~ 64	75 ~ 76	86	91	92 ~ 94
Silty soils with low liquid limit(ML)	41 ~ 42	61 ~ 62	76 ~ 79	85 ~ 88	90 ~ 92	92 ~ 95
Clayey soils with low liquid limit (CL)	39 ~ 51	58 ~ 69	85 ~ 74	86 ~ 92	91 ~ 95	94 ~ 97

Notes: 1. For sands (SW, SP), the equilibrium moisture is inversely proportional to D60;
2. For the other fine-grained soils, the equilibrium moisture is proportional to the passing percentage of particles less than 0.075mm.

The second method is the soil consistence-based method: This method is usually used to evaluate wet or dry conditions of existing road subgrade soils. Through experimental tests, one can measure the average water content (w), the liquid limit(w_L), and the plastic limit (w_P), of roadbed soils. The soil specimens are sampled at 0.8 meter beneath from the roadbed surface. With the measured parameters, the soil consistence (w_C) can be computed in Equation 3-1.

$$w_C = \frac{w_L - w}{w_L - w_P} \qquad (3-1)$$

For a specific soil, the higher value of consistence represents the less moisture content. In the previous national design specification of asphalt pavement[14], with this consistency-based method the subgrade moisture conditions can be classified into four types, namely dry, moist wet, wet, and over-wet as shown in Table 3-5.

Table 3-5 Subgrade consistence and the corresponding moisture condition

	Dry	Moist Wet	Wet	Over-wet
	$w_c \geq w_{c1}$	$w_{c1} > w_c \geq w_{c2}$	$w_{c2} > w_c \geq w_{c3}$	$w_c < w_{c3}$
Clayey Sands	$w_c \geq 1.20$	$1.20 > w_c \geq 1.00$	$1.00 > w_c \geq 0.85$	$w_c < 0.85$
Clayey Soils	$w_c \geq 1.10$	$1.10 > w_c \geq 0.95$	$0.95 > w_c \geq 0.80$	$w_c < 0.80$
Silty Soils	$w_c \geq 1.05$	$1.05 > w_c \geq 0.90$	$0.90 > w_c \geq 0.75$	$w_c < 0.75$

The third method is the critical height-based: this method is suitable to the new-built road pavement design since it is impossible to measure the subgrade water contents during the preliminary design. As is well known, subgrade moisture is pertinent to the water table height and capillary rise. Therefore, the height from the subgrade surface to the water table, denoted by H_0, is employed to characterize subgrade moisture types. The height at the cut-off point between dry and moist wet is denoted by H_1, the one at the cut-off point between moist wet and wet is denoted by H_2, and the one at a cut-off point between wet and over-wet is denoted by H_3. The H_1, H_2, and H_3 are called the critical subgrade heights which are used to distinguish subgrade moisture types.

3.3 Subgrade Bearing Capability

3.3.1 Roadbed Resilient Modulus

As well known, subgrade soils are not elastic, but experience some permanent deformation after each load application. However, when the loading is small enough, the deformation under each loading repetition is almost completely recoverable. If that is the case, the soil material can be considered as an elastic

material. As shown in Fig. 3-5, the strain of a soil specimen under a repeated load test has the following features:
- At the initial stage of loading applications, the permanent deformation is considerably large;
- With the number of repetitions increasing, the plastic strain due to each load repetition decreases;

After hundreds of repetitions, the plastic deformation due to each load repetition is almost equal to zero. In other words, the deformation is recoverable under each loading cycle. The resilient modulus is referred to the deviator stress divided by the recoverable strain when the permanent deformation due to each loading cycle is small enough.

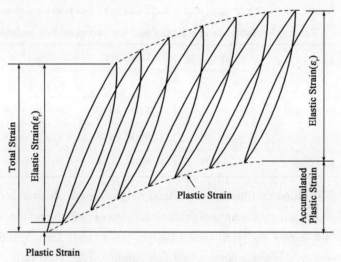

Fig. 3-5 Strain under repeated loading

Roadbed is the top part of a subgrade structure with the thickness of 80cm or 120cm according to the national design specification[13]. As the pavement supporting structure, the roadbed takes traffic loads transferred from the upper pavement layers and its stress-strain relation plays an important role in impacting road pavement performance. Evidently, the roadbed permanent deformation is increasing with the loading repetitions, but the increasing rate depends on the applied load. Under the lower load, the roadbed is gradually compacted into its dense state. As a result, the increasing rate of the accumulated permanent deformation is decreasing until the roadbed reaches its stable conditions. Under a higher load, however, the roadbed is in an un-stable condition during the load applications. As a result, the increasing rate of the accumulative deformation is increasing until the roadbed reaches its failure. Therefore, in the roadbed and pavement design, it is important that the loading on the roadbed surface should be small enough compared with its strength.

There are different types of testing methods for evaluating the resilient modulus, including the triaxial testing, the uniaxial testing, the plate loading testing, and field testing. Details of those testing methods will be founded in the design specifications[2,3,13-14] and some of them will be introduced in Chapter 6.

3.3.2 Roadbed Reaction Stiffness

Another parameter for characterizing the soil material mechanical property is the roadbed reaction stiffness which is also called R-value. When the subgrade is simulated with the Winkler model, the vertical load is proportional to the vertical displacement as shown in the Equation 3-2:

$$K = \frac{P}{W} \tag{3-2}$$

In the equation, P is the applied load, W is the displacement, and K is the reaction stiffness or R-value. The unit is MN/m^3.

3.3.3 Roadbed California Bearing Ratio (CBR)

The California Bearing Ratio (CBR) is an important parameter for determining the relative strength of soil with respect to the standard macadam. The CBR value can be obtained through a penetration test. Details about the testing method can be found in laboratory testing standards and the value can be calculated with the Equation below:

$$\text{CBR} = \frac{p}{p_s} \times 100\% \tag{3-3}$$

In the equation, p and p_s are the pressures of the testing specimen and the standard macadam at penetration displacement $d = 2.54$mm or 5.08mm. The value of p_s is known: when $d = 2.54$mm, $p_s = 7030$kPa; when $d = 5.08$mm, $p_s = 10550$kPa.

3.4 Materials Used in Pavement Engineering

Four categories of pavement materials will be mainly discussed, namely unbound granular or block materials, hydraulically-bound mixtures, asphalt mixtures, and Portland cement concrete. In addition to the four categories of pavement materials that are conventionally used in road construction engineering, reclaimed or recycled pavement materials are also introduced, which include reclaimed asphalt pavement (RAP), cycled cement concrete, etc.

3.4.1 Unbound Granular or Block Materials

Unbound granular or block materials may include improved soils, crushed stones, crushed sands, graded crushed stones, graded gavels, block stones, etc. As shown in Table 2-2, this type of material is mainly used in cushion, base, or subbase layers. Of course, subgrade materials can also be categorized into this type of material. Followed is a brief discussion on definitions and basic requirements pertinent to four different types of unbound materials:

(1) **Graded crushed or gravel stone mixture** is composed of crushed stones or gavels with a specially designed gradation. As shown in Fig. 3-6, the main differences between crushed stones and gravels are particle shapes: the crushed stones have larger angularities than the gravels.

a)Gravels   b)Crushed Stones

Fig. 3-6　Gravels and Crushed Stones

(2) **Water-mixed Stone** is one kind of crushed stone mixtures. Water is used during construction to facilitate the compaction process. This type of materials is mainly used in base or cushion layers.

(3) **Slurry-stabilized Stone** is another kind of crushed stone mixture. Different from water-mixed stones, a Slurry-stabilized stone mixture is composed of crushed stones as coarse aggregates and slurry as filler and binder materials.

(4) **Block materials** include block stones and precast concrete bricks as shown in Fig. 3-7. This type of material mainly used in pavements of streets and pedestrian roads in cities.

a)Precast concrete bricks   b)Block stones

Fig. 3-7　Block Materials

3.4.2 Hydraulically-Bound Mixtures

Hydraulically-bound mixtures (HBM) have been highly used as base or subbase layers in asphalt pavements of expressways, class-one highways and class-two highways. The most popularly used HBM include cement bound mixtures (CBM), lime bound mixtures (LBM), and lime fly-ash bound mixtures (LFBM) as listed in Table 3-6.

Table 3-6 List of semi-rigid base materials used in pavement engineering

Material Type	Source Materials
Cement bound mixtures (CBM)	Cement, water, and granular materials which include graded crushed stones, gravels, and sands and untreated crushed stones, sands, gavels, or soils
Lime bound mixtures (LBM)	Lime, water, and granular materials which include soils, natural gravel soils, crushed stone soils, graded gravels (no soils), graded crushed stones, and slag
Lime-fly ash bound mixtures (LFBM)	Lime, fly ash, water, and granular materials which include soils, cussed stones, gravel sands, sands, and slag

Since cement, lime, fly-ash, and slags are inorganic binders, HBM is also called the inorganic binder stabilized material (IBSM) in Chinese specifications[2,14,28].

3.4.3 Asphalt Materials

Due to the better performance and easy to recycle, asphalt materials have been extensively used in current paving practices. Asphalt materials in paving engineering may include asphalt binders and asphalt mixtures:

(1) **Asphalt Binders** may refer to Petroleum Asphalt, Natural Asphalt, Modified Asphalt, etc. and can be used in asphalt mixtures or directly used in pavement layers. For instance, liquid asphalt binders can be directly used in paving primer layers, tack coats, or seal coats.

(2) **Asphalt Mixtures** are composed of coarse aggregates, fine aggregates, mineral fillers, asphalt, and some additives. Different from unbound mixtures and HBM, asphalt mixtures are mainly used in the surface and base courses of pavement structures. Details of asphalt mixtures are included in the course of *Road Construction Materials*.

In pavement design, attentions should be given to max particle size, time-dependent, temperature-dependent, and water-related properties of asphalt mixtures. For instance, fine-grained asphalt mixtures are used in the upper layer of the asphalt surface course, since the upper surface layer has a smaller thickness. In terms of time-dependent, temperature-dependent, and water-related properties, pavement designers should select asphalt mixture types and proportion design methods based on local conditions.

3.4.4 Concrete Materials

Concrete is composed of aggregates, cement, water, supplementary cementitious and chemical admixtures, and airs. The combination of water and cement is referred as paste, while the combination of paste and fine aggregates is referred as mortar.

Different from asphalt materials, concrete performance is mainly determined by cement hydration which refers to the reaction of cement and water leading to the hardening of the paste. Since the complete hydration, also called curing, may take about one month or longer, special attention should be paid when selecting cement concrete as paving materials:

(1) **Long construction period**: Since concrete curing may take a month or more, there are various factors that may affect the curing process. As a result, concrete properties will be significantly impacted if inadequate hydration occurs during the curing period. For instance, a variation of temperature or water contents may result in thermal stresses in concrete. Therefore, it should be careful when selecting concrete materials under rapid changes in temperatures or moistures.

(2) **Difficult in recycling**: since the cement concrete has high stiffness, it becomes very difficult in recycling concrete materials. This is one of the drawbacks when selecting concrete materials in pavement design.

3.4.5 Recycled Materials

Researchers, designers, and practitioners are paying more and more attentions to the development and application of sustainable pavements. The use of recycled materials is one of the sustainable applications. The recycled materials may include the reclaimed asphalt pavements (RAP), the recycled electronic wastes, the recycled engine oils, the recycled truck tires, the recycled building materials, etc. Details about these recycled materials are out of the scope of this textbook.

3.5 Material Structural Characterization

Paving materials are composed of coarse aggregates, fine aggregates, and binder materials (original binders + filling materials). Different percentages of those three constituents result in different material structures.

1) **Binder Materials Identify Mixture Names.**

Binders used in pavement engineering may include asphalt mastic, hydraulically cements, cement mortar, and clay. Asphalt mastic is composed of asphalt binder and filling materials, which is the binder material of asphalt mixture. Hydraulically cements may include Portland cement, fly ash, lime, slags, etc, which is the binder materials of hydraulically-bound mixtures. Cement mortar is composed of Portland cement and filling materials, which is the binder of cement concrete. Clay is the tiny particles in an unbound mixture. Obviously, paving materials may be divided into asphalt mixtures, HBM, cement concrete and unbound mixtures in terms of the binder materials.

2) Fine and Coarse aggregates Characterize Mixture Structures.

Fine and coarse aggregates are major components of paving mixtures, which take over 80% ~ 95% of the mixture mass. Based on the percentage of coarse aggregates, paving mixtures may be divided into the skeleton structure and the suspension structure; while based on the percentage of fine aggregates, paving mixtures may be divided into the dense structure and the voided structure. Combining fine and coarse aggregates, paving materials may be voided skeleton structure, dense skeleton structure, and dense suspension structure.

In summary, as shown in Fig. 3-8 the binder materials may distinguish the material types into unbound materials (binder is clay), asphalt mixtures (binder is asphalt mastic), concrete material (binder is cement mortar), and HBM (hydraulically bound binder). According to the aggregate structure, the mixture structure may be one of the dense skeleton structure, the dense suspension structure, the voided skeleton structure.

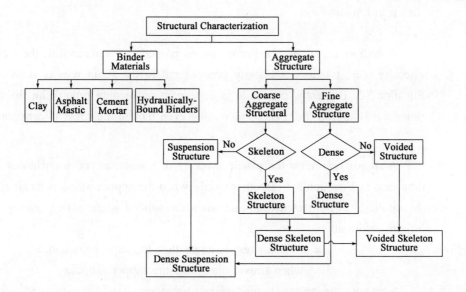

Fig. 3-8 **Structural characteristics of paving materials**

3.6 Material Mechanical Characterization

3.6.1 Mechanical Models for Pavement Materials

Under traffic loads, stresses and strains may be developed within the pavement structure. The relation between stress and strain tells the pavement material capability of bearing traffic loads in terms of deformation. In order to better understand material stress-strain relationship, mechanical models are employed to simulate materials. Spring, dashpot, and slipper, as shown in Fig. 3-9 are the three basic mechanical elements that represent elastic, viscous, and plastic properties of materials, respectively.

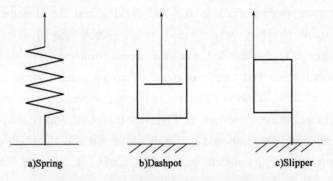

a)Spring   b)Dashpot   c)Slipper

Fig. 3-9 Three Basic Mechanical Elements

The spring element represents the linear elastic property of a material. If the material's Young's modulus is E, its strain is linearly proportional to the stress as shown in Equation 3-4.

$$\sigma = E\varepsilon \tag{3-4}$$

A dashpot represents the linear viscous property of a material. If the material's viscosity is η, its stress is linearly proportional to the strain rate as shown in the Equation 3-5. Evidently, the strain is dependent on loading time. With the loading time increasing, the strain keeps increasing even though the stress is constant.

$$\sigma = E\dot{\varepsilon} \tag{3-5}$$

A slipper represents the plastic property of a material and its behavior can be described in Equation 3-6. In other words, when the applied stress is small enough, the material has no deformation and when the applied stress is large enough it has infinite deformation.

$$\varepsilon = \begin{cases} \infty & \text{when stress is larger than the slipper resistance} \\ 0 & \text{when stress is less than the slipper resistance} \end{cases} \tag{3-6}$$

Most of the material mechanical behaviors can be simulated with the combinations of those three basic elements. Followed is a brief introduction to the

mechanical models of pavement materials:
- *Mechanical model for unbound paving materials*: As stated in section 3.5, an unbound mixture consists of mineral particles and voids. Therefore, the mixture deformation may be from the deformation and moving of particles. The spring element can be used to simulate the elastic deformation of particles while the slipper element can be used to simulate the moving of particles. The mechanical model of an unbound mixture may be simulated with the combination of springs and slippers.
- *Mechanical model for HBM*: As stated in section 3.5, a HBM consists of particles voids and the binder material. Therefore, HBM's deformation may be from the deformation and moving of particles as well as the deformation of the binder material. The spring element can be used to simulate the elastic deformation of particles while the slipper element can be used to simulate the moving of particles. If the binders within the HBM microstructure still work, it does not allow moving of particles. In this case, springs are used to simulate HBM elastic behaviors. After millions of repetitions of axle loads, the binders fail to work well, both springs and slippers should be combined to simulate HBM mechanical behaviors.
- *Mechanical model for concrete material*: A concrete material consists of particles and the cement binder. It is evident that most particles in a cement concrete are completely fixed by the cement mortar. Therefore, springs are commonly used to simulate the elastic behaviors of cement concrete mixtures.
- *Mechanical model for asphalt binders*: Asphalt binder has both elastic, viscous, and viscoelastic properties. It can be simulated with combinations of springs and dashpots. The two common combinations are the Kelvin Model where one spring and one dashpot are connected in parallel and the Maxwell Model where one spring and one dashpot are connected in series as shown in Fig. 3-10. The Kelvin model is also called the viscoelastic element.

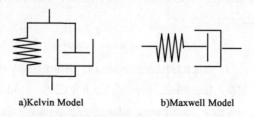

a) Kelvin Model   b) Maxwell Model

Fig. 3-10 Rheological models for asphalt binders

- *Mechanical model for asphalt mixtures*: Since asphalt binder has viscous, elastic, and viscoelastic behaviors, asphalt mixture has viscous, elastic, viscoelastic, and plastic properties. Therefore, the mechanical model should combine springs, dashpots and slippers.

3.6.2 Deformation Characteristics of Pavement Materials

3.6.2.1 Deformation Features of Mechanical Elements

As mentioned above, all paving materials can be simulated with the combinations of springs, dashpots, and slips. In terms of deformation, the three mechanical elements have the following features:

- Deformation from a spring element is independent on loading time and proportional to the applied stress. Therefore, the elastic deformation is recoverable under cyclic loading conditions.
- Deformation from a slip is dependent on the magnitude of the applied load. Once the applied load is large enough, the plastic deformation will occur and unrecoverable. If the applied load is not large enough, plastic deformation will not occur.
- Deformation from a dashpot is dependent on loading time. In other words, the strain may keep increasing even though the stress is constant and the strain is unrecoverable.
- Deformation from a Kelvin model is a viscoelastic deformation and also dependent on loading time. This type of deformation is recoverable and dependent on the rest time. When the rest time is long enough, the deformation can be completely recoverable. Otherwise, part of deformation becomes permanent deformation since it cannot be recovered within the given period.

Evidently, the deformation may be elastic, viscous, plastic, and viscoelastic. The elastic deformation can be immediately recovered at the time of unloading, while the plastic deformation cannot be recovered once it occurs. The viscous and viscoelastic deformation is dependent on time and the viscous deformation is unrecoverable while the viscoelastic deformation can be recoverable if the rest time is long enough.

3.6.2.2 Deformation Features of Unbound Mixtures

In order to characterize the deformation of unbound mixtures, resilient modulus (MR), California bearing ratio (CBR) and reaction modulus (R-value) are the three key parameters that are popularly used in pavement engineering. In the national design specification[13], MR is recommended. Details about the determination of MR will be introduced in the asphalt pavement and concrete pavement design.

Since springs and slips are the basic mechanical elements of unbound materials, the elastic deformation from aggregate particles and the plastic deformation from relative moving between adjacent particles are the basic components of the total deformation of this type of materials. Therefore, it is important to keep the unbound material under the relative low stress conditions for the purpose of reducing the plastic deformation.

3.6.2.3 Deformation Features of HBM Materials

In order to characterize the deformation of HBM, resilient modulus (MR) and elastic modulus are the two popularly-used parameters in pavement engineering. The concepts of those parameters can be found in the previous sections of this chapter or many references. Since the resilient modulus is no longer used in both asphalt pavement and concrete pavement design specifications[2,3] of China, the deformation features of HBM material are represented through the elastic modulus. Testing methods and determination of the HBM elastic modulus will be introduced in Chapter 8 and Chapter 9.

Similar to the unbound mixtures, springs and slippers are the basic mechanical elements of HBM. The major difference between those two types of materials is that HBM has hydraulically bounds between aggregate particles. As a result, the relative displacements between particles cannot occur before the bounds break. Therefore, the deformation is elastic in the earlier stage of service life and it is plastic in the later stage of the service life. In other words, the permanent deformation is not a failure indicator of the HBM.

3.6.2.4 Deformation Features of Concrete Materials

Concrete can be considered as elastic materials and Young's modulus is used to characterize its deformation features. It should be noted, however, that the stress-strain curve can be considered as a linear curve when the applied load is below 30% of the ultimate load. When the applied stress is between 30% and 50%, the stress-strain curve can be approximately considered as a linear curve. Thus, Young's modulus testing is conducted under a stress level between 30% and 50% of the compressive strength.

Similar to HBM materials, springs and slips are the basic mechanical elements of concrete materials and there are bounds between particles. The major difference is that plastic deformation is negligible throughout its service life. Even if the concrete material is in the failure condition, the plastic deformation is not from the relative displacement between particles.

3.6.2.5 Deformation Features of Asphalt Materials

Asphalt materials may include asphalt binders and asphalt mixtures. Even though asphalt materials have elastic, viscoelastic, plastic, and viscous deformations, they are usually considered as viscoelastic materials and the parameters for characterizing their deformation features include resilient modulus, dynamic modulus, creep stiffness, relaxation modulus, and stiffness modulus, etc. In the national design specification[2], the dynamic modulus is used as the design parameter which will be detailed in Chapter 8. Followed is a brief introduction to the concepts of dynamic modulus, creep stiffness, and relaxation modulus.

Dynamic modulus is a viscoelastic parameter under the dynamic loading condition. Fig. 3-11 shows a typical result of dynamic modulus testing. Obviously, strain lags stress by a phase angle. As a result, the stress reaches its peak value earlier than that of the strain. The dynamic modulus value, however, is computed through the peak stress divided by the peak strain. In practice, both the dynamic modulus value and the phase angle should be considered simultaneously. The value represents the magnitude of deformation and the phase angle represents the time-dependent property.

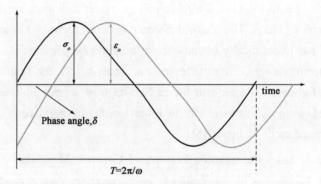

Fig. 3-11　Stress and strain of dynamic modulus testing

Creep stiffness is viscoelastic parameter which is measured through applying a constant load on the sample and computed through stress divided by the strain. Since the strain keeps increasing even through the stress is constant for a viscoelastic material, the creep stiffness is decreasing with the loading time increasing.

Fig. 3-12 shows a creep-recovery test. It is evident that the creep strain is nonlinearly increasing in the loading phase and it is nonlinearly recovered in the unloading phase. Therefore, the creep stiffness is not a constant but dependent on the loading time.

Relaxation stiffness is another viscoelastic parameter which is measured through applying a constant strain on the sample and computed through stress divided by the strain. Since stress keeps decreasing even through the strain is constant for a viscoelastic material, the relaxation stiffness is decreasing with the loading time increasing as shown in Fig. 3-13.

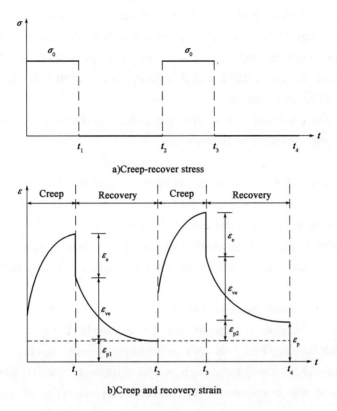

Fig. 3-12 Stress and strain of creep-recovery testing

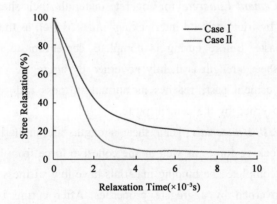

Fig. 3-13 Stress relaxation of a viscoelastic material

3.6.3 Strength Characterization of Pavement Materials

Strength is the ultimate stress under which a material reaches its failure conditions. Strength properties can be characterized in compressive strength, shear strength, tensile strength, and flexural strength. Road paving materials usually have larger compressive strength values compared with the shear, tensile, and flexural strengths. Therefore, shear, tensile, and flexural strengths are often employed as key inputs in pavement stress analysis and design. The shear strength can be used to characterize all paving materials including both granular and bounded mixtures, while the tensile and flexural strengths are mainly used to characterize bounded mixtures including HBM, asphalt mixtures, and cement concrete materials.

1) Shear Strength

Shear strength of road materials is theoretically expressed with Mohr Coulomb theory as computed in Equation 3-7.

$$\tau = c + \sigma\tan\varphi \tag{3-7}$$

in which c and φ are the cohesive fore and the internal friction angle.

(a) *Unbound materials*: for unbound materials, their shear strengths are governed by the frictional coefficient between adjacent particles, particle interlocking effects, and adhesive force. Therefore, particle size, surface texture, morphology, mixture density, water contents, and loading conditions are factors that may impact the unbounded materials' shear strength.

(b) *Asphalt mixtures*: for asphalt mixtures, their shear strength is governed by not only frictional and interlocking forces, but also the cohesive force provided by asphalt binder. Frictional and interlocking forces significantly impact alsphalt mixture shear strengths at high temperatures and cohesive forces mainly govern them at low temperatures. Additionally, different types of asphalt mixtures, the effects of aggregate particles and asphalt binders are different.

(c) *Cement Concrete*: for concrete materials, their shear strengths are similarly governed by frictional and interlocking forces as well as the cohesive force from the cement paste. Before curing is complete, cement paste has a low stiffness and concrete shear strength is mainly governed by aggregate properties. After curing is complete, cement paste reaches its normal stiffness and concrete shear strength is mainly governed by the cement paste.

(d) *HBM materials*: Their shear strengths are similarly governed by frictional and interlocking forces as well as the cohesive force from binding materials. Before curing is complete, the binding materials have low stiffness and the shear strength is mainly governed by aggregate properties. After curing is complete, the binding materials reach their normal stiffness and HBM mixture shear strengths are mainly governed by the binding materials.

2) Tensile and flexural Strength

Tensile and flexural strength are important inputs in both asphalt and concrete pavement design. There are three basic methods to characterize tensile strength properties of paving materials, namely the direct tensile strength from the direct tensile tests, the indirect tensile strength from the diametral compression tests (also called indirect tensile tests), and the flexural tensile strength measured by the bending beam tests or estimated from diametral compression tests. Details about the testing procedures are not provided in this chapter. Followed is discussion on tensile strength properties of pavement materials:

(a) **Asphalt concrete**: In the national asphalt pavement design specification, the flexural tensile strength used to characterize asphalt concrete strength properties. The diametral compression testing method is employed to measure the flexural tensile strength whose typical values are recommended by the national pavement design specification.

(b) **Concrete materials**: The tensile strengths of concrete materials are mainly characterized by the flexural and direct tensile strength which can be measured by the bending beam tests and the diametral compression tests. In the national rigid pavement design specification, the flexural tensile strength is used and their typical recommended values are also provided. Details will be given in Chapter 9.

(c) **HBM materials**: Similar to asphalt mixtures and concrete materials, the flexural tensile strength is used in the national pavement design specification[2] and the typically recommended values for different HBM materials are also recommended.

3.6.4 Fatigue Characterization of Pavement Materials

Fatigue is a pavement performance indicator to evaluate pavement failure under a cyclic load which is far less than the ultimate strength. The cyclic load is called fatigue strength and the period from the loading applied to the material failure is called fatigue life. The ratio of fatigue strength to the ultimate strength is called stress ratio. Fig. 3-14 shows the fatigue testing result of pavement materials. It is evident that with the stress ratio increasing, the fatigue life becomes shorter. In other words, fatigue life is dependent on fatigue strength. When fatigue strength is small enough, the fatigue life is infinite. The small fatigue strength is called fatigue limit.

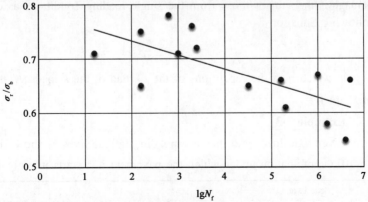

Fig. 3-14 Fatigue life vs stress ratio

For different types of pavement materials, there are various models for predicting fatigue life as demonstrated in the following Equations:

For asphalt materials, there are three models as shown in the Equations below:

$$N_f = a\left(\frac{1}{\sigma_r}\right)b \qquad (3\text{-}8)$$

$$N_f = c\left(\frac{1}{\varepsilon_r}\right)d \qquad (3\text{-}9)$$

$$N_f = k\left(\frac{1}{\varepsilon_r}\right)a\left(\frac{1}{S_m}\right)b \qquad (3\text{-}10)$$

In the three Equations, a, b, c, d, k are material properties which can be determined through laboratory tests; N_f is the fatigue life; ε_r is the controlled constant strain or fatigue strength; S_m is the stiffness modulus of asphalt concrete.

For concrete and HBM materials, the fatigue model is shown in Equation 3-11:

$$s = \frac{\sigma_r}{\sigma_b} = \alpha - \beta \lg(N_f) \qquad (3\text{-}11)$$

in which is the ultimate strength of concrete or semi-rigid materials, α and β are the material properties determined through laboratory tests.

Example 3-2:

Given a concrete slab has its ultimate flexural strength of 4.5MPa, the internal stress within the slab is 2.25MPa, and the material parameter of α and β are 1.0 and 0.057. Determine the fatigue life of this concrete slab.

Solution:

Submit $\alpha = 1.0$, $\beta = 0.057$ into Table 5-2, $\sigma_b = 4.5$MPa, $\sigma_r = 2.25$MPa, $\lg N_f = (1 - 2.25/4.5)/0.057 = 14.8$, therefore, $N_f = 5.91 \times 10^8$ (times of load applications).

As mentioned above, the fatigue test in the laboratory is performed under a repeated constant load. In the field, however, the pavement experiences various axle loads. In order to apply the laboratory testing data for predicting the actual fatigue of the pavement structure, the M. A. Miner principle is commonly used for analyzing metal materials. Based on the Miner principle, the fatigue damage from each single loading condition can be linearly accumulated. In other words, the overall fatigue damage is the sum of those from the single loading conditions as computed in the following Equation:

$$\sum_{i=1}^{k} \frac{n_i}{N_i} = 1 \qquad (3\text{-}12)$$

in which n_i is the repetitions of the ith load of the k loads, N_i is the fatigue life of ith load.

Example 3-3:

Given axle loads and its corresponding fatigue lives as shown in Table. Design a traffic combination under which the pavement just starts its fatigue failure.

Axle Load	L1	L2	L3	L4
Fatigue life	5000	2000	1000	100

Solution:

The combination can be 5000 repetitions of axle load L1, 2500 L1 + 1000L2, or 1000L1 + 400L2 + 200L3 + 20L4. There are other options.

3.7 Summary

This chapter has presented concepts, classifications, and characteristics of subgrade soils and pavement materials. The key points are summarized as follows:

(1) For subgrade soil classifications, USCS and AASHTO methods are introduced. The USCS method is currently used in the national specification[11], while the AASHTO method is commonly used in the highway engineering field in American and most European countries.

(2) Subgrade moisture may significantly impact subgrade soil performance. According to the current subgrade design specification[13], the subgrade soil moisture conditions can be classified into dry, moist, and wet based on the equilibrium moisture conditions.

(3) In order to characterize subgrade bearing capability, MR, CBR, and R-value are introduced. The CBR is commonly used to determine the soil property in the laboratory, while the MR is the key input parameter in the pavement structure design. Details will be provided in the subgrade design.

(4) A total of five types of pavement materials are introduced in this chapter, namely unbound granular materials, asphalt materials, HBM materials, cement concrete, and recycled materials.

(5) Based on the coarse and fine aggregates road mixture may be the voided skeleton structure, the dense skeleton structure, and the dense suspension structure.

(6) The basic mechanical elements and their mechanical features are introduced and the pavement material deformation, strength, and fatigue properties are discussed. Finally, the miner principle is introduced.

Problems

1. Classify the following soils by the AASHTO classification system. Given the group index for each soil.

Soil	Sieve Analysis-Percent Finer			Liquid Limit	Plasticity Index
	No. 10	No. 40	No. 200		
A	90	74	32	28	9
B	86	56	8	NP	
C	42	28	12	18	13
D	92	68	30	42	18
E	90	48	22	31	5

2. According to the climatic zoning and soil types of your hometown, determine the soil saturation degree in your hometown if the subgrade moisture is in the dry condition.

3. If the capillary rise is 1.0m and roadbed thickness is 1.2m, determine the critical heights (the moisture conditions are dry, moist, and wet).

4. Tell differences between MR, CBR, and R-values in evaluating the subgrade soil capability.

5. What are your understandings of the pavement material structural characteristics?

6. Compare differences between HBM, cement concrete, and asphalt mixtures in terms of the structural characteristics.

7. What are the creep and relaxation of asphalt materials?

8. A pavement material fails after 20000, 40000, 50000 and 90000 repetitions of axle loads of 100kN, 60kN, 40kN, and 30kN. Please calculate the overall fatigue damage when the repetitions are 10000, 20000, 30000, and 50000 of those axle loads?

9. There are two types of subgrade soils whose MR, CBR, and R-values are MR_1 and MR_2, CBR_1 and CBR_2, R_1 and R_2. Given $CBR_1 = 5$, $CBR_2 = 150$, could you estimate MR_1 and MR_2, R_1 and R_2?

10. Could you tell why pre-compaction is very important for unbound granular materials, asphalt mixtures, and HBMs?

11. Resilient modulus, Young's modulus, and dynamic modulus are commonly used for characterizing pavement materials' deformation characterizations. According to the current asphalt pavement design specification of China, _____ is used for characterizing asphalt mixtures' deformation features, _____ is used for HBM, _____ is used for concrete, and _____ is used for unbound mixtures.

12. AADT = 250000 for a very-busy expressway. According to the current pavement design specification, the traffic loading condition belongs to the extremely heavy traffic level. Since this expressway is significantly important to Chinese economic development, it is undesirable to make frequent maintenance and reconstruction is not allowable. The only solution is to build a long-lasting pavement. Could you tell how to design such a long-lasting pavement using the concepts of fatigue strength, fatigue life, and fatigue limits?

4. Highway Drainage System

Drainage is one of the most important factors which should be seriously concerned in engineering design and construction: inadequate drainage may eventually result in serious damage to the highway infrastructures. In addition, the accumulated water on pavement may impact traffic flow and cause accidents due to hydroplaning and loss of visibility from splash and spray. In fact, more than 25 percent of highway construction cost is spent on facilities of drainage and erosion control, such as culverts, bridges, channels, and ditches, etc. The purpose of this chapter is to provide a discussion of the highway drainage system which is pertinent to subgrade and pavement design. Detailed computations of the drainage facility design are not presented in this chapter. Readers may refer to the textbook of *Highway Hydraulics and Hydrology*[15].

4.1 Introduction

4.1.1 Water Sources and Effects

In Highway Engineering two sources of water are primarily concerned: The first one is from rain, snow, adjacent lakes or rivers, while the other one is the ground water which flows in underground streams. Effects of those two sources of water may include: washing away the soil (erosion and scouring), making the road body less resistant to traffic (i. e. weakening the load bearing capacity), depositing soils (silting) which may obstruct the passage of water, washing away entire sections of the road or its structures. Drainage for these two sources of water are referred to as the surface drainage and the subsurface drainage.

4.1.2 Highway Drainage Design

As shown in the Fig. 4-1, the highway drainage system is divided into two subsystems: the surface drainage includes pavement surface drainage, central reserve drainage, slope drainage, and other surface drainage while the subsurface drainage includes the pavement internal drainage and subgrade internal drainage. There are various surface drainage facilities which may enable the water to flow off the road surface (crown slopes, longitudinal slopes, and ditches), collect and lead the water away from the road (side ditches, miter ditches), catch surface water before it reaches the road (catch water drains), lead the water from the side drains under the road to the other side (culverts), and allow the road to cross rivers and streams in a controlled manner throughout the seasons. The subsurface drainage facilities (blind ditches, seepage ditches, well systems) intercept water before it gets to the road, lower the water table, and remove excess free moisture. In the subsequent sections of this chapter typical drainage facilities of Highway Engineering will be introduced.

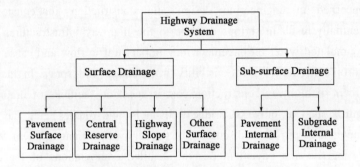

Fig. 4-1 Highway Drainage System

4.1.3 General Requirements

According to the national highway drainage design specification, the following considerations should be paid to in design highway drainage facilities:

First of all, investigation or survey should be performed on hydrology, weather, topography, highway classes, and functional requirements in the overall design of the highway drainage system.

Secondly, drainage design should be consistent with the main structure and natural environmental conditions. Of course, different drainage facilities should also be consistent.

Thirdly, water from roads is not allowed to drain into farmland or irrigation facilities. Highway drainage facilities should be separated from the farmland irrigation facilities.

Fourthly, the drainage design should be environment-friendly and minimize effects of pollutions on natural environments.

Finally, the drainage system should be economic, easy to construct, convenient to maintain, and durable.

4.2 Surface Drainage

Surface drainage is referred to all means by which surface water is removed from the highway subgrade, pavement, and right of way (Row) or streets.

Fig. 4-2 illustrates the different types of surface drainage facilities. Details will be provided in the subsequent contents of this section.

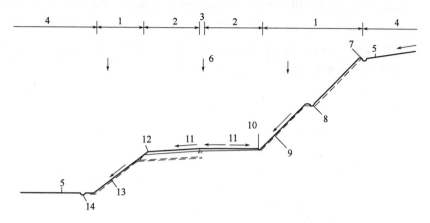

Fig. 4-2 **Highway Surface Drainage System**

1-Slope Drain; 2-Pavement Drain; 3-Central Reserve Drain; 4-Other Drainage; 5-Road Boundary; 6-Rainfalls; 7-Interception Ditch; 8-Drainage Channel; 9-Vertical Drainage Pipe; 10-Side Drainage Ditch; 11-Crown Slope or Cross Slope; 12-Catch Water Strap; 13-Vertical Drainage Ditch; 14-Slope Foot Drainage Ditch

4.2.1 Drainage with Cross Slopes

One of the most important surface drainage methods is to drain water through cross slopes. According to the different engineering conditions, there are three types of the cross slopes, namely the crown slope, the outward slope, and the inward slope as shown in Fig. 4-2. The crown slope is the most popular cross slope which is roof shaped with the highest point at the road center line, with a descending gradient towards the road shoulders as shown in Fig. 4-3a). The inward slope is usually used in some roads in mountainous terrain for safety reasons since the cross-slope faces the hillside of the road as shown in Fig. 4-3b). The outward slope is used sometimes in low-cost roads to drain the water away from the hillside of the road. The advantage of the outward cross is that the side drains can be omitted and the road carriage way can be moved closer to the side slope. The major drawback with this design, however, is that 'out-sloped' roads with clayey soils may become slippery during rains and then a safety hazard. To address this problem, interception drains may be used.

As required in the national design specification[16], in the cut sections cross slopes may be used to drain the surface runoff into side ditches as shown in Fig. 4-4a), while in the fill sections cross slopes may be used to drain the surface run off into road shoulder and then out of road surface through side slopes as shown in Fig. 4-4b).

The cross slope is about 1% ~ 4% and the value is 1% ~ 2% for asphalt or concrete pavements. Since the surface water may be drained through the fill slopes, additional conditions should be met to avoid the side slope erosion in designing the cross slope of the fill sections: ①The first condition is the flat longitudinal slope and small water-collecting amount; ②The second is the low embankment with anti-erosion side slope; ③The third done is the high embankment, but with slope-protection treatments.

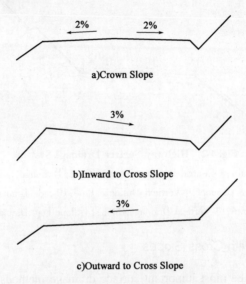

Fig. 4-3 Three types of cross slopes

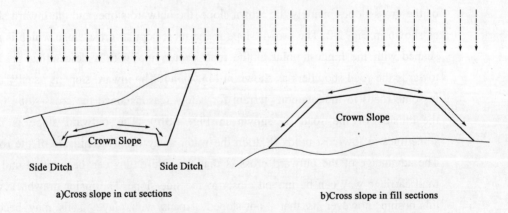

Fig. 4-4 Illustration of surface water drainage through cross slopes

4.2.2 Concentrated Drainage System

For the high embankments without slope protection measures or the low embankments with the slopes vulnerable to erosion, the concentrated drainage system may be recommended. The system consists of cross slope, longitudinal slope (larger than 0.3%), catchwater strap, outfalls, and chutes, as shown in Fig. 4-5.

Fig. 4-5 Illustration of the concentrated drainage system

4.2.3 Central Reserve Drainage System

The central reserve drainage system may be open-form for the reserve wider than 3.0 meters or closed-form for the reserve narrower than 3.0 meters. As demonstrated in Fig. 4-6a), the open-form central reserve consists of impermeable geotextile, the permeable geotextile, the longitudinal permeable pipe, the

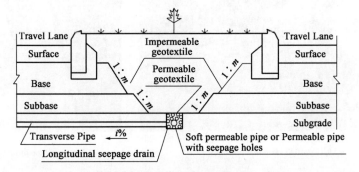

a) Open-form Central Reserve

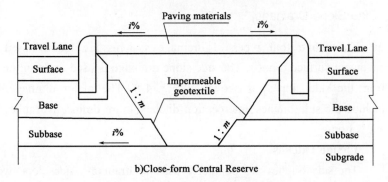

b) Close-form Central Reserve

Fig. 4-6 Central Reserve Drainage System

longitudinal seepage drains, and the transverse drainage pipes. As demonstrated in Fig. 4-6b), the closed form central reserve is mainly composed of the impermeable geotextile and pavement on the central reserve (the same slope with the travel lane slope).

4.2.4 Drainage at Superelevation Sections

At superelevation sections, the special drainage measures should be taken. In the national specification for drainage design of highway[16], there are two major types of measures for drainage at superelevation sections, namely the inward cross slope drainage and the sub-surface drainage as illustrated in Fig. 4-7. When the annual rainfall is less than 400mm and the highway has four-lanes, the inward cross slope may be used to drain the water from the outside to the inside. When the annual rainfall is more than 400mm and the highway has more than four-lanes, the drainage measure is the sub-surface drainage which drains water through cross slope to the longitudinal catchwater channel, then to the catchwater well, and out of the pavement through the transverse pipe and chutes.

a) Inward cross slope drainage   b) Subsurface drainage

Fig. 4-7 Superelevation Drainage System

4.2.5 Side Slope Drainage

The above four types of drainage systems are mainly used to drain the pavement surface runoffs. The side slope drainage is used to drain the surface water from the side slopes, as shown in Fig. 4-8. The major drainage facilities may include the side ditches, interception ditches, mitre drains, hydraulic drops, chutes, and so on.

1) Side Ditches

The side ditches are popularly used to drain the side slope water and have various types: The first one is the V-shape which can be easily constructed by a motor-grader and easily maintained by heavy equipment. However, this type of ditches carries a lower capacity than other cross-section shapes. The next one is the rectangular shape which requires less space but needs to be lined with rock or concrete to maintain its shape. This shape is often used in urban areas where there is limited space for drainage. The third one is the trapezoid shaped side drain which carries a high flow capacity and by carefully selecting the right gradients for its side slopes. Of course, there are other shapes of side ditches that are not included in this textbook.

For designing the side ditches, special considerations should be given on erosion and silting control to maintain the good quality of the side drains. The best way to control erosion and silting is by installing sufficient numbers of mitre drains, interception drains and culverts to reduce the amount of water flowing through the drain or to empty the side drains frequently.

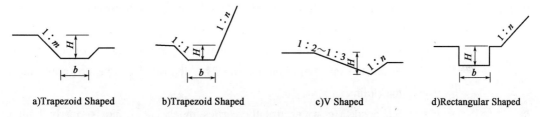

a)Trapezoid Shaped   b)Trapezoid Shaped   c)V Shaped   d)Rectangular Shaped

Fig. 4-8 Side Slope Drainage System

2) Mitre Drain

A mitre drain is also called an offshoot drain which is an open drain designed to divert runoff from a table drain or road shoulder away from a road as illustrated in Fig. 4-9. When designing a mitre drain, the following considerations should be given:

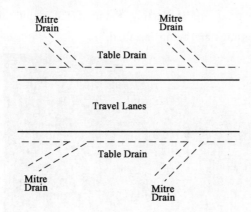

Fig. 4-9 Illustration of Mitre Drains

- The location of a mitre drain is dependent on local terrain and should be no less than 2m away from the pavement subgrade;

78 ROAD SUBGRADE AND PAVEMENT ENGINEERING

- Trapezoid shapes are popularly used as the mitre drain cross-sections with the side slope of 1 : 1 ~ 1 : 1.5 and the height or width of no less than 0.5m.
- The longitudinal slope of a mitre drain should be ranging from 0.3% to 3% (0.5% to 1% in most engineering applications).
- The angle between the mitre drain and the side drain should never be greater than 45 degrees (an angle of 30 degrees is recommended). If it is necessary to take water off at an angle greater than 45°, it should be done in two or more bends so that each bend is less than 45°.

3) Interception Ditches

Instead of draining water, interception ditches are used to catch and lead away from the surface water coming from higher lying areas before it reaches the road or to direct water to where it can safely cross the road as illustrated in Fig. 4-10. Followed are a few considerations in designing interception ditches:

- Interception ditches usually have a trapezoidal cross-section and the excavated material should always be deposited on the downhill side of the drain.
- Since surface water usually carries much silt, if not properly built or timely maintained, the interception ditch may silt up quickly.
- Since the interception ditches are off the road, they may receive less maintenance especially when they are difficult to reach.
- Sometimes, the interception ditches may be ploughed up or blocked off by people using the land.
- Intercept ditches can also be used for diverting minor streams away from the road and collecting them at the points where the major drainage crossings are being installed.

Fig. 4-10 Illustration of interception ditches

4) Hydraulic Drops and Chutes

Hydraulic drops and chute are specially applied in abrupt slopes whose longitudinal slopes are greater than 10% and water head height differences are greater than 1.0 m.

Hydraulic drop is the structure through which the water from the upstream channel (may be the river, ditch, reservoir, pond, or drainage area, etc.) may flow and fall into the downstream channel (may be the river, ditch, reservoir, pond, drainage area, etc.) over a drop. Generally, a hydraulic drop is composed of five parts: inlet, drop shaft, stilling basin, control weir, and outlet. According to the drop heights, a hydraulic drop may be a single-stage structure or a multi-stage structure. Fig. 4-11 shows an example of the single-stage drop which is used for draining the water from side ditches.

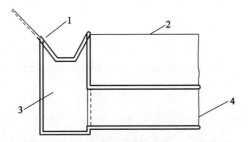

Fig. 4-11   An example of single-stage drop
1-Side ditches; 2-Subgrade; 3-Drop shaft; 4-Culvert

Chute refers to the channel on a steep slope, and it is also known as the suspended ditch. This type of drainage facility is usually used for leading pavement water into the fill subgrade side ditches or leading the water from the catch water drains into a drainage channel or side ditches.

4.2.6   Other Facilities for Draining Surface Water

In addition to the commonly-used drainage facilities for draining the side slope water, there are many other facilities, such as drifts, vented fords, inverted siphons, and aqueduct.

Drifts are normally constructed to pass river streams which are dry during long periods of the year. If the waterway has continuous flow of water throughout the year, the use of other cross-drainage solutions such as culverts, vented fords or bridges should be considered. During rains, most drifts carry shallow flows of water through which vehicles can pass.

Occasionally, deep drifts are flooded with in short periods and the road will be closed for traffic. Fig. 4-12 shows an example of drifts.

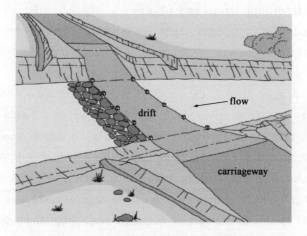

Fig. 4-12 Demonstration of a drift

Vented fords can provide a cost-effective alternative to culverts and bridges. While drifts are appropriate for streams that dry out during periods of the year, vented fords are commonly used for crossing rivers and streams that carries a minimal flow of water through the dry season. Fig. 4-13 shows an example of vented fords.

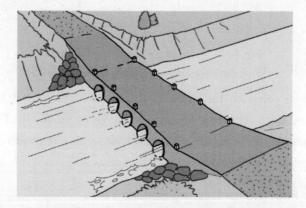

Fig. 4-13 Demonstration of a vented ford

Siphons or inverted siphons are used to convey water across a natural depression, under a road, or under a canal. Use potential energy to force water flow to the other side of the subgrade through an underground pipes. Siphons are usually made of circular concrete pipe or PVC, connecting two canal reaches in series. Some siphons have rectangular cross-sections. Siphons may have a straight lateral alignment, or have changes in direction.

Aqueduct is an artificial (man-made) channel that is constructed to convey water from one location to another over a road.

Evaporation ponds are artificial ponds with very large surface areas that are designed to efficiently evaporate water by sunlight and exposure to the ambient temperatures.

4.3 Subsurface Drainage

4.3.1 Subgrade Internal Drainage

The facilities of subgrade internal drainage include the underdrains, seepage drains, and seepage wells. Followed is a brief introduction:

An underdrain is a drainage system installed under a road or road ditch to collect and transport subsurface water. These buried conduits come in a variety of shapes and sizes and are usually wrapped in geotextile fabric which allows water to enter the conduits while keeping sediment out. Fig. 4-14 shows two examples of underdrains.

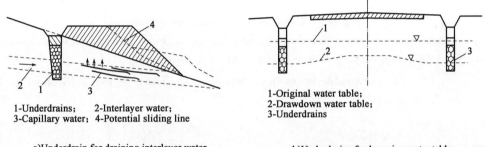

1-Underdrains;   2-Interlayer water;
3-Capillary water;   4-Potential sliding line

1-Original water table;
2-Drawdown water table;
3-Underdrains

a) Underdrain for draining interlayer water

b) Underdrains for lowering water table

Fig. 4-14 Examples of underdrains

A seepage ditch collects underground water to the ditch by way of seepage and eliminates the water to a designated location through channels. Its function is reducing or intercepting ground water. Seepage ditch is suitable for groundwater buried shallow and layers without fixed aquifers.

A seepage well is a vertical direction underground drainage facility going through the impermeable layer to discharge the underground water from the top of the embankment to deeper water carrier, so that the upper underground water can be reduced or eliminated.

4.3.2 Pavement Internal Drainage

In the following three conditions, a pavement internal drainage system is needed: First of all, when the annual rainfall is larger than 600mm and subgrade permeability coefficient is less than 4~10mm/s, then it is necessary to consider the pavement internal drainage for class-I highway, expressway, or some important class-II highways. Secondly, if there is perched water in subgrade sides for a very long time, it is necessary to consider the pavement internal drainage. Thirdly, in frozen areas, it is recommended to consider the pavement internal drainage to minimize the frost-thaw effects.

There are three types of pavement internal drainage methods, namely the edge drainage system, the drainage base, and the drainage cushion layers. Followed is a brief introduction:

The edge drainage system is employed to drain free water along the pavement edges (shoulders). Two examples are shown in Fig. 4-15.

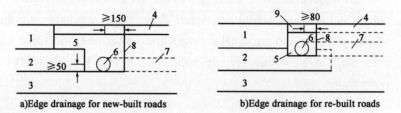

a) Edge drainage for new-built roads   b) Edge drainage for re-built roads

Fig. 4-15 Examples of edge drainage systems

1-Surface; 2-Base; 3-Cushion layer; 4-Shoulder pavement; 5-Catchwater channel; 6-Longitudinal drainage pipes; 7-Transverse outfall pipe; 8-Inverse geotexture filter; 9-Backfill shoulder pavement

The permeable bases have two types as shown in Fig. 4-16 and Fig. 4-17, respectively.

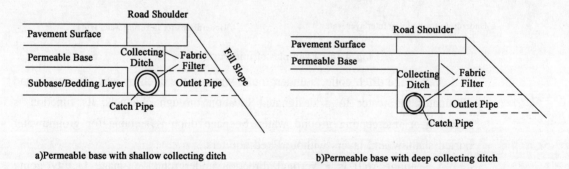

a) Permeable base with shallow collecting ditch   b) Permeable base with deep collecting ditch

Fig. 4-16 Permeable Base I

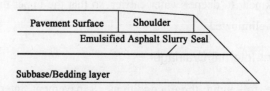

Fig. 4-17 Permeable Base II

Drainage cushion layer is used sometimes to drain free water as shown in Fig. 4-18.

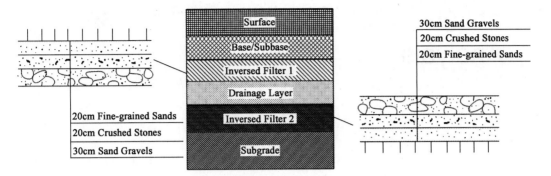

Fig. 4-18 Drainage cushion layer

4.4 Summary of Chapter 4

This chapter provides an introduction to the highway drainage system. It covers three major sections: introduction, surface drainage, and subsurface drainage. Followed are key points:

1. Overall introduction to road drainage, but main focus on subgrade and pavement drainage.

2. This chapter was prepared based on the national design specification for road drainage, textbooks, and www.icourses.cn.

3. Students should refer to the national design specification[2] for design purposes.

Problems and Questions

1. What are the primary sources and effects of water in a pavement?

2. What are the components of surface drainage systems?

3. What are the components of surface and subsurface drainage systems?

4. In a rainy area, what are your suggestions for the surface drainage design? (list your suggestions and reasons).

5. Permeable bases are commonly used as the pavement internal drainage approaches. List and compare the permeable bases.

6. Underdrains, seepage ditches, and seepage wells are the three subgrade internal drainage methods. Could you tell some examples of those three drainage methods? (If possible, find some engineering examples).

7. Since there are many concepts or definitions in this chapter, could you list them and try to find their relations?

5. Subgrade Serviceability and Stress Analysis

Since the main function of the subgrade soil layer is to support the pavement structural layers, there is a strong need for highway engineers to enforce a certain construction requirement or mechanical characteristics of the subgrade to ensure the quality performance of the pavement structure. The serviceability of subgrade refers to the capability of the subgrade to resist detrimental effects of traffic loading and environmental conditions to meet the service requirements. The main service ability of subgrade mainly includes permanent deformation resistance, high strength, stability, durability and permeability. Section 5.1 introduces the subgrade service ability requirements and the corresponding distresses when it fails to meet the requirements. In order to better understand the mechanical behaviors of subgrade soils under the integrated effects of traffic loading and environmental conditions, the stress analysis methods will be introduced in section 5.2, 5.3 and 5.4 respectively for determining the working zone, the slope stability, and retaining wall stability.

5.1 Subgrade Serviceability and Distresses

Subgrade construction quality depends on geological conditions, local natural conditions, design plans, construction techniques, construction quality inspection and management levels. If all these factors are carefully considered, a good serviceability will be achieved. Otherwise, if any of these are compromised, various subgrade distress will be induced. This section will introduce the subgrade serviceability parameters and distresses.

5.1.1 Permanent Deformation Resistance and Distresses

Under environmental and traffic loading conditions, subgrade may have the recoverable and un-recoverable deformation. The un-recoverable deformation is called permanent deformation or settlement which should be controlled or treated before subgrade damage. The resistance to the permanent deformation is one of the important subgrade serviceability indicators.

Fig. 5-1 shows three typical distresses including the permanent deformation due to improper construction methods causing inadequate low degree of compaction, un-

uniform deformation due to the use of improper subgrade fill materials, or soft ground soils without a proper treatment.

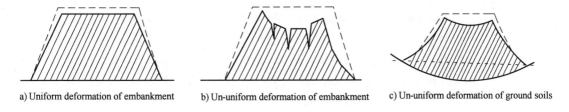

a) Uniform deformation of embankment   b) Un-uniform deformation of embankment   c) Un-uniform deformation of ground soils

Fig. 5-1   Typical Deformation-induced Distresses of Subgrad

5.1.2   Instability Resistance and Distresses

Under effects of the intrinsic and external factors, shear strength of subgrade soils decreases while the internal shear stress increases. The intrinsic factors may include the inadequate shear strength of subgrade soils and the improper design of subgrade shapes and the external factors may be from environmental effects, traffic loading, earthquake, and human activities. As a result of those detrimental effects, subgrade may fail to meet the stability requirements. The capability of subgrade to survive from the stability requirements is called the instability resistance. For subgrade that has an inadequate instability resistance, the distresses, such as sliding and collapse as shown in Fig. 5-2 will be induced.

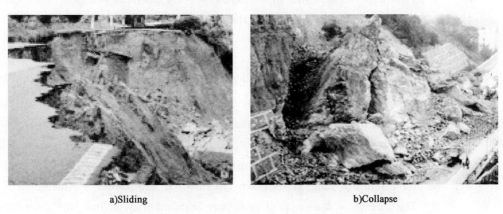

a)Sliding   b)Collapse

Fig. 5-2   Typical Instability-induced Distresses of Subgrade

5.1.3   Durability and Distresses

Durability is the ability of subgrade structure to remain functional without requiring excessive maintenance or repair. The major unit may be used to measure the subgrade durability is years of its service life. The factors which impact the durability may include traffic, temperature, water, materials, geology, compaction, regular maintenance, and so on. Followed are a few examples with problems of durability:

Water-related damage: Subgrade is prone to damages under the soaking and erosion of rivers along the highway. Meanwhile, if the highway drainage system is not efficient enough or there is a large amount of rainfall, the runoff on the pavement surface and slope surface cannot be quickly drained out, and then it will cause erosion to the slope surface.

Weathering: Subgrade is prone to damages under weathering. As a result, the soil subgrade may have the distress of peeling while the rock subgrade may have the distress of spalling as shown in Fig. 5-3.

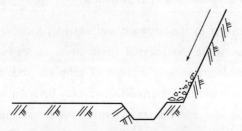

Fig. 5-3 Typical Distress of Spalling

Frost-thaw: In the winter time, subgrade is frozen while in the spring time the frozen subgrade is melt. Under the cyclic frost-thaw effects, the subgrade may lose its serviceability and result in various distresses, such as pumping, non-uniform deformation, and so on. Eventually, the durability will get weakened.

5.1.4 Permeability and Distresses

Pavement is a layered structure seated on the subgrade and its layer material are mixtures with air voids. Therefore, pavement is not impermeable. As a result, surface water may seep into subgrade through voids, cracks, joints, and so on. The seepage water will be accumulated at the interface between subgrade and pavement if the subgrade permeability is not sufficient. Obviously, it is important to consider the permeability of subgrade in designing subgrade and pavement structures.

The distresses due to inadequate permeability may include the frost-heave, pumping, non-uniform deformation, etc.

5.1.5 Measures for Improving Subgrade Serviceability

In order to guarantee the subgrade serviceability, special considerations should be given in design, construction, and maintenance. During the design phase, the fill or cut cross-sections, drainage, and effects of temperatures should be paid special attentions to. In the construction phase, it is important to select the better filling materials (stabilization if necessary), proper construction methods, and the adequate compaction. Finally, the timely maintenance is also crucial to maintain the subgrade serviceability.

5.2 Subgrade Stress Analysis and Working Area

5.2.1 Subgrade Stress Analysis

As mentioned in the Chapter 2, the traffic loading is the pavement-tire interaction pressure which directly applied to the pavement surface and then transferred onto the underlying layers. Therefore, in order to characterize the stresses within the pavement subgrade, the mechanical model should consider not only the subgrade itself, but also all layers of the pavement as shown in Fig. 5-4a).

The Boussinesq theory developed in 1885 is used for the subgrade stress analysis in China. It considers the whole structure (including pavement and subgrade) as a homogenous, isotropic and elastic half space, and the wheel loading is simplified with a concentrated load (denoted by P). The pavement layers, however, have the larger stiffness and density values compared with those of the subgrade. Therefore, it needs to convert the pavement layer thicknesses into the equivalent thicknesses of the subgrade through the Equation below:

$$h_e = \sum h_i \sqrt[2.5]{\frac{E_i}{E_0}} \quad (5\text{-}1)$$

In the Equation, h_e is the equivalent thickness of the pavement structure; E_0 is the subgrade surface modulus and also is the equivalent modulus of pavement layers; h_i is the pavement layer thickness; E_i is the original pavement layer modulus.

Fig. 5-4b) shows the Boussinesq model for the road structure under the wheel load. The stress of z direction under the wheel load of P is calculated with the Equation 5-2.

$$\sigma_{zt} = \frac{3P}{2\pi z^2} = k\frac{P}{z^2} \quad (5\text{-}2)$$

In addition to the traffic-induced stress determined with Equation 5-2, the gravitational stress is also produced due to the gravitational forces of pavement layers and subgrade soils. It can be easily computed with Equation 5-3.

$$\sigma_{zg} = \gamma z \quad (5\text{-}3)$$

The total stress is the sum of σ_{zg} and σ_{zt}. It should be noted that the densities of pavement layers are different from subgrade soils. The calculation from Equation 5-3 is an approximate solution.

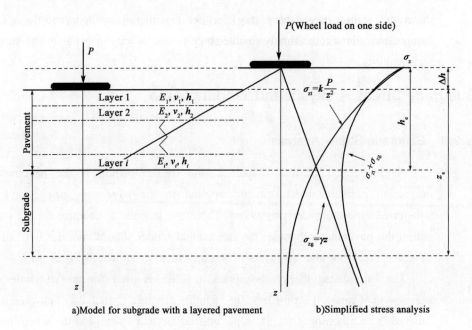

a) Model for subgrade with a layered pavement   b) Simplified stress analysis

Fig. 5-4 Subgrade model and the simplified stress analysis method

5.2.2 Subgrade Working Area

As discussed above, Traffic loading and gravitational force are two types of loads which may impact the subgrade internal stress. As shown in Fig. 5-4, the stress induced by the gravitational force (σ_{zg}) increases with the depth (z), while the stress induced by traffic loading (σ_{zt}) decreases with the depth (z). At certain depth (z_a), where the ratio of between two types of stresses (σ_{zt}/σ_{zg}) is small enough (less than 10%), the traffic loading effect can be ignored. The subgrade within the depth z_a is called the subgrade working area. Within the working area, both traffic loading and gravitational force considerably impact the subgrade internal stresses, while out of the working area, the traffic loading effects can be ignored. Fig. 5-5 shows the method which is used in Chinese practice to determine the working area depth, z_a. It should be noted that this is an approximate solution and can be used for estimating the working area depth.

5.2.3 Applications of Working Area in Pavement Engineering

As discussed in Chapter 3, it is critical for a subgrade to behave elastically throughout its service life. Therefore, special considerations should be paid to the working area in the subgrade design, through selecting better materials, improving the compactness of soils, adding sufficient drainage measures, and so on.

As shown in Fig. 5-6a), when the embankment thickness (H) is higher than the working area depth (z_a), the specially considerations should be paid to the filling materials within the working area.

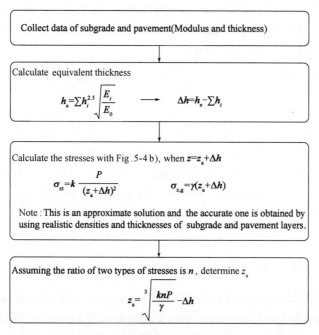

Fig. 5-5 Method for determining the working area depth z_a

As shown in Fig. 5-6b), if the embankment is lower than the working area, the working area is composed of filling materials and ground soils. If that is the case, the ground soils should be treated or improved to meet the overall quality requirements.

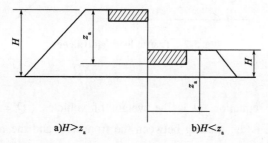

a) $H > z_a$ b) $H < z_a$

Fig. 5-6 Relation between working area depth (z_a) and subgrade height (H)

5.3 Side Slope Stability Analysis

5.3.1 Stability Coefficient

The side slope stability is dependent on the subgrade soil shear strength property, geometry of the side slope, and traffic loading. For the subgrade lower than 8.0m for soil slopes or lower than 12.0m for the rocky slopes, it is unnecessary to perform the stability analysis and the side slope may be designed using the recommended value.

The stability coefficient is defined as the ratio of the shear stress developed along the most likely rupture surface to the shear strength of soils. It can be computed with the Equation 5-4.

$$K = \frac{R}{T} \tag{5-4}$$

In the Equation 5-4, K is the stability coefficient; R is the resistance of subgrade materials; and T is the sliding force. When $K = 1$, the subgrade is in state of the limit equilibrium; when $K > 1$, the subgrade is in stable condition; and when the $K < 1$, the subgrade is in instable condition. The target of side slope stability analysis is to determine whether the subgrade is stable through calculating the stability coefficient, K. According to the sliding or rupture surface, there are different stability analysis methods in subsequent sections.

5.3.2 Equivalency of Vehicular Loading

In addition to the subgrade soil properties (cohesion, angle of internal friction, and unit weight), the traffic load should be considered for the fill subgrade stability analysis. As shown in Fig. 5-7, the traffic load can be equivalent to the thickness of the subgrade soil, h_0, which can be determined in Equation 5-5.

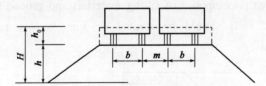

Fig. 5-7 Traffic load equivalency

$$h_0 = \frac{NQ}{BL_\gamma} \tag{5-5}$$

In the equation, Q is the weight of vehicles ($Q = 550$kN for the standard vehicle); L is the spacing between the front axle and the rear axle ($L = 12.8$m for the standard vehicle); N is the number of vehicles in parallel ($N = 2$ for two lanes and $N = 1$ for one lane in the one direction); γ is the unit weight of subgrade soil; B is the width of the equivalent subgrade soil which can be determined in Equation 5-6.

$$B = Nb + (N-1)m + d \tag{5-6}$$

Where b is the wheel spacing of rear axle ($b = 1.8$m); m is the rear wheel spacing of the two adjacent vehicles ($m = 1.3$); d is the width of the tire imprint ($d = 0.6$m). With the default values of the variables, $B = N \times 1.8 + (N-1) \times 1.3 + 0.6 = 3.1N - 0.7$.

5.3.3 Stability Analysis for Straight-line Sliding

This method is suitable for conditions where the sliding surface is linear. Fig. 5-8 shows three typical linear sliding examples, namely the high fill subgrade, the steep cut subgrade, and the embankment on a steep slope. It should be noted that the sliding surface of Fig. 5-8c) is the slope of the steep surface and the sliding surface should be found for the other two examples.

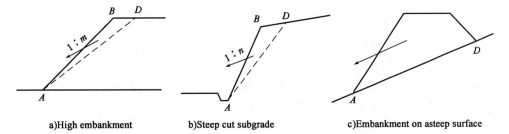

a) High embankment b) Steep cut subgrade c) Embankment on asteep surface

Fig. 5-8 Subgrade with the linear sliding surface

As shown in Fig. 5-9, assuming the sliding surface's slope angle is ω and the sliding soil weight (Q) can be divided into two forces along and perpendicular to the sliding surface (T and N). As a result, the stability coefficient (K) can be computed through Equation 5-7, where c and L are cohesion, angle of internal friction, and the total length of sliding surface (AD in the figure).

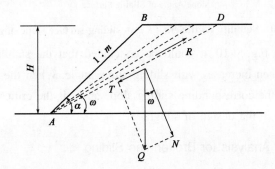

Fig. 5-9 Force system analysis on the linear sliding surface

$$K = \frac{R}{T} = \frac{N \cdot f + cL}{T} = \frac{Q \cdot \cos\omega \tan\varphi + cL}{Q\sin\omega} \tag{5-7}$$

The sliding soil weight (Q) can be easily calculated with the Equation 5-8.

$$Q = \frac{0.5\gamma LH\sin(\alpha - \omega)}{\sin\alpha} \tag{5-8}$$

Substitute Q of Equation 5-8 into the Equation 5-7, it becomes:

$$K = \tan\varphi \cdot \cot\omega + \frac{2c}{\gamma H} \cdot \frac{\sin\alpha}{\sin(\alpha - \omega) \cdot \sin\omega} \tag{5-9}$$

Example 5-1:

For a cut slope with the side slope of 1:0.5 and height $H = 6.0m$, determine the sliding surface angle and the stability coefficient if the angle of internal friction $\varphi = 25°$, cohesion $c = 14.7kN$, and unit weigh $\gamma = 17.64 kN/m^3$.

Solution:

With the information above, $\sin \alpha = \dfrac{1}{\sqrt{0.5^2 + 1}} = 0.894$ and $\alpha = 63.43°$; $\tan \varphi = 0.466$; $\dfrac{2c}{\gamma H} = \dfrac{2 \times 14.7}{17.64 \times 6} = 0.278$; Then, the Equation 5-9 becomes $K = 0.466 \cot \omega + \dfrac{0.248}{\sin(63.43° - \omega) \cdot \sin \omega}$; In Microsoft Excel, it can easily plot the curve of K vs. as shown in Fig. 5-10. It is evident that the minimum value of K is 1.53 and the corresponding sliding surface slope angle at $w = 38°$.

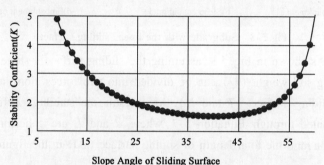

Fig. 5-10 Stability coefficient (K) vs sliding surface slope angle (ω)

From Fig. 5.10, it could be concluded that the stability coefficient decreases first and then increases with sliding slope angle. When the minimum value of K is achieved, the corresponding sliding slope angle is the critical angle which should be controlled in the design of subgrade.

5.3.4 Stability Analysis for Broken-line Sliding

When an embankment is built on the land with broken-line slopes as shown in Fig. 5-11a), the straight-line sliding analysis method is not suitable. In this section will introduce the **Residual Thrust Method** which may be used for instability analysis of broken-line sliding. Followed are the assumptions:
- Locations and shapes of sliding surfaces are given;
- The slide stability problem is treated as a plane strain problem;
- Sliding power is concentrated on the sliding surface, with shear stress parallel to the slide surface and normal stress perpendicular to the sliding surface;
- Slide is treated as a rigid plastic material, no tension;
- The damage of sliding surface is subject to Mohr-Coulomb failure criterion;

- The direction of residual pushing force is parallel with sliding surface and residual pushing force is taken zero when residual pushing force is negative.

Followed are steps of stability analysis for a broken-line sliding:
- The first step is to divide the embankment into several sections and number them from top to bottom;
- The second step is from top to bottom to calculate the residual sliding force which is equal to the sliding force minus the resistance force;
- The last step is to determine whether the embankment is stable or not according to the residual sliding force of the last soil section.

The residual sliding force can be determined with the Equation 5-10 by analyzing the force system of the soil section in Fig. 5-11b).

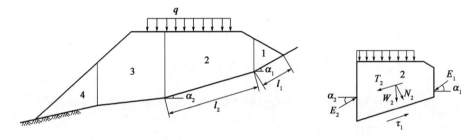

a) Model for stability analysis   b) Force Analysis on Element 2

Fig. 5-11   Embankment on a sloped ground with broken-lines

$$E_i = W_i \sin\alpha_i + Q_i \cos\alpha_i - \frac{1}{F_s}(W_i \cos\alpha_i - Q_i \sin\alpha_i \tan\varphi_i) + E_{i-1}\psi_{i-1} \quad (5\text{-}10)$$

In the equation, ψ_{i-1} is the thrust coefficient and can be determined in Equation 5-11.

$$\psi_{i-1} = \cos(\alpha_{i-1} - \alpha_i) - \frac{\tan\varphi_i}{F_s}\sin(\alpha_{i-1} - \alpha_i) \quad (5\text{-}11)$$

where:

W_i is vertical force including weight of slide i and vehicular loads;

Q_i is horizontal force including earthquake forces;

E_i is residual thrust passed from the previous slide, parallel to the section $i-1$;

α_i, α_{i-1} is the intersection angle of slide $i, i-1$ with the horizontal plane;

φ_i, c_i, l_i is angle of internal friction, cohesion, length of sliding surface;

F_s is factor of safety.

Example 5-2:

An embankment seated on a broken-line slope as shown in Fig. 5-12, the intersection angle of slide 1, 2, and 3 are 45°, 0°, and 14.02°; the angle of internal friction $\varphi = 15°$, cohesion $c = 10 \text{kN}$, and unit weigh $\gamma = 18 \text{kN/m}^3$; and the stability coefficient $F_s = 1.25$. Determine whether this embankment is stable.

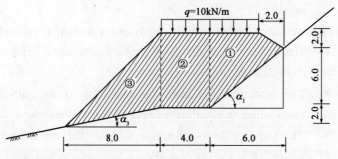

Fig. 5-12 Embankment on a sloped ground with broken-lines(m)

Solution:

(1) Solve the residual sliding force E_1

Area of slide 1 = $(4.0 + 6.0) \times 2.0/2 = 28 (\text{m}^2)$

Weight of slide 1 = $18 \times 28 = 504 (\text{kN/m})$

$$E_1 = W_{Q1} \cdot \sin\alpha_1 - \frac{1}{F_s}(c_1 l_1 + W_{Q1} \cdot \cos\alpha_1 \cdot \tan\varphi_1)$$

$$= 504 \times \sin 45° - \frac{1}{1.25}(10 \times 6.0 \times \sqrt{2} + 504 \times \cos 45° \times \tan 15°)$$

$$= 212 (\text{kN/m})$$

(2) Solve the residual sliding force E_2

Area of slide 2 = $4.0 \times 8.0 = 32 (\text{m}^2)$

Weight of slide 2 = $18 \times 32 = 576 (\text{kN/m})$

$$\psi_1 = \cos(\alpha_1 - \alpha_2) - \frac{1}{F_s}\sin(\alpha_1 - \alpha_2)\tan\phi_2$$

$$= \cos(45° - 0) - \frac{1}{1.25}\sin(45° - 0)\tan 0.2618$$

$$= 0.707 - 0.8 \times 0.707 \times 0.268 = 0.555$$

$$E_2 = W_2 \cdot \sin\alpha_2 - \frac{1}{F_s}(c_2 l_2 + W_2 \cdot \cos\alpha_2 \cdot \tan\phi_2) + E_1\psi_1$$

$$= 576 \times \sin 0 - \frac{1}{1.25}(10 \times 4.0 + 576 \times \cos 0 \times \tan 15°) + 212 \times 0.555$$

$$= -38 (\text{kN/m}) < 0$$

(3) Solve the residual sliding force E_3

Area of slide 3 = $8.0 \times 8.0/2 = 32 (\text{m}^2)$

Weight of slide 3 = $18 \times 32 = 576 (\text{kN/m})$

$$E_3 = W_{Q3} \cdot \sin\alpha_3 - \frac{1}{F_s}(c_3 l_2 + W_{Q2} \cdot \cos\alpha_2 \cdot \tan\phi_2) + E_1\psi_1$$

$$= 576 \times \sin 14.02° - \frac{1}{1.25}\left(10 \times \frac{8.0}{\cos 14.02°} + 576 \times \cos 14.02° \times \tan 15°\right)$$

$$= -45 (\text{kN}) < 0$$

Since E_3 is negative, this embankment is stable.

5.3.5 Stability Analysis for Curve-line Sliding

In reality, the sliding surface is not linear, but a curve-line. The first step of determining the stability coefficient is to find the critical sliding surface. Assuming that the critical sliding surface is a circle line passing through the slope toe, there are two methods for determining the circle center, namely method of 4.5H and method of 36° Angle. Followed are the brief introduction of these two methods:

5.3.5.1 Determine Circle Center

1. Method of 4.5H: Fig. 5-13 shows the method of 4.5H. The key steps for the stability analysis are as follows:

- The first step is to find the point E through drawing a line from A to G and a line from G to E (GE = 4.5H);
- The second step is to find F through two angles β_1 and β_2 which is shown in Table 5-1;
- The third step is to draw circles whose centers are along the line of EF;
- The fourth step is to determine the stability coefficient K_i for each circular curve-line sliding surface;
- The last step is to find the minimum value of the stability coefficient and the corresponding sliding circular curve.

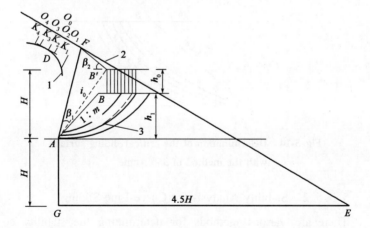

Fig. 5-13 Determination of the critical sliding surface with the method of 4.5H

Table 5-1 Reference Values for method of 4.5H

Side Slope	Slope Angle	β_1	β_2
1 : 0.5	60°00′	29°	40°
1 : 1	45°00′	28°	37°
1 : 1.5	30°40′	26°	35°

continue

Side Slope	Slope Angle	β_1	β_2
1:2	26°34′	25°	35°
1:3	18°26′	25°	35°
1:4	14°03′	25°	36°
1:5	11°19′	25°	37°

2. Method of 36° Angle: As shown in Fig. 5-14, the key steps for the stability analysis are as follows:

- The first step is to find the straight line at the angle of 36 from point B;
- The second step is to draw circles whose centers are on the straight line;
- The third step is to determine the stability coefficient K_i for each circular curve-line sliding surface;
- The last step is to find the minimum value of the stability coefficient and the corresponding sliding circular curve.

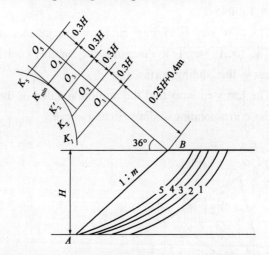

Fig. 5-14 Determination of the critical sliding surface with the method of 36° Angle

5.3.5.2 Stability Analysis for Curve-Line Sliding

There are various methods for determining the stability coefficient of the critical sliding surface. Followed are the two commonly used methods based on the slice method, namely method of Fellenius and method of Bishop:

1. Method of Fellenius: It is also called the Swedish circle method. It is the simplest method that was developed in 1927. In this method, the sliding surface is a circle line and the interactions between the adjacent slices are neglected as shown in Fig. 5-15. The stability coefficient is computed in Equation 5-12.

5. Subgrade Serviceability and Stress Analysis

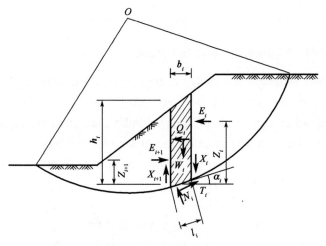

Fig. 5-15 Stability analysis with the method of Fellenius

$$K_s = \frac{\sum_{i=1}^{n}(c_i l_i + W_i \cos\alpha_i \tan\varphi_i)}{\sum_{i=1}^{n} W_i \sin\alpha_i} \quad (5\text{-}12)$$

2. Method of Bishop: As shown in Fig. 5-16, the key steps for the stability analysis are as follows:

- The first step is to divide the embankment into small sides with assuming the center and radius of the circular sliding surface;
- Calculate the stability coefficient with the Equation 5-13 and determine the corresponding sliding surface.

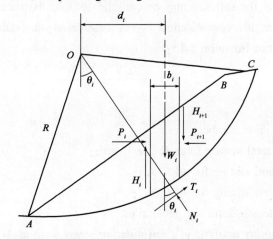

Fig. 5-16 Stability analysis with the method of Bishop

$$K_s = \frac{\sum_{i=1}^{n} \frac{1}{m_{\theta_i}}(c_i l_i \cos\theta_i + W_i \tan\varphi_i)}{\sum_{i=1}^{n} W_i \sin\theta_i} \quad (5\text{-}13)$$

Where:

$$m_{\theta_i} = \cos\theta_i + \frac{\sin\theta_i \tan\theta_i}{K_s} \tag{5-14}$$

5.3.6 Stability Analysis for Soft Subgrade

Soft subgrade is mainly referred to the embankment seated on soft ground soils. The soft soils may be composed of mud and vegetation, which has high natural water content, high compressibility, low bearing capacity and low shear strength. Under traffic or gravitational loading conditions, the soft subgrade might have lateral sliding failure and large settlement as shown in Fig. 5-17.

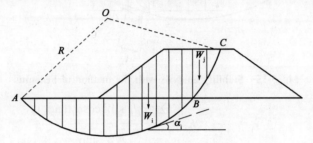

Fig. 5-17 Stability analysis of soft subgrade

To perform the stability analysis for a soft subgrade, the curve-line stability analysis methods as mentioned above can be employed. In the laboratory tests of soil shear strengths, there are two types of methods, namely the vane shear test and the quick direct shear. There are two methods for analyzing the subgrade stability.

1. Stability analysis of total stress method: Under the gravitational force and traffic loads, the soft soil may be consolidated and the shear strength increases with time. When this consolidation is not considered, the stability coefficient can be determined in Equation 5-15:

$$F_s = \frac{\sum S_i + \sum (S_j + P_j)}{P_T} \tag{5-15}$$

where:

i, j is slide number;

P_T is total sliding force for each slice;

S_i is anti-sliding for ARC AB;

S_j is anti-sliding for ARC BC;

P_j is tensile force for geotextile.

2. Stability analysis of Consolidation stress method: When this consolidation is considered, the stability coefficient can be determined in Equation 5-16:

$$F_s = \frac{\sum (S_i + \Delta S_i) + \sum (S_j + P_j)}{P_T} \tag{5-16}$$

Where the additional strength due to consolidation is calculated in the Equation 5-17:

$$\Delta s_i = W_{li} U_i \cos \alpha_i \tan\varphi_{gi} \qquad (5\text{-}17)$$

In addition to the two methods of the stability analysis, the critical height of filling materials is also employed to evaluate the soft subgrade stability:

3. *Critical height for subgrade with thin soft soil layer*: When the soft soil layer is very thin, it can be replaced or treated. Without any treatment or replacement, the critical height of embankment can be estimated with the Equation 5-18:

$$H_c = \frac{c}{\gamma} \cdot N_w \qquad (5\text{-}18)$$

Where N_w is the stability factor which is dependent on the side slope (α) and the depth factor (λ) and can be found through Fig. 5-18.

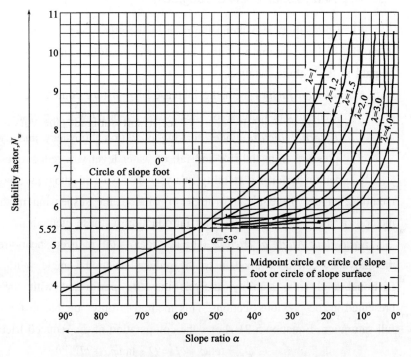

Fig. 5-18 Chart for determining the stability factor

Steps for determining the critical height are as follows:
- Assuming the embankment height is H;
- Determine the depth factor through $\lambda = \dfrac{d+H}{H}$, where d is the depth of soft soil;
- Through the Fig. 5-18, the stability factor can be determined;
- Finally, the critical height can be determined.

***Critical height for subgrade with thick soft soil layer*:** When the soft soil layer is very thick, the critical height can be determined in Equation 5-19:

$$H_c = 5.52 \frac{c}{\gamma} \tag{5-19}$$

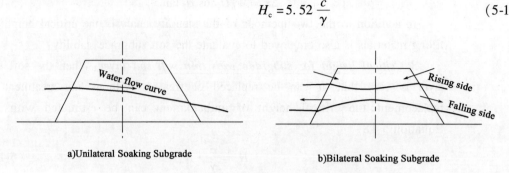

a) Unilateral Soaking Subgrade b) Bilateral Soaking Subgrade

Fig. 5-19 Water level diagram of soaked subgrade

5.3.7 Stability Analysis for Soaked Subgrade

When the subgrade is along the river or the other long-standing water sources, it may be soaked seasonally. If that is the case, the following considerations should be paid in the stability analysis:

- *Internal factors*: with the increase of moisture content, decrease of shear strength, and increase of shear stress, stability will decrease;
- *External factors*: under soaking condition, buoyancy and hydrodynamic pressure from the rise and fall of water level will reduce the stability.

In order to perform a stability analysis of a soaked subgrade, there are three methods, namely the equivalent angle of friction, the suspension method, and the method of slices. Followed is a brief introduction to those methods:

Equivalent Angle of friction: The key idea is the reduced shear strength due to the buoyancy can be equivalent to the reduced frictional angle. With the reduced frictional angle, the stability analysis may be performed with the approaches presented in the previous sections. This method is only suitable to the condition of full saturation. Equation 5-21 shows the computation of the reduced frictional angle:

$$Q_B \cdot \tan\varphi + cL = Q \cdot \tan\varphi_B + cL \tag{5-20}$$

Therefore,

$$\tan\varphi_B = \frac{Q_B}{Q} \cdot \tan\varphi = \frac{\gamma_B}{\gamma} \cdot \tan\varphi \tag{5-21}$$

Suspension Method: The key idea is the hydrodynamic pressure may be balanced by the buoyancy:

- For calculating anti-sliding moment, the reduced frictional angle is used to consider the buoyancy effects.
- For calculating the sliding moment, the buoyancy is not considered since it is balanced by hydrodynamic pressure.

As a result, the stability coefficient can be calculated in Equation 5-22:

$$K_s = \frac{M_y}{M_{01}} = \frac{[(Q-W)\cos\alpha_0 \tan\varphi + cL]R}{(F_1+F_2)\gamma\alpha} \quad (5\text{-}22)$$

Method of Slices: The key idea is the subgrade is divided into the soaked part and the dry part, with considering both the buoyancy and hydrodynamic pressures. Details are not presented in this textbook.

5.4 Stress Analysis for Retaining Wall Design

5.4.1 Theories for Soil Pressure Computation

Rankine's theory: The soil pressure is determined through analyzing the ultimate stress states in an elastic half space. Therefore, this method is also called the **ultimate stress method**.

Coulomb's theory: The sliding surface is considered a plane and the mechanical equilibrium of the sliding soil block is the basis of this theory. Therefore, this theory, is also called the **Mechanical Equilibrium of Sliding Block**.

Details about those two theories have been taught in the course of ***Soil Mechanics***. Students should carefully review the corresponding contents before they study this chapter.

5.4.2 Force System on a Retaining Wall

As shown in Fig. 5-20, the major forces on a retaining wall may include the retaining wall weight (G), the supporting forces from the underlying soils (N and T), the active or static soil pressure behind the wall (E_a or E_c), and the passive soil pressure in the front of the wall (E_p). In addition to the major forces, there are other forces from environmental effects or earthquake.

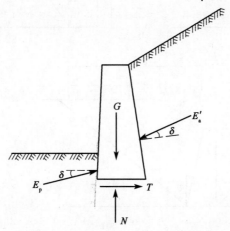

Fig. 5-20 Force system on a retaining wall

5.4.3 Active Soil Pressure under Normal Conditions

There are three normal conditions, namely the sliding surface intersected at the internal side slope (Fig. 5-21), the sliding surface intersected at the subgrade surface (Fig. 5-22), and the sliding surface intersected at the external side slope (Fig. 5-23).

The detailed equation deducting may be found in many references. Followed are the step-by-step procedures for determining the active soil pressure for these three conditions as shown in Fig. 5-21 ~ Fig. 5-23.

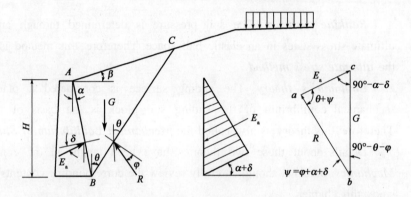

Fig. 5-21 The sliding surface intersected at the internal side slope

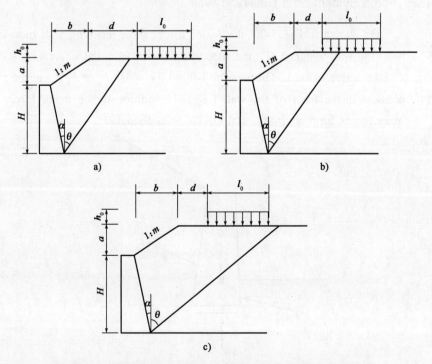

Fig. 5-22 The sliding surface intersected at the subgrade surface

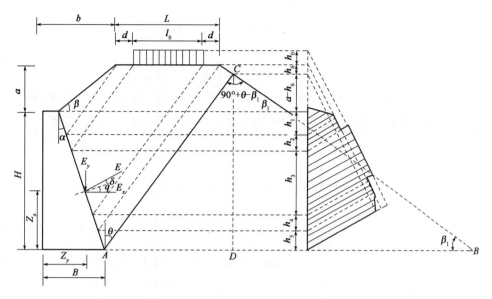

Fig. 5-23 The sliding surface intersected at the external side slope

Active Soil Pressure when the sliding surface is intersected at the internal side slope: The steps for determining the active soil pressure are as follows.

$$E_a = \frac{1}{2}\gamma H^2 K_a$$
$$= \frac{1}{2}\gamma H^2 \frac{\cos^2(\varphi - \alpha)}{\cos^2\alpha \cos(\alpha + \delta)\left[1 + \sqrt{\frac{\sin(\varphi + \delta)\sin(\varphi - \beta)}{\cos(\alpha + \delta)\cos(\alpha - \beta)}}\right]^2} \quad (5\text{-}23)$$

Active Soil Pressure when the sliding surface is intersected at the subgrade surface: Step #1 is to determine the parameters of A_0 and B_0 as follows.

- For the condition in Fig. 5-22a)

$$A_0 = \frac{1}{2}(a + H)^2 \quad (5\text{-}24)$$

$$B_0 = \frac{1}{2}ab - \frac{1}{2}H(H + 2a)\tan\alpha \quad (5\text{-}25)$$

- For the condition in Fig. 5-22b)

$$A_0 = \frac{1}{2}(a + H + 2h_0)(a + H) \quad (5\text{-}26)$$

$$B_0 = \frac{1}{2}ab + (b + d)h_0 - \frac{1}{2}H(H + 2a + 2h_0)\tan\alpha \quad (5\text{-}27)$$

- For the condition in Fig. 5-22c)

$$A_0 = \frac{1}{2}(a + H)^2 \quad (5\text{-}28)$$

$$B_0 = \frac{1}{2}ab - l_0 h_0 - \frac{1}{2}H(H + 2a)\tan\alpha \quad (5\text{-}29)$$

The step #2 is to determine the angle of the $\tan\alpha$ and the active soil pressure.

$$\tan\theta = -\tan\psi \pm \sqrt{(\cot\varphi + \tan\psi)\left(\frac{B_0}{A_0} + \tan\psi\right)} \quad (5\text{-}30)$$

$$E_a = \gamma\left[A_0\frac{\cos\theta}{\text{con}(\theta-\beta_1)} + B_0\right]\frac{\cos(\theta+\varphi)}{\sin(\theta+\psi)} \quad (5\text{-}31)$$

Active Soil Pressure when the sliding surface is intersected at the external side slope: step #1 is to determine the parameters of A_0 and B_0 as follows.

$$A_0 = -\frac{1}{2}[b+L+(H+\alpha)\cot\beta_1 - H\tan\alpha]^2\sin\beta_1 \quad (5\text{-}32)$$

$$B_0 = \frac{1}{2}\{(H+a)[2(b+L)+(H+a)\cot\beta_1] - ab - H^2\tan\alpha\} + l_0 h_0 \quad (5\text{-}33)$$

$$\tan\theta = \frac{-Q \pm \sqrt{Q^2 - 4PR}}{2P} \quad (5\text{-}34)$$

$$P = -A_0\sin\beta_1\sin\varphi\cos\psi + B_0\cos(\psi-\varphi)\sin^2\beta_1 \quad (5\text{-}35)$$

$$Q = 2A_0\sin\beta_1\cos\varphi\cos\psi + B_0\cos(\psi-\varphi)\sin^2\beta_1 \quad (5\text{-}36)$$

$$R = \cos\beta_1\cos(\psi-\varphi)(A_0 + B_0\cos\beta_1) + A_0\sin^2\beta_1\cos\varphi\sin\psi \quad (5\text{-}37)$$

$$E_a = \gamma\left[A_0\frac{\cos\theta}{\cos(\theta-\beta_1)} + B_0\right]\frac{\cos(\theta+\varphi)}{\sin(\theta+\psi)} \quad (5\text{-}38)$$

5.4.4 Passive Soil Pressure under Normal Conditions

The force system is shown in Fig. 5-24 and the passive soil pressure can be calculated with the Equations below:

$$E_p = \frac{1}{2}\gamma H^2 K_p \quad (5\text{-}39)$$

$$K_p = \frac{\cos^2(\varphi+\alpha)}{\cos^2\alpha\cos(\alpha-\delta)\left[1 - \sqrt{\dfrac{\sin(\varphi+\delta)\sin(\varphi+\beta)}{\cos(\alpha-\delta)\cos(\alpha-\beta)}}\right]^2} \quad (5\text{-}40)$$

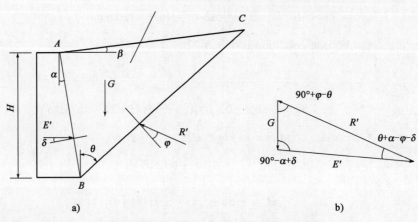

Fig. 5-24 Passive soil pressure calculation

5.4.5 Active Soil Pressure under Non-normal Conditions

The calculation methods above are suitable to the sandy soils and without considering effects of soaking, dynamic water pressure, buoyancy, and earthquake. In this section, the soil pressure calculation methods will be introduced with considering those effects:

Active pressure of clayey soils

When the soil behind the retaining wall is clayey soil, the cohesive strength (c) should be considered in addition to the angle of friction. In order to consider the effects of c, an amplified angle of friction (φ_D) is commonly used based on the equivalency of shear strength as demonstrated in the Equation below:

$$c + \sigma\tan\varphi = \sigma\tan\varphi_D \tag{5-41}$$

With the amplified angle of friction (φ_D), the active pressure of clayey soils can be determined with those methods as mentioned in the previous sections.

Active pressure of soaked sandy soils

Since soaking gives little effects on angle of friction for a sandy soil, the soil pressure coefficient (K_a) keeps a constant before and after soaking. Assuming the active pressure of soaked soils is denoted by E_b, the Equation below shows the determination of E_b:

$$E_b = E_a - \Delta E_b \tag{5-42}$$

Where E_a is the soil pressure under normal conditions and ΔE_b is the reduced pressure due to effects of buoyancy which can be determined in Equation 5-43:

$$\Delta E_b = \frac{1}{2}\{\gamma - [\gamma_d - (1-n)\gamma_w]\} \tag{5-43}$$

In the equation, γ_d and γ_w are the unit weights of dry soil and water, while n is porosity of filling soil.

Active pressure of soaked clayey soils

Since moisture conditions give effects on both the friction angle and the cohesive strength, the soil pressure is divided into the two parts: E_1 above the water table and E_2 beneath the water table. E_1 can be directly determined with the approaches in the previous sections, while E_2 is determined with considering the soil weight above the water table. The equivalent soil thickness can be determined in Equation below:

$$h_b = \frac{\gamma}{\gamma_d - (1-n)\gamma_w}\{h_0 + H - H_b\} \tag{5-44}$$

Where H is the retaining wall height, H_b is thickness of soaked soil, and h_0 is the equivalent soil thickness of the applied traffic load.

5.4.6 Traffic Load Equivalency

In calculating retaining wall, the traffic load acting on the pavement surface may be equivalent to the thickness of the subgrade soil (h_0). Equation below may be used to determine the equivalent thickness:

$$h_0 = \frac{q}{\gamma} \tag{5-45}$$

Where q is the traffic load-induced pressure which is dependent on the retaining wall height as shown in Table 5-2.

Table 5-2 Traffic load-induced pressure

Retaining wall height (m)	q (kPa)
≤2.0	20.0
2.0 < H < 10	Interpoation between 10.0 and 20.0
≥10.0	10.0

5.5 Summary of Chapter 5

This chapter provides an introduction to the subgrade serviceability and stress analysis. Followed are the key points discussed in this chapter:

1. Subgrade serviceability may be characterized with permanent deformation, stability, durability, and permeability;

2. In section 2, the vertical stress analysis within a subgrade is performed and the working area is introduced;

3. In section 3, the stability analysis methods are introduced, which include the straight-line sliding method, the broken-line sliding method, and curve-sliding methods. With the three typical methods, the subgrade side slopes under different conditions are analyzed;

4. In the last section, the retaining wall stress analysis is performed. Since the basic theories have been discussed in the soil mechanics. In this chapter, only a few applications are introduced.

Problems and Questions

1. List the subgrade distresses and present the corresponding measures to minimize those distresses.

2. A pavement is constructed on a subgrade and its MR equals to 50 MPa. The pavement surface layer has a modulus of 2000 MPa and its thickness is 20cm, the base layer has a modulus of 3000 MPa and its thickness is 36cm. The subbase has a modulus of 1500 MPa and its thickness equals to 20cm. The unit weight of subgrade

soil is 20kN/m³ and a standard axle load (100kN) is applied on the subgrade. Assuming n equals to 10, please estimate the subgrade working area depth Z_a.

3. The subgrade height is 2m. If the unit weight of subgrade soil is 20kN/m³, $n = 10$, vehicular load = 100kN. How deep the working depth Z_a is? What should you consider during the design and construction?

4. For a cut slope with the side slope of 1:0.5 and height $H = 10.0$m, determine the sliding surface angle ω and the stability coefficient. If the angle of internal friction $\varphi = 30°$, cohesion $c = 15$kPa, and unit weigh $\gamma = 18$kN/m³.

5. An embankment seated on a broken-line slope as shown in the figure below. The intersection angle of slide 1, 2, and 3 are 18.4°, 0°, and 32°, respectively. The angle of internal friction $\varphi = 15°$, cohesion $c = 10$kPa, and unit weigh $\gamma = 18$kN/m³; and the stability coefficient $F_s = 1.45$. Determine whether this embankment is stable.

6. In term of stability analysis, what are differences between a normal subgrade and a soaked subgrade?

6. Pavement Serviceability and Stress Analysis

Due to the interacting damaging effects of traffic and the environment, pavements are deteriorating over time. In order to evaluate the capability of pavement structures serving the public, the AASHTO design guide uses the concept of the serviceability index to represent pavement performance during the design life. In English dictionary, serviceability is the quality of being able to provide good service. In this textbook, the pavement serviceability is defined as the capability of a pavement to resist traffic and environmental effects or a functionality requirement.

In the mechanistic-empirical pavement design method, the stress analysis is employed to capture the mechanical responses under various traffic loading conditions. It is critical to evaluate whether a pavement structure meets the serviceability requirements. The major objective of this chapter is to provide a discussion on pavement serviceability and stress analysis.

6.1 Asphalt Pavement Serviceability and Distresses

For asphalt pavements, the concept of serviceability is referred to temperature stability, durability, and functionality. The temperature stability includes the high-temperature stability and the low-temperature stability. The durability is referred to water stability, fatigue resistance, and aging. The functionality includes skidding resistance and permeability. Failing to meet the serviceability requirements may result in pavement distresses which can be categorized into five types: cracking, patching and potholes, surface deformation, surface defects, and miscellaneous distresses as listed in Table 6-1. Some details of those distresses will be discussed in the subsequent sections and readers may find more details in the distress identification manual for the LTPP[17].

Table 6-1 Asphalt pavement distresses types

	DISTRESS TYPE	UNIT OF MEASURE
A	Cracking	
	1. Fatigue Cracking Square	Square Meters
	2. Block Cracking Square	Square Meters

continue

	DISTRESS TYPE	UNIT OF MEASURE
A	3. Edge Cracking	Meters
	4a. Wheel Path Longitudinal Cracking	Meters
	4b. Non-Wheel Path Longitudinal Cracking	Meters
	5. Reflection Cracking at Joints	Not Measured
	Transverse Reflection Cracking	Not Measured
	Longitudinal Reflection Cracking	
	6. Transverse Cracking	Number, Meters
B	Patching and Potholes	
	7. Patch/Patch Deterioration	Number, Square Meters
	8. Potholes	Number, Square Meters
C	Surface Deformation	
	9. Rutting	Millimeters
	10. Shoving	Number, Square Meters
D	Surface Defects	
	11. Bleeding Square	Square Meters
	12. Polished Aggregate	Square Meters
	13. Raveling Square	Square Meters
E	Miscellaneous Distresses	
	14. Lane-to-Shoulder Dropoff	Not Measured
	15. Water Bleeding and Pumping	Number, Meters

6.1.1 High-temperature Stability and Distresses

High-temperature stability is referred to resistance to surface deformation and surface defects at high temperatures. Failing to meet the high-temperature stability may result in distresses of C (surface deformation) and D (defects) including shoving, bleeding, slippage, and rutting:

(1) **Shoving**: shoving is one type of asphalt surface deformation and can be defined as a longitudinal displacement of a local area of the pavement surface. It is generally caused by braking or accelerating vehicles, and is usually located at curved road sections or intersections. Fig. 6-1 shows a typical example of shoving.

(2) **Slippage**: slippage is another high temperature-related distress which is similar to shoving, but the slippage's deformation is often in horizontal direction. A typical example is shown in Fig. 6-2.

(3) **Bleeding**: Excess bituminous binder occurs on the pavement surface, and it is usually found at the wheel paths with the three severity levels: discoloration, loss

of surface texture, and aggregate obscured. In the discoloration level, the pavement surface is discolored relative to the remainder of the pavement as shown in Fig. 6-3a). In the loss of surface texture level, the pavement surface is losing surface texture because of excess asphalt which is shown in Fig. 6-3b). In the level of aggregate obscured, the aggregate may be obscured by excess asphalt possibly with a shiny, glass-like, and reflective surface that may be tacky to the touch as shown in Fig. 6-3c).

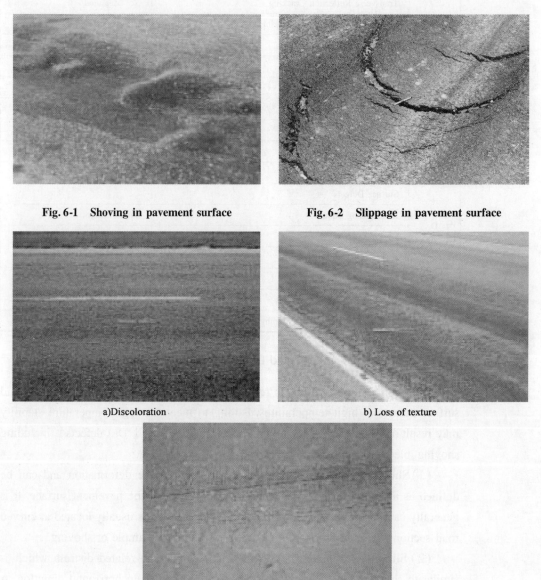

Fig. 6-1 Shoving in pavement surface   Fig. 6-2 Slippage in pavement surface

a) Discoloration   b) Loss of texture

c) Aggregate obscured

Fig. 6-3 Bleeding in pavement surface

(4) **Rutting**: Rutting is a typical pavement distresses, especially at high temperatures. A rutting is defined as a longitudinal surface depression in the wheel path. It may have associated transverse displacement. In Chinese practice, rutting can be categorized into four types, namely instability rutting, structural rutting, consolidation rutting, and polishing rutting. As shown in Fig. 6-4a), an instability rutting is mainly attributed to the instable deformation of asphalt materials at high temperature. This type of rutting usually occurs within the top two layers of asphalt concrete. The structural rutting is due to the lower stiffness of the entire pavement structure as shown in Fig. 6-4b). In the flexible pavement design, it should be carefully considered. As shown in Fig. 6-4c), the polishing rutting is due to the aggregate polishing resistance while the consolidation rutting is due to the inadequate compaction during the construction phase.

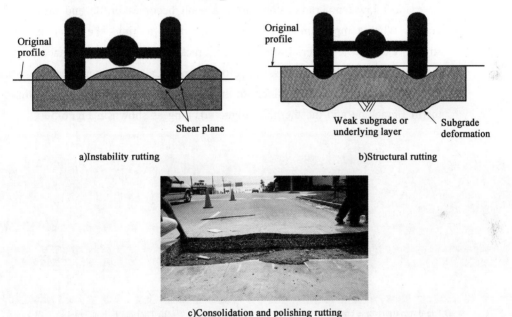

c) Consolidation and polishing rutting

Fig. 6-4 Rutting in pavement surface

To evaluate the high-temperature stability, there are various methods, which include field tests and laboratory tests. Field tests are reliable and persuasive, but they are expensive and time-consuming. In order to save time and costs, the laboratory tests are the valid alternatives and commonly used in pavement engineering. Till now, dozens of laboratory testing methods have been put into practice, including lab track tests, accelerated load facility (ALF) tests, Marshall flow tests, creep tests, rutting tests, direct shear tests, and so on. More new testing methods will be developed to meet the emerging high-temperature stability requirements since the traffic and environmental conditions are changing.

According to engineering experience accumulated over years, the following measures should be taken in design of asphalt pavement materials or structures: First of all, the major pavement distresses should be identified before any measures are selected. Since the major rutting type is the instability rutting in China, the following two considerations should be taken in to select the measures for solving the high-temperature stability issues:

- In term of the aggregate section, more fractured surface, high stiffness, better surface texture or roughness, skeleton gradation, and sufficient compaction are recommended;
- In term of the asphalt section, high viscosity, modified asphalt, addition of fibers, and asphalt contents should be paid special attentions to.

6.1.2 Low-temperature Stability

Under low-temperature conditions, asphalt becomes brittle and prone to have cracks. When temperatures are various from time to time, the additional thermal stresses exceed the material strength and cracks happen. The resistance of asphalt pavements to the thermal stress or deformation is called low-temperature stability. The two typical distresses pertinent to the low-temperature stability are the top-down thermal cracking and the thermal fatigue cracking as shown in Fig. 6-5.

 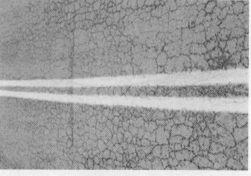

a) Top-down transverse cracks　　　　　　b) Thermal fatigue cracks

Fig. 6-5　Two types of low temperature cracks

To evaluate or predict the low-temperature stability, there are dozens of methods including indirect tension tests, direct tension tests, creep tests, thermal stress tests on restrained strain, stress relaxation tests, and bending beam tests. Details about these testing methods are out of scope of this textbook and readers can refer to the testing specifications[2,29] or publications for more details.

To control the low temperature distresses, the key is to make the proper design for the low temperature stability. Followed are the main considerations for this purpose:

- When selecting source materials, modified asphalt binders are preferred and they should be with lower viscosity, less sensitivity to temperature,

less wax contents, and better stress relaxation properties;
- In the mix proportion design, it is recommended to add fibers into asphalt mixtures and fine-grained mixture types are preferred;
- In the pavement structural combination design, it is recommended to add a stress absorption layer to release the thermal stresses.

6.1.3 Water Stability

Water is one of the most important environmental factors which significantly impact pavement performance. Obviously, the water stability which is the resistance to water-related damage is one of the important pavement serviceabilities. Failing to meet the water stability may result in the pavement distresses of striping/raveling, pothole, skidding, and damage to subgrade.

As shown in Fig. 6-6, the mechanism of water stability may be interpreted as follows: First of all, since water invades into asphalt film, reduces asphalt binder's adhesive strength, decreases asphalt mixture's strength, and eventually causes pavement distresses. Secondly, water invading into the interface between asphalt and aggregates prevents asphalt binding to aggregates. As a result, bounds between asphalt and aggregates are decreasing and distresses of striping/raveling may be induced. Thirdly, water may be trapped in asphalt mixtures or at the pavement interface. Under the vehicular loading, the dynamic hydraulic loads may induce cyclic erosion to pavement materials and structure.

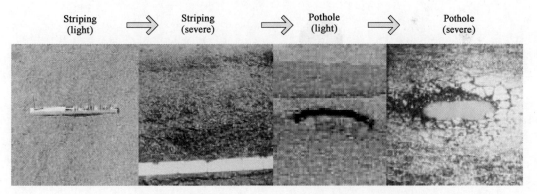

Fig. 6-6 Pavement distresses of stripping and potholes

To evaluate the water stability, laboratory tests can be categorized into three types: The first is to measure adhesion of asphalt to aggregates through boiling the samples. The second is to measure the strength ratios through the immersion Marshall method, immersion indirect tension tests, and immersion rutting tests. The third is address the frost-thaw effects through the frost-thaw table tests and the frost-thaw compression tests.

114 ROAD SUBGRADE AND PAVEMENT ENGINEERING

To prevent pavement damaging due to inadequate water stability, the following considerations should be paid:
- The most important measure is to improve the drainage system and reduce moisture conditions surrounding asphalt mixtures;
- The second measure is to select asphalt with better viscosity and aggregates with a larger content of silicon dioxide (SiO_2);
- The third measure is to dry aggregates during construction.

6.1.4 Load-induced Fatigue Resistance

As mentioned above, there are various reasons for pavement fatigue and traffic loading is the most important one. As shown in Fig. 6-7, at the point A of the top surface, the stress is compressive when the wheel is just on it and becomes tensile when the wheel is approaching or leaving; while at the point B of the bottom surface, the stress is tensile when the wheel is just on it and becomes compressive when the wheel is approaching or leaving. Obviously, in one cycle of traffic loading, the tension and compression stresses appear alternately even at the same location and the stress values are also various from time to time. After many loading cycles, the pavement may fail due to the accumulative damages from the cyclic loading. The capability of a pavement structure resisting this damage is called the load-induced fatigue resistance, which is one of the important pavement serviceability indicators.

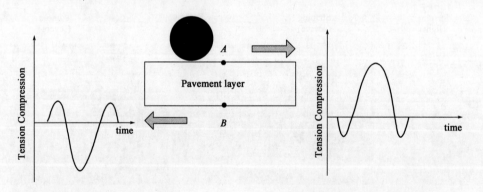

Stress at point B: when Approaching, the stress is compressive, when arriving at the point B, the stress is tensile, and when leaving the stress is compressive

Stress at point A: when Approaching, the stress is tensile, when arriving at the point A, the stress is compressive, and when leaving the stress is tensile

Fig. 6-7 Pavement stresses under cyclic loading

Failing to meet the load-induced fatigue resistance may result in cracks which may be the longitudinal cracking, alligator cracking, and pattern cracking as shown in Fig. 6-8.

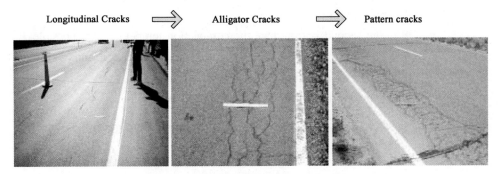

Fig. 6-8　Asphalt pavement fatigue cracks

In order to evaluate the load-induced fatigue resistance, there are various laboratory tests, and the most popular test is the bending beam fatigue test. Details about the laboratory testing methods are not provided herein.

In order to minimize the load-induced fatigue cracking, the following measures should be considered:

- The first is to control the traffic loading conditions which directly impact the fatigue life;
- The second is to select proper paving materials and it is recommended to use lower-stiffness asphalt binders and the dense graded mixtures;
- The third is to optimize the pavement structural combinations and it is recommended to increase asphalt pavement thickness and binding strength between the adjacent layers.

6.1.5　Aging Resistance

Aging is the process of becoming older. Asphalt mixture becomes stiffer due to the oxidization of asphalt constituents in the service life, but its flexibility and relaxation capability decrease. Obviously, aging is undesirable since it may increase the probability of cracking and stripping at moderate or low temperatures. It is also desirable since it may decrease the probability of rutting at high temperatures. The so-called aging resistance herein is referred to the pavement service ability for resisting aging-induced cracks and stripping.

In order to evaluate the aging resistance, asphalt binders usually are tested through *Pressure Aging Vessel* (PAV) and *Rolling Thin Film Oven* (RTFO) for simulating the long-term aging and short-term aging, respectively. The asphalt mixtures with RTFO or PAV binders will be tested through resilient modulus testing, indirect tension testing, dynamic modulus testing, and creep testing to evaluate effects of aging on mixture performance.

In order to minimize the aging effects, the following measures should be considered:

- The first is to select proper asphalt binders which have the better aging

resistance;
- The second is to reduce the compaction temperatures if possible;
- The third is to optimize the mix proportion design and select the dense graded mixtures;
- The fourth is to timely maintain asphalt pavements.

6.1.6 Functional Requirements

If the five serviceability indicators above represent how strong an asphalt pavement structure is, the functional requirements then represent how well it serves the public. In fact, more and more attentions have been paid worldwide on the asphalt wearing layer design to meet the functional requirements. The two major serviceability indicators are the skidding resistance and permeability. Failing to meet the skidding resistance or permeability may result in lower acceleration and longer brake distance which are closely related to traffic accidents.

In design of a pavement structure, the following considerations should be paid to:
- The first is to select proper aggregate gradations and the coarse-grained mixtures are preferred for improving the skidding resistance.
- The second is to specially design the wearing layer which can be considered as a functional layer for protecting the pavement structure and provide proper functionality requirements.

6.2 Concrete Pavement Serviceability

For concrete pavements, the concept of serviceability is referred to load-induced bending stress resistance, thermal stress resistance, joint efficiency, durability, and functional requirements. Durability may be further divided into water resistance and fatigue resistance. Failing to meet the serviceability requirements may result in pavement distresses which can be categorized into cracking, joint deficiencies, surface defects, and miscellaneous distresses. Some details of those distresses will be discussed in the subsequent sections and readers may find more details in the distress identification manual for the LTPP[17].

6.2.1 Load-induced Bending Stress Resistance

Since concrete slab has larger stiffness and takes most of the traffic loads, the major task of concrete pavement design is to analyze and evaluate concrete slabs. Therefore, the load-induced bending stress resistance is referred to the capability of the concrete slab in resisting the load-induced bending stresses, which includes the load-induced fatigue resistance and the maximum thermal stress resistance. Failing to meet the serviceability requirements may result in transverse or longitudinal cracks.

In order to evaluate this serviceability, the rupture strength and Young's modulus of concrete slab should be measured through the laboratory testing. Readers may find details about this testing in the national specification[18].

In addition to the concrete slab strength and modulus, there are other factors which impact the bending stress. Followed are the major considerations to improve this serviceability of a concrete pavement:

- The first is to select a proper concrete slab thickness and joint spacing which directly impact the bending stress value;
- The second is to properly design subgrade, base, and subbase which determine the integrated modulus of the underlying layers and finally impact the bending stress value;
- The third is properly calculating traffic loading which directly impact the bending stress values;
- The fourth is to determine the critical loading conditions through stress analysis;
- The fifth is to select proper concrete material whose modulus and strength should meet the specification requirements.

6.2.2 Thermal Stress Resistance

For concrete pavements, there are two types of thermal stresses: they are the curling stress which is induced by the temperature differences between the top and bottom of a slab and the direct tension or compression stress which is induced by the volume change of a concrete slab. Since air temperatures are various from time to time, the internal thermal stress values in concrete are also various from time to time. Therefore, the pavement may be damaged by the accumulative effects of the cyclic thermal stresses or through one application of the maximum thermal stresses. Therefore, both the load-induced fatigue resistance and the load-induced maximum thermal stress resistance should be considered in measuring the concrete pavement serviceability. When a concrete pavement structure fails to meet either the thermal fatigue resistance or the maximum stress resistance, it may result in distresses, which include fatigue cracks, joint deficiency, fragments due to excessive compression, and blowups.

In order to improve the thermal stress resistance, the following factors should be considered:

- Modulus: larger modulus may result in larger thermal stresses.
- Bending strength: higher bending strength' higher thermal stress resistance.
- Thermal coefficients: larger value results in the lower resistance.
- Combined effects: curling stresses may be superposed with traffic load-

induced stresses.

6.2.3 Joint Efficiency

For jointed concrete pavement design, it is important to maintain the joints efficiency during the pavement life. However, due to environmental effects, traffic loading and other conditions, joint may become deficient. The distresses associated with the joint deficiency include the faulting, joint seal damage, joint spalling, cracks, and slab fragments as well as pumping and water bleeding. Details about the distresses are not provided herein and followed are the factors which should be considered to reduce the joint deficiency:
- The first is to properly design joints including the joint spacing, sealing materials, dowel bars, and tie bars;
- The second is to properly design the underlying layers for providing sufficient supporting and efficient erosion resistance;
- The third is to reduce the amount of free water at the joints.

6.2.4 Water Resistance

The water sources associated with the concrete pavement serviceability may include surface runoff, seepage water, and capillary water. A concrete pavement structure should have sufficient resistance to avoid effects from these water sources. The surface runoff may be accumulated at joints to affect the joint seal durability and eventually damage the joints. With deterioration of joint seal materials, joints become deficient and water may seepage into pavement structure. As a result, pumping, faulting, cracking, and fragments may happen. The capillary water from the underlying layers may accumulate at the interface between concrete and its foundation. This type of water may be frozen in winter and thawed in spring. As a result, the associate distresses may happen.

6.2.5 Functional Requirements

If the four serviceability indicators above represent how strong a concrete pavement structure is, and the functional requirements represent how well it serves the public. The basic functional requirements may include the skidding resistance, noise reduction, and comfortability. During designing a pavement structure, the following considerations should be paid to meet the functional requirements:
- The first is to properly design the surface textures for improving the skidding resistance and noise reduction;
- The second is to consider an asphalt overlay for improving the skidding resistance, noise reduction, and comfortability;

- The third is to consider the continuously-reinforced concrete pavement for eliminating effects of joints.

6.3 Stresses and Strains in Flexible Pavements

As discussed in the chapter 1, the earliest asphalt pavements have very thin paved surface. As a result, most of the traffic loading is mainly taken by the pavement subgrade. Therefore, it is reasonable to model asphalt pavements with semi-infinite elastic space and analyze their stress-strain responses through the Boussinesq (1885) model[19]. With the invention of automobiles, traffic loads were dramatically increasing. As a result, thicker pavement layers were used and the two-layer elastic system theory was developed by Burmister in 1943[20] to perform the pavement stress analysis. With the rapid development of traffic loads after the World War II, pavement structures became thicker and thicker. Three-layered elastic system[21], multilayered elastic systems, and the corresponding computational programs were developed to meet the increasing traffic needs. In order to better understand the underlying mechanism of asphalt pavement failure and improve the quality of asphalt pavement design, this section herein presents flexible stress analysis methods with single-layered model, two-layered model, three-layered model, and multi-layered model. Fig. 6-9 illustrates the development of these mechanical models for analyzing flexible pavements.

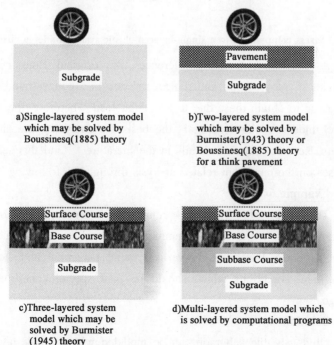

Fig. 6-9 Typical Models for Asphalt Pavement Stress Analysis

6.3.1 Stress in a Single-layered Elastic System

A single-layered elastic system is referred to an elastic, homogeneous, and isotropic half-space. Even though subgrade soils have both elastic and plastic behaviors, they may be considered as elasticity at the low stress conditions. Additionally, a vehicular load can be considered as a circular load as discussed in Chapter 2. Therefore, it is reasonable to simulate a subgrade without pavement or with very thin pavement as a single-layered elastic system under a circular load. Since both the system and the circular load are symmetric, the nine stress components can be reduced into the four stress components as shown in Fig. 6-10.

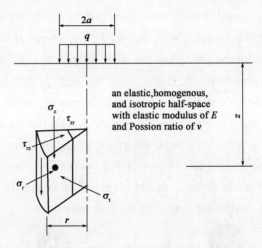

Fig. 6-10 Stress components in a single-layered elastic system under a circular load

As illustrated in many references, the original Boussinesq (1885) model provides stresses, strains, and deflections due to a concentrated load which can be integrated to obtain those due to a circular load. Therefore, the Boussinesq (1885) model under circular loading is the basis for analyzing the single-layered elastic system. Readers may find details in the literature[25] and this section herein mainly focuses on the pavement-related analysis through the following examples.

Example 6-1:

The tire pressure of a truck running on a newly-built subgrade is q and the imprint circular radius is a. Assuming the subgrade resilient modulus and Possion ratio is E and v. Determine the vertical, radial, tangential, and shear stresses and find the critical conditions which should be paid special conditions in the subgrade design.

Solution:

Obviously, the subgrade can be modeled with a single-layered elastic system and the computational model is shown in Fig. 6-10. In order to simplify the calculation, the Possion ratio $v = 0.5$ (The actual value for a subgrade soil is about 0.4). With the Boussinesq model, the stress analysis was performed and the corresponding stresses were plotted in Fig. 6-11. The following findings were observed:

(1) The four stresses components are independent on the Young's modulus and can be linearly related to the tire pressure q. In other words, no matter how different the subgrade soils are, the stresses are identical if the loading conditions are identical.

(2) The vertical and horizontal stresses reach their maximum values when $r = 0$ and z is approximately equal to zero. When z is larger than $4a$, the vertical stresses

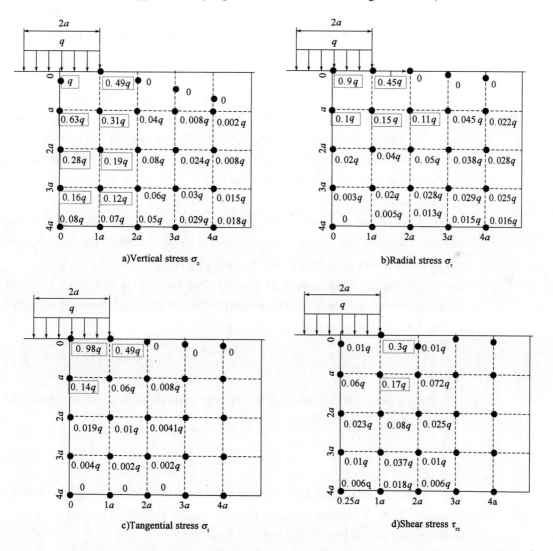

Fig. 6-11 Stresses in a single-layered elastic system due to circular loading

are less than 8% of the tire pressure q, the radial stresses are less than 0.5% of q, and the tangential stresses are zero. The stresses higher than $0.1q$ are marked with red boxes. Evidently, the critical area where the vertical stresses are larger than 10% of q is located at the square with vertices of $(0,0)$, $(2a,0)$, $(2a,4a)$, and $(0,4a)$; the critical area where the radial stresses are larger than 10% of q is located at the square with vertices of $(0,0)$, $(3a,0)$, $(3a,2a)$, and $(0,2a)$, and the critical area where the tangential stresses are larger than 10% of q is located at the square with vertices of $(0,0)$, $(2a,0)$, $(2a,2a)$, and $(0,2a)$.

(3) The shear stress reaches its maximum value when $r=a$ and z is approximately equal to zero. When z is larger than $2a$, the shear stresses are less than 8% of the tire pressure q. The stresses higher than $0.1q$ are marked with red boxes. Evidently, the critical area where the shear stresses are larger than 10% of q is located at the square where r is approaching to a and z is between 0 and $2a$.

Example 6-2:

The tire pressure of a truck running on a newly-built subgrade is q and the imprint circular radius is a. Assuming the subgrade resilient modulus and Possion ratio is E and v, determine and analyze the subgrade surface deflection. If the loading condition is a non-uniform pressure $q(r)$ instead of the uniform pressure q, determine and analyze the surface deflection.

Solution:

Obviously, the subgrade can be modeled with a single-layered elastic system and the computational model is shown in Fig. 6-10. Followed are solutions for different conditions according to the Boussinesq theory:

(1) When the loading plate is flexible (tire pressure is similar to a flexible plate), the pressure is uniform. The vertical deflection at the symmetry of the traffic loading can be determined with the Equation 6-1.

$$\omega = \frac{1+v}{E}qa\left\{\frac{a}{(a^2+z^2)^{0.5}} + \frac{1-2v}{a}\left[(a^2+z^2)^{0.5} - z\right]\right\} \tag{6-1}$$

On the subgrade surface, $z = 0$, and the vertical surface deflection can be determined with Equation 6-2:

$$\omega_0 = \frac{2pa(1-v^2)}{E} \tag{6-2}$$

(2) When the loading plate is rigid (the field plate testing), the deformation under the plate is uniform, but the pressure is non-uniform. The vertical surface deflection ω_0 can be determined with the Equation 6-3:

$$\omega_0 = \frac{\pi qa(1-v^2)2}{E} \tag{6-3}$$

A comparison of Equation(6-2) and Equation(6-3) indicates that the vertical surface deflection under a rigid plate is less than that under a flexible plate. The ratio is about 79%. This is reasonable because the pressure under the rigid plate is smaller near the center of the loaded area but greater near the edge. The pressure near the center has a greater effect on the surface deflection at the center. With this finding above, the field rigid plate loading testing results should be revised by increasing the measured value through multiplying by a coefficient.

6.3.2 Stress in Two-layered Burmister Model

Pavements are layered structures with better materials on top and cannot be represented by a homogeneous mass. Therefore, the Boussinesq theory is not applicable unless the pavement layer is very thin. In 1943, Burmister first developed solutions for a two-layered system[20] and then extended them to a three-layered system in 1945[21]. With the advent of computers, the Burmister theory was applied to a multi-layer system with any number of layers by Huang in 1967[22] and 1968[23]. This section first provides a brief introduction to the assumptions of the Burmister model and then focuses on the stress analysis on a two-layered Burmister model through examples.

Fig. 6-12 shows an n-layer system. The basic assumptions to be satisfied are as follows:

(1) Each layer is homogeneous, isotropic, and linearly elastic modulus E and a Possion ratio v.

(2) The layer materials are weightless and infinite in areal extent.

(3) Except the lowest layer (usually is the subgrade layer) is infinite in thickness, each layer has a finite thickness h_i.

(4) A uniform pressure q is applied on the top of the surface over a circular area of radius a.

(5) The continuity conditions should be satisfied at the layer interfaces. The vertical stresses, shear stresses, vertical displacements, and radial displacements are identical at both sides of the interface. For frictionless interface, the continuity of shear stress and radial displacement are replaced by zero shear stress at each side of the interface.

The exact case of a two-layer Burmister model is the full-depth asphalt pavement that a thick asphalt layer is placed directly on the subgrade. However, an asphalt pavement is composed of surface course, base course, subbase course, and bedding layers. Therefore, it is necessary to combine different layers into a single layer for computing stresses and strains. Followed are a few examples:

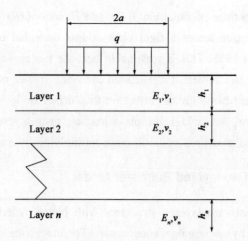

Fig. 6-12 An n-layer Burmister model subjected to a circular load

Example 6-3:

An asphalt pavement is placed on the subgrade with Young's modulus of E_0 and Poisson ratio of v_0. Determine the vertical stresses at the top surface of subgrade.

Solution:

Since the goal is to determine the stresses on the subgrade surface, the resilient modulus of asphalt pavement layers should be combined into a single modulus E_1. With the Burmister theory (readers may find details in the references[24,25]), the vertical stresses are determined when the ratio of E_1 to E_0 is ranging from 1 to 100 as shown in Fig. 6-13. The following findings were observed:

(1) With the modulus ratio increasing, the vertical stress dramatically decreases.

(2) With the asphalt layer thickness increases, the vertical stress decreases.

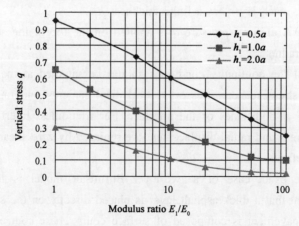

Fig. 6-13 Effects of modulus ratio on vertical stress at the subgrade top surface

With the findings above, a designer may minimize effects of traffic loads on subgrade through increasing the pavement thickness and the modulus ratio. It should be noted that increasing subgrade modulus results in larger stress on the subgrade top surface. Therefore, a balance should carefully be considered when a designer tries to improve the subgrade capability by increasing the subgrade stiffness.

Example 6-4:

An asphalt pavement is placed on the subgrade with Young's modulus of E_0 and Poisson ratio of v_0. The pavement layers are combined into a single layer with modulus E_1 and Poisson ratio of v. Since the vertical surface deflection has been used as a criterion of pavement design in many specifications, could you help a designer determine the vertical deflection at the pavement surface.

Solution:

Similar to the vertical stress solution, the pavement surface defection is a function of the modulus ratio and can be expressed in the following two Equations:

When the loading plate is flexible,

$$\omega_0 = \frac{1.5qa}{E} F_2 \quad (6-4)$$

When the loading plate is rigid,

$$\omega_0 = \frac{1.18qa}{E} F_2 \quad (6-5)$$

In two Equations above, F_2 is dependent on the modulus ratio and asphalt pavement thickness h_1. The typical values of F_2 is listed in Table 6-2.

Table 6-2 Typical Values of F_2

	$h_1 = a$	$h_1 = 2a$	$h_1 = 3a$	$h_1 = 4a$
$E_1/E_2 = 2$	0.8	0.68	0.65	0.6
$E_1/E_2 = 5$	0.6	0.41	0.36	0.31
$E_1/E_2 = 10$	0.4	0.3	0.26	0.22

6.3.3 Stress in a Multilayer System

As mentioned in the previous chapters, a pavement consists of the upper surface, mid-surface, bottom surface, upper base, lower base, subbase, and bedding layers. Each layer has stand alone properties and it is difficult to combine those layers into a single layer. Therefore, in most cases, a multilayer elastic system should be used for modeling an asphalt pavement. Of course, it is not accurate to perform the stress analysis on such a multilayer system, so the computer program or software is essential. There are various methods, including Bitumen Stress Analysis in Road (BISAR) developed by Shell Research in the 1970s, Highway Pavement Design System (HPDS) developed by Southeast University in the 2000s, and Good pave developed in 2017.

6.4 Concrete Pavement Stress Analysis

6.4.1 Theory of Thin Plate System on Elastic Foundation

Different from the asphalt pavement, a concrete pavement takes most of the loads since the stiffness ratio between concrete slab and the underlying layer depth is very large. Therefore, the focus of a concrete pavement stress analysis is to compute the load-induced and thermal induced stresses in the concrete surface.

In terms of design or stress analysis theories, geotechnical or structural design theories are commonly employed to perform the concrete pavement structure analysis. The most popular theory is the theory of the thin plate system on an elastic foundation. Followed are the basic assumptions:

(1) The concrete slab is a very thin plate and strain in z direction is so small that it can be neglected.

(2) The normal vector of the neutral surface is always perpendicular to the neutral surface and shear strain in horizontal directions is equal to zero.

(3) Displacement within the neutral surface is zero.

With three assumptions, all the displacement, strain, and stress components can be expressed as functions of the vertical displacement. In other words, once the vertical displacement is given, the corresponding displacements, strains, and stresses can be solved with the methodology as shown in Fig. 6-14.

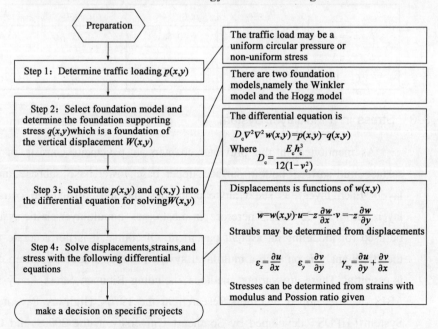

Fig. 6-14 Flowchart for determining the load-induced stresses

6. Pavement Serviceability and Stress Analysis

In the process of the load-induced stress analysis shown in Fig. 6-14, one of the key steps is to determine the foundation supporting stress $q(x,y)$. The Winkler and the elastic half-space foundations are two commonly used models as shown in Fig. 6-15.

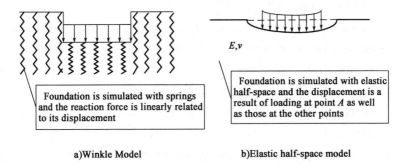

a) Winkle Model   b) Elastic half-space model

Fig. 6-15 Two types of foundation models for concrete pavement stress analysis

According to the Winkler model, the foundation underlying the concrete slab may be simulated with springs and the reaction force is linearly related to its displacement as expressed in the Equation (6-6).

$$q(x,y) = Kw(x,y) \qquad (6-6)$$

where K is the reaction modulus of the foundation; $w(x,y)$ is the vertical displacement, and the $q(x,y)$ is the foundation reaction stress.

According to the elastic half-space model, the foundation underlying the concrete slab is simulated with the elastic half-space with Young's modulus E and Poisson ratio v. The reaction force is not linearly related to its displacement, but a function of the vertical displacement $w(x,y)$.

6.4.2 Load-induced Stress in concrete pavements

6.4.2.1 Methods Developed for Concrete Pavement Stress Analysis

Based on the theory of thin plate system on an elastic foundation, three methods can be used to determine the stresses and deflections in concrete pavements: closed-form formulas, influence charts, and finite element computer program. Based on the Winkler foundation model, Westergaard developed solutions to the deflections and moments of concrete slabs under three typical vehicular loading conditions, while Hogg analyzed the stresses and strains of the infinite plate on the elastic half-space foundation in 1938. Pickett and Rey (1951)[26] developed influence charts which can be applied to multiple wheel loads of any configuration. With the advent of computers, finite element solutions have become more and more popular with the following advantages:

(1) Instead of the infinite concrete slab, dimensions of slabs can be determined;

(2) Stress analysis may be performed under complex and realistic boundary conditions, such as various loading combinations, load transfer coefficient, faulting effects, and so on;

(3) Stress, strain, and displacements at any points within the pavement structure could be documented and analyzed.

The focus of this section, however, is not to explore the existing stress analysis methods, but to present methods which are currently used in national design specifications[3]. They are developed based on the thin plate system on elastic foundations and named with a single-layered plate system on elastic foundation, the two-layered plate system on elastic foundation, and the composite plate system model.

In the single-layered plate system on the elastic foundation, the plate system is the concrete slab, while the foundation is the underlying pavement layers and subgrade as shown in Fig. 6-16a).

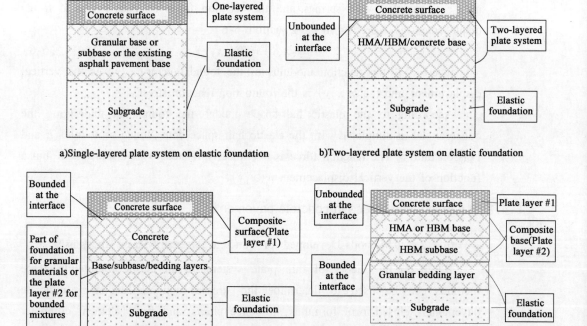

Fig. 6-16 The three models for concrete stress analysis in the national design specification[3]
(Notes: *the composite plate system on elastic foundation is further divided into the composite surface on elastic foundation and the composite base on elastic foundation*)

In the two-layered plate system on elastic foundation, the plate system consists of two unbounded plate layers: the top plate layer is the concrete surface while the bottom plate layer is another rigid material which can be hot mix asphalt (HMA), hydraulically bounded mix (HBM), or cement concrete. The foundation consists of the remaining pavement layers and subgrade.

The composite plate system model is further divided into two types, namely the composite surface model and the composite base model. As shown in Fig. 6-16c), the composite surface consists of the concrete surface and the concrete base which can be the existing concrete surface as the base or the newly-built lean or the rolled concrete base layer. As shown in Fig. 6-16d), the composite base is composed of the HMA or HBM base seated on an HBM subbase. It should be noted that a composite surface or a composite base can be considered as a single plate layer in the stress analysis. For instance, a pavement structure of a concrete surface paved on a composite base can be analyzed with the model of the two-layered plate system on an elastic foundation.

6.4.2.2 Critical Loading Position and Solutions to Load-induced Stress

In the national design specification[3], load-induced stress solutions are provided at the critical load position as described below:

Critical Loading Position. Within the concrete structure, stresses are various from one position to another. It is unnecessary to calculate all of them and only the critical stress at the critical position should be captured for design purpose. The critical loading position is located at the center of the longitudinal joints and the critical stress is located at the bottom of the concrete slab. The base layer has the identical critical loading position to that of the concrete surface.

A Solution to Single-layered Plate System on Elastic Foundation. In order to simplify the calculation, the concrete slab is considered as a free plate without restraints in the horizontal directions. Fig. 6-17 shows the process for determining the load-induced bending stress: First of all, a concrete pavement structure is initialized and the key parameters ($h_i, E_i, h_c, E_c, v_c, E_0$) are determined; Then, the equivalent modulus of the foundation (E_t) is calculated through operating the parameters of h_i, E_i, and E_0; Then, the concrete bending stiffness (D_c) is determined through concrete modulus (E_c) and Poisson ratio (v_c); Then, with the calculated D_c and E_t, the relative stiffness radius r can be determined; Finally, the bending stress due to the axle load p_s can be determined through inputting r, h_c, and p_s.

Solution to Two-layered Plate System on Elastic Foundation. Similar to the single-layered plate system on elastic foundation, the concrete slab is considered as a free plate without restraints in the horizontal directions. Fig. 6-18 shows the process for determining the load-induced bending stress: First of all, a concrete pavement structure is initialized and the key parameters ($h_i, E_i, h_c, E_c, h_b, E_b, v_c, E_0$) are determined; Then, the equivalent modulus of the foundation (E_t) is calculated through operating the parameters of h_i, E_i, and E_0; Then, the concrete surface bending stiffness (D_c) is determined through concrete modulus (E_c) and Poisson ratio (v_c); Then, the base layer (the second plate) bending stiffness (D_b) is determined through base modulus (E_b) and Poisson ratio (v_b); Then, with the calculated D_c, D_b and E_t, the relative stiffness radius r_g can be determined; Finally, the bending stress of concrete surface σ_{ps} can be determined through inputting r_g, h_c, D_c, D_b and p_s. With the similar way the bending stress of base layer (σ_{bps}) can be determined through inputting r_g, D_c, D_b and p_s.

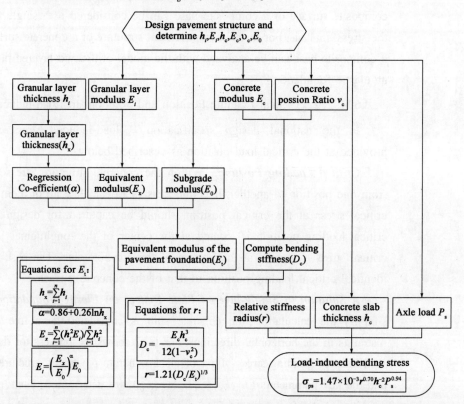

Fig. 6-17 Flowchart for load-induced bending stress of the single-layered plate system on Elastic foundation

Solution to Composite Models. Since a composite model can be considered as one plate layer in the stress analysis, the bending stress solutions can be achieved through the flowcharts shown in Fig. 6-17 and Fig. 6-18. The key inputs are the composite bending stiffness and the equivalent thickness.

For the composite surface model, the composite bends stiffness and the equivalent thickness are calculated through the Equations 6-7 ~ 6-9.

As expressed in the equations below:

$$\widetilde{D_c} = \frac{E_{c1}h_{c1}^3 + E_{c2}h_{c2}^3}{12(1-v_{c2}^2)} + \frac{(h_{c1}+h_{c2})^2}{4(1-v_{c2}^2)}\left(\frac{1}{E_{c1}h_{c1}} + \frac{1}{E_{c2}h_{c2}}\right) \qquad (6-7)$$

$$d_x = \frac{1}{2}\left[h_{c2} + \frac{E_{c1}h_{c1}(h_{c1}+h_{c2})}{E_{c1}h_{c1}+E_{c2}h_{c1}}\right] \quad (6\text{-}8)$$

$$\widetilde{h}_c = 2.42\sqrt{\frac{\widetilde{D}_c}{E_{c2}d_x}} \quad (6\text{-}9)$$

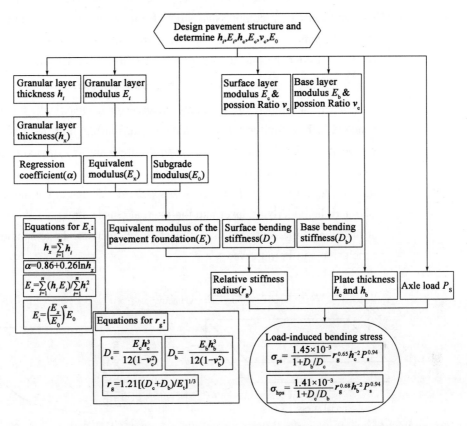

Fig. 6-18 Flowchart for load-induced bending stress of the two-layered plate system on Elastic foundation

For the composite base model, the composite bending stiffness is determined through Equation 6-10 and the bending stress is determined through Equation 6-11:

$$D_{b0} = \frac{E_{b1}h_{b1}^3}{12(1-v_{b1}^2)} + \frac{E_{b2}h_{b2}^3}{12(1-v_{b2}^2)} \quad (6\text{-}10)$$

$$\sigma_{bps} = \frac{\widetilde{\sigma}_{bps}}{1+D_{b2}/D_{b1}} \quad (6\text{-}11)$$

Where $\widetilde{\sigma}_{bpr}$ is determined through substituting D_{b0} into the model of two-layered plate system on elastic foundation.

6.4.3 Thermal Stress in concrete pavements

In addition to the traffic loading, environmental conditions are also critical in impacting concrete pavement deterioration. The environmental impacts may come from temperature and moisture conditions in two different ways, namely the bending effect from temperature or moisture differentials between the top and bottom of a slab and tensile or compressive stress from concrete slab volume change. In this textbook, temperature-induced thermal analysis is presented in this section and readers consider the moisture-induced stress in the similar way.

6.4.3.1 Effects of Volume Change on Concrete

When air temperature gradually increases or decreases, the temperature within a concrete slab is uniformly increasing or decreasing. Fig. 6-19 shows a concrete pavement subject to a decrease in temperature. Due to symmetry, the slab tends to move from both ends toward the center, but the underlying layer prevents it from moving. As a result, the frictional stresses are developed at the interface between the slab and the underlying layer and the internal tensile stress is induced within the slab at the same time. For the slab subject to an increase in temperature, the inverse conclusion can be observed.

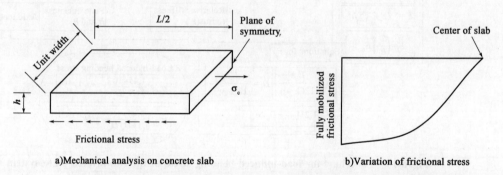

a) Mechanical analysis on concrete slab   b) Variation of frictional stress

Fig. 6-19 Thermal stress analysis due to uniform temperature change

Evidently, the slab is free to move if the interface frictional coefficient is zero, while the slab remains stationary if the interface frictional force is larger than the thermal stress. Followed are the methods for determining thermal stresses within the slab and frictional stress at the interface.

When the temperature increases or decreases by Δt and the thermal coefficient is equal to α, the strains in a concrete slab can be expressed in Equations 6-12 and 6-13.

$$\varepsilon_x = \frac{1}{E}(\sigma_x - v\sigma_y) + \alpha \Delta t \tag{6-12}$$

$$\varepsilon_y = \frac{1}{E}(\sigma_y - v\sigma_x) + \alpha \Delta t \tag{6-13}$$

For conditions where strains in both x and y directions are equal to zero, the stresses in x and y directions can be determined in Equation 6-14. For instance, the larger reinforced concrete slab used in airport pavement can be considered as a condition meets this requirement.

$$\sigma_x = \sigma_y = -\frac{E\alpha\Delta t}{1-v} \tag{6-14}$$

For the conditions where strain in x direction is equal to zero and the stress in y direction is equal to zero, the stresses in x direction can be determined in Equation 6-15. One practical example is the thermal stress in the middle of concrete slab edge with restraints from underlying base course. Another example is the thermal stress in a long narrow concrete slab with restraints from underlying base course.

$$\sigma_x = -E\alpha\Delta t \tag{6-15}$$

In reality, the underlying layer's restraints may not be enough to present moving of a slab with finite dimensions. Therefore, the strains are not equal to zero and the two equations above are not be used for determining the thermal stresses. If that is the case, the thermal stress is determined by the frictional force as shown in Equation 6-16.

$$\sigma_x = \frac{L}{2}\gamma f \tag{6-16}$$

Where L is the slab length, f is the average frictional coefficient at the interface; γ is the unit weight of the concrete.

Fig. 6-20 shows the procedure for determining the thermal stresses due to the temperature changing with time.

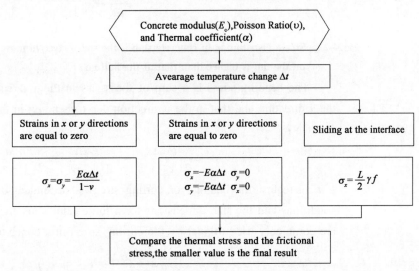

Fig. 6-20 Procedure to determine the thermal stress due to temperature changing

6.4.3.2 Effects of Temperature Differentials

As mentioned above, the temperature changing with time results in a concrete slab volume changing and eventually induces direct compressive or tensile stress. In fact, the temperature distribution is not uniform within a slab, but varies from one location to another. During the day, temperature on the top of the slab is higher than that at the bottom. The top tends to expand while the bottom tends to contract. However, the slab is restrained by the slab weight, dowel bars, and tie bars. As a result, the compressive stress is induced on the top and tensile stress at the bottom. At the night time, the temperature at the bottom is higher than that on the top. The bottom tends to expand and the top tends to contract. Thus, tensile stress is induced on the top and the compressive stress is induced at the bottom.

When the temperature differential between the top and the bottom is Δt (the temperature at the top is higher than that at the bottom) and the thermal coefficient is α, the strain distribution is shown in Fig. 6-21. When the slab is completely restrained and prevented from moving, the compressive strain at the top and the tensile strain at the bottom will be induced. The maximum strain is:

$$\varepsilon_x = \varepsilon_y = \frac{\alpha \Delta t}{2} \tag{6-17}$$

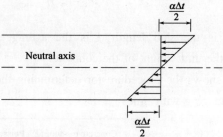

Fig. 6-21 Strain distribution in concrete slab if the slab is free to move (temperature on the top is higher than that at the bottom)

The bending stress is a sum of the stress in the x direction due to bending in the x direction and that in the y direction due to bending in the y direction. The final result is:

$$\sigma_x = \frac{E\alpha\Delta t}{2(1-v^2)} + v\frac{E\alpha\Delta t}{2(1-v^2)} = \frac{E\alpha\Delta t}{2(1-v)} \tag{6-18}$$

In reality, the bending or curling stress is dependent on the underlying layer conditions and the slab dimensions for a finite slab. Thus, the Equations 6-19 ~ 6-22 are commonly used to analyze the curling stress in a concrete slab.

$$\sigma_x = \frac{E\alpha\Delta t}{2(1-v^2)}(c_x + vc_y) \tag{6-19}$$

$$\sigma_y = \frac{E\alpha\Delta t}{2(1-v^2)}(c_y + vc_x) \qquad (6\text{-}20)$$

$$\sigma_x = \frac{E\alpha\Delta t}{2}c_x \qquad (6\text{-}21)$$

$$\sigma_y = \frac{E\alpha\Delta t}{2}c_y \qquad (6\text{-}22)$$

It should be noted herein that the Equation 6-19 and Equation 6-20 are employed to calculate the curling stresses at the center of a slab, while the remaining two Equations are used to calculate the curling stresses at the edge of slab.

In the four Equations above, c_x and c_y are correction factors for a finite slab, which is dependent on the slab dimensions and the relative stiffness radius as shown in Fig. 6-22.

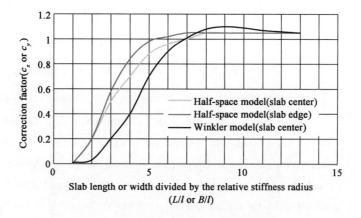

Fig. 6-22 **Stress correction factor for finite slab**

The relative stiffness radius is dependent on elastic foundation models and can be determined with the following Equations:

If the foundation is the Winkler model, the relative stiffness radius is:

$$l = \left[\frac{Eh^3}{12(1-v^2)}\right]^{\frac{1}{4}} \qquad (6\text{-}23)$$

where h is the slab thickness, E is the slab modulus, and v is the slab Poisson ratio, and k is the reaction modulus of the Winkler foundation.

If the foundation is the half-space model, the relative stiffness radius is:

$$l = h\left[\frac{E_c(1-v_s^2)}{6E_{tc}(1-v_c^2)}\right]^{\frac{1}{3}} \qquad (6\text{-}24)$$

where h is the slab thickness, E_c is the slab modulus, and v_c is the slab Poisson ratio, E_{tc} is the modulus of the half-space foundation, v_s is the foundation's Poisson ratio.

Fig. 6-23 shows the procedure to determine the curling stresses due to temperature gradient within a concrete slab.

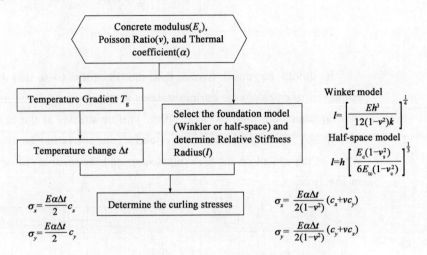

Fig. 6-23 Procedure for determining curling stresses

6.4.3.3 Solutions to Maximum Curling Stresses in National Design Specification

With the methods presented in section 6.4.3.2, the curling stress can be solved in idealized conditions. In reality, however, the impact factors are various from the underlying frictional forces, the internal stress conditions, the pavement models, loading positions, and so on. Therefore, the national design specification[3] presents solutions to maximum curling stresses at the critical loading position for different types of pavement structures as demonstrated below:

Maximum Curling Stress in a Single-layered Plate System. Since the critical loading position is located at the center of the longitudinal joints, the solution should be theoretically solved in Equation 6-21. In the design specification[3], the thermal curling stress coefficient c_x is substituted by B_L which is determined by the following Equation:

$$B_L = 1.77 e^{-4.48 h_c} C_L - 0.131(1 - C_L) \qquad (6-25)$$

In Equation 6-25, the thermal curling stress coefficient can be determined below:

$$C_L = 1 - \frac{\sinh t \cos t + \cosh t \sin t}{\cos t \sin t + \sinh t \cosh t} \qquad (6-26)$$

Where the parameter t is dependent on the concrete slab length (L) and the relative stiffness radius (r) of the concrete slab as determined in Fig. 6-17.

$$t = \frac{L}{3r} \qquad (6-27)$$

Assuming the Maximum temperature gradient is T_g, the temperature difference

$\Delta t = T_g h_c$ and the maximum thermal curling stress at the critical loading position can be determined in Equation 6-28:

$$\sigma_{t,max} = \frac{E_c \alpha_c T_g h_c}{2} \quad (6-28)$$

Maximum Curling Stress in a two-layered Plate System. The two layered plate system consists of the upper plate and bottom plate. Since temperature influence on the upper plate are much larger than that on the lower plate, the curling stress in the bottom plate is not considered in the design specification[3]. The curling stress at the critical position of the upper plate can be determined with the Equation 6-28, but the thermal curling stress coefficient can be determined in Equation 6-29:

$$C_L = 1 - \left(\frac{1}{1+\xi}\right) \quad (6-29)$$

$$t = \frac{L}{3 r_g} \quad (6-30)$$

$$\xi = \frac{(k_n r_g^4 - D_c) r_\beta^3}{(k_n r_\beta^4 - D_c) r_g^3} \quad (6-31)$$

$$r_\beta = \frac{D_c D_b}{(D_c + D_b) k_n} \quad (6-32)$$

$$k_n = \frac{1}{2}\left(\frac{h_c}{E_c} + \frac{h_b}{E_b}\right) \quad (6-33)$$

Maximum Curling Stress in a Composite Plate System. For the composite base model, the thermal stress in the base layer is not calculated and that in the concrete surface can be calculated using the method of the single-layered plate system model. For the composite surface model, the maximum thermal curling stress can be determined in Equation 6-34:

$$\sigma_{t,max} = \frac{E_{c2} \alpha_c T_g (h_{c1} + h_{c2})}{2} B_L \zeta \quad (6-34)$$

$$\zeta = 1.77 - 0.27 \ln\left(\frac{E_{c1} h_{c1}}{E_{c2} h_{c2}} + 18 \frac{E_{c1}}{E_{c2}} - 2 \frac{h_{c1}}{h_{c2}}\right) \quad (6-35)$$

Where B_L can be determined through Equation 6-25 through substituting h_c with $h_{c1} + h_{c2}$. It should be noted that C_L should be determined through the corresponding equation for the single-layered plate system model and the two-layered plate system model.

6.5 Summary of Chapter 6

Pavement serviceability indicates the capability of a pavement structure resisting effects of traffic and environmental conditions, while the stress analysis is an approach to explore effects of traffic and environmental conditions. This chapter presents introduction and discussion on both the serviceability and the stress analysis methods. Followed are the key points:

(1) Asphalt pavement serviceability includes high temperature stability, low temperature stability, water stability, load-induced fatigue resistance, aging and functional requirements. The corresponding distresses may include the permanent deformation under high temperature conditions, the thermal cracking at low temperatures, the fatigue cracking under cyclic loads, and so on.

(2) Concrete pavement serviceability includes the load-induced bending stress resistance, thermal stress resistance, joint deficiency, water resistance, and functional requirements. Once any serviceability cannot well satisfied, distresses may be induced, which include cracking, faulting, pumping, and so on.

(3) In terms of stress analysis in a flexible pavement, the focus is on the load-induced stresses. There are various models, including the single-layered elastic system model, the two-layered elastic model, and multi-layered elastic system model.

(4) In terms of stress analysis in a rigid pavement, the focus is on both the load-induced stress and the environment-induced stresses. The theory for stress analysis is the thin plate system on an elastic foundation. In the national design specification[3], the three models are also induced in this chapter.

Problems

1. A class-two highway is planned in the natural zone II. The subgrade soil is clay with a low liquid limit, the water table is 1.2m beneath the roadbed surface, the granite aggregate is used, and the pavement width is 7 meters. The jointed plain concrete pavement (JPCP) is selected. The standard axle P_s = 100kN and the maximum axle load P_m = 165kN. The annual average daily truck traffic (ADTT) of the first year is 200 standard axles in the design lane and the annual increasing rate of the traffic volume is 7%. According to the conditions above, a concrete pavement structure as shown in Fig. p6-1. Determine the load-induced bending stress within the concrete slab.

240mm Concrete Slab $E = 30$GPa, $v = 0.15$, $f_r = 4.5$MPa
200mm graded stones, $E_r = 350$MPa
200mm graded gravels, $E_r = 200$MPa

Fig. p6-1 Concrete pavement structure

2. Temperature is an important factor which should be considered in pavement design. Could you explain the differences between asphalt and concrete pavement serviceability in terms of effects from temperatures?

3. Due to the temperature difference along concrete slab depth, curling stress

may be developed; In the daytime the top surface has the higher temperature while in the night time, the bottom has the higher temperature. Could you explain how the curling stresses are induced?

4. Explain the reasons for the accumulative permanent deformation of an asphalt mixture under the cyclic traffic loading.

5. Given a continuously-reinforced pavement has compressive modulus of 30GPa, thermal coefficient of 1E-5/℃, and Poisson's ratio of 0.15. Frictional coefficient of the interface between concrete and its underlying layer is 1.5. The concrete unit weight or specific gravity is 0.024MN/m^3.

(1) if concrete temperature gradually decreases by 15℃ due to air temperature changing, determine the max thermal stress;

(2) if the continuously-reinforced concrete pavement is replaced with a jointed concrete pavement and the transverse joint spacing is 6 meters, determine the max thermal stress.

6. A concrete slab with length $L = 6\text{m}$, width $W = 3.75\text{m}$, and thickness $d = 28\text{cm}$, Young's modulus $E_c = 29\text{GPa}$, Poisson ratio, and $a_t = 9 \times 10^6/℃$ is placed on a foundation whose relative stiffness radius $l = 0.75$, the temperature gradient $T_g = 89℃/\text{m}$, determine the curling stress at the concrete slab center and at the middle points of the slab edges.

7. Please list major distresses for both asphalt pavement and concrete pavement and specify the causes of the distress, load induced? Temperature induced? Moisture induced? Or the combination of several factors?

8. Please explain the effects of moisture on performance of both asphalt pavement and concrete pavement.

9. A uniformly distributed load of intensity q is applied through a circular area of radius a on the surface of an incompressible ($v = 0.4$) homogeneous half-space with an elastic modulus E. In terms of q, a, and E, determine the vertical displacement, three principal stresses at a point below the surface under the edge of the loaded area as shown in Fig. P6-2.

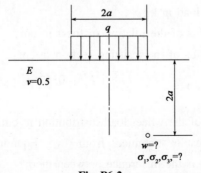

Fig. P6-2

10. A 25kN wheel load exerting contact pressure of 0.7MPa is applied on an elastic two-layer system. Layer 1 has elastic modulus 1500MPa and thickness 20 cm. Layer 2 has elastic modulus 750MPa. Both layers are incompressible, with Poisson ratio of 0.5. Assuming that the loaded area is a single circle, determine the maximum surface deflection, interface deflection, and interface stress.

11. A pavement configuration is same as in the Problem 10. Two wheel loads are applied on the top of the pavement surface. Each wheel loads weights 25kN with a contact pressure of 0.7MPa. The distance between the centers of two loads is 3 times of the loading contact radius. Please determine the maximum surface deflection, maximum interface deflection. Using software to determine the maximum deflection at the depth of 5 times of the loading contact radius.

12. A concrete slab with length $L = 6$m, width $W = 3.75$m, and thickness $d = 28$cm, Young's modulus $E_c = 2.9 \times 10^9$ Pa, Poisson ratio 0.15, and $a_t = 9 \times 10^{-6}/°C$ is placed on a foundation whose relative stiffness radius $l = 0.75$. The temperature gradient in the concrete slab is 90°C/m. Please determine the curling stress at the concrete slab center and at the middle points of the slab edges.

13. A concrete slab with length $L = 6$m, width $W = 3.75$m, and thickness $d = 28$cm, Young's modulus $E_c = 2.9 \times 10^9$ Pa, Poisson ratio 0.15, and $a_t = 9 \times 10^{-6}/°C$ is placed on a foundation whose relative stiffness radius 0.75m. The standard axle load is 100kN. Pleased determine the critical stress at the bottom of the slab in the center of the long edge using equations listed in the Appendix B in JTG D40-2011. Assuming a 25kN wheel load with contact pressure of 0.7MPa is applied, determine the critical stress at the bottom of the slab in the center of the long edge using Equations listed below (same as those used in the textbook *Pavement Analysis and Design*):

$$\sigma_e = \frac{0.572P}{h^2}\left[4lg\left(\frac{l}{b}\right) + 0.359\right]$$

where:

h is slab thickness in cm;

P is wheel load in kg;

l is the radius of the relative stiffness in cm;

b is the radius of the resisting section in cm:

$$b = \begin{cases} \sqrt{1.6a^2 + h^2} - 0.675h & (a < 1.724h) \\ a & (otherwise) \end{cases}$$

a is radius of the wheel load distribution in cm.

Compare the results obtained from two Equations and components of two Equations, what is the difference between them?

7. Highway Subgrade Design

A subgrade design is the process of creating and evaluating a subgrade structure model which is the basis for construction. The model may be altered according to the construction requirements. The focus of this chapter is to discuss how to design such a structure model and the Chapter 10 will induce the construction methods.

7.1 Design Methodology

According to the national subgrade design specification[13], a subgrade design includes the roadbed design, cross-section design, drainage requirements, protection and retaining structure design, and design of subsidiary facilities. Fig. 7-1 shows the general design methodology which includes not only the key subjects in each design step but also the chapters covering the appropriate subjects. It should be noted that the design procedure in Fig. 7-1 is focused on a newly-built subgrade. If one wants to design on a widened or re-built subgrade, Chapter 6 of the national design specification[13] may be referred.

Followed are explanations of Fig. 7-1:

(1) A subgrade design starts from the design preparation which includes the design data from the design assignment, the key requirements from specifications[2,3,13], and other relevant information.

(2) Traffic analysis has been discussed in Chapter 2 which focuses on determining the equivalent single axle loads (ESAL). In addition to ESAL, the traffic load equivalency methods are also introduced for subgrade vertical stress analysis and stability analysis on side slopes or retaining walls.

(3) Environmental conditions in this chapter are mainly referred to the climatic conditions, which may include temperature, annual rainfall, adjacent water source, and etc.

(4) Other inputs may include the natural hydrology, geology, earthquake, filling material sources, and so on.

(5) It is important to have a potential pavement structure before the subgrade design since pavement and subgrade should be integrally designed. Pavement thickness may impact the thickness of a filling subgrade height. The requirements of

roadbed are also dependent on the pavement types. The key contents of pavement structure design will be introduced in Chapters 8 and 9.

(6) With the information from Chapter 3 and 5, the step after the pavement structure initialization is to determine subgrade soil types and identify the key serviceability requirements. This step will be introduced in the roadbed design of this textbook.

(7) With the method discussed in Chapter 5, the vertical stress analysis may be performed and the depth of the working area is determined by the information of pavement layer materials and subgrade soils.

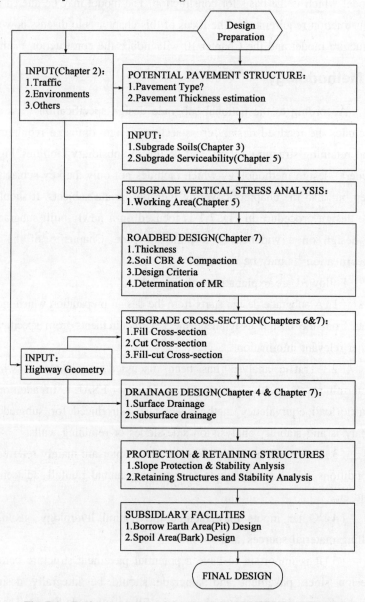

Fig. 7-1 Design procedure for a newly-built Highway subgrade

(8) Based on the working area depth, the roadbed thickness may be determined. Based on the national subgrade design specification[13], the roadbed soils should meet the CBR and compaction requirements and the roadbed structure capability should be evaluated with the roadbed surface resilient modulus as the design criteria. It should be noted that the roadbed requirements are independent on the subgrade cross-section types.

(9) Both subgrade cross-sections and drainage design are pertinent to the highway geometric design. In this chapter, the main focus is on the structural or performance requirements of subgrade cross-sections which may include fill, cut, and fill-cut cross-sections.

(10) In order to guarantee the subgrade stable and durable, it is necessary to design protection and retaining structures. This step is a supplement to the cross-section design: Some subgrade cross-sections are stable and durable without any protection or retaining structures, while some others need those additional structures.

(11) The last step is to design the subsidiary facilities which include the pit design and bank design. The locations of pits and banks are designed during the highway geometric design. This chapter mainly focuses on structural or performance requirements.

7.2 Design Principles or Basic Requirements

In the national design specification[13], the following basic requirements are specified:

(1) Subgrade design should rely on various datas along the highway, including weather, hydrology, geology, earthquake, and construction materials, etc. Reconnaissance of geological conditions and subgrade material availability along the highway should be performed. Meanwhile, geotechnical properties, thickness, distribution and relative physical properties of soil layers should be obtained.

(2) Deep cut and high fill subgrades should be avoided if possible. If the fill height is more than 20m or the cut depth is more than 30m, the subgrade approach should be compared with the bridge, tunnel or separate subgrade approaches.

(3) For subgrade constructed along the river or soaked subgrade, the design height of the subgrade edge should be higher than the summation of water level based on flood frequency (Table 7-1) calculation, water level rise due to backwater, water level rise due to waves and 0.5m safety height.

(4) Subgrade cross section type and slope grade should be selected based on the local natural conditions and engineering geological conditions. For subgrades constructed along the river, the river channel should not be occupied. Meanwhile,

slope protection and reinforcement projects should be constructed if necessary based on the erosion conditions. In addition, redundant earthwork from the subgrade construction should not lead to riverbed blockage, river diversion, or destruction of structures, farmland and houses along the highway.

Table 7-1 Subgrade Design Flood Frequency

Highway Class	Expressway	Class-I Highway	Class-II Highway	Class-III Highway	Class-IV Highway
Flood Frequency	1/100	1/100	1/50	1/25	Dependent on local conditions

Note: If the highway is exclusive, one grade higher standard should be used.

(5) Subgrade fill materials should meet the requirements of subgrade strength and resilient modulus. Earthwork distribution should be designed based on the comparison of cut and fill balance, concentrated earthwork disposal and earthwork borrow, and subgrade fill material improvement.

(6) Settlement after construction should be kept in mind throughout the subgrade design process. Uneven settlement should be well controlled for the transition area between subgrade and structures of bridges and culverts, transition area between cut and fill, high embankment, and subgrade with steep slopes.

(7) The effects of water and freezing should be included during the design process. Meanwhile, a complete water drainage system and necessary anti-freezing facilities should be constructed.

7.3 Roadbed Design

As shown in Fig. 7-1, it is necessary to initialize the pavement structure and perform the vertical stress analysis before designing the roadbed. In this section, the concept of roadbed will be introduced followed by thickness design, filling material requirements, design criteria and resilient modulus determination.

7.3.1 Roadbed Definition and Thickness Design

Roadbed can be defined as the subgrade part that is 80cm or 120cm below the pavement structure, which can be further divided as the upper and lower roadbed layers. The upper roadbed lager is 30cm. The lower roadbed layer is 50cm for light, medium and heavy traffic or 90cm for the very heavy and extreme heavy traffic. For some highways with special axle loads (roads in a forest area, for instance), the working area should be calculated and the roadbed thickness should be determined based on the working area instead of 80cm or 120cm.

7.3.2 Requirements on CBR and Compaction of Roadbed Soils

California Bearing Ratio (CBR) is employed to characterize the roadbed soil mechanical property. Table 7-2 lists the minimum requirements according to the national design specification[13], which are dependent on the highway classification, location, and traffic loading levels. In general, the CBR value in the Table 7-2 is measured according to the national soil engineering testing specification[11]. When the annual rainfall is less than 400mm and the subgrade has a good drainage system, the CBR testing conditions and quality control requirements can be different from the Table 7-2: ①the CBR testing can be performed with the water content in the balanced moisture condition; ②the minimum CBR requirements for roadbed soils can be determined according to the local climate and traffic canditions.

Table 7-2 Minimum Requirements of Subgrade Fill Materials

Roadbed Components		Depth from Roadbed Surface	Minimum value of CBR (%)		
			Expressway or Class-I Highway	Class-II Highway	Class-III or Class-IV Highway
Upper Roadbed		0~0.3	8	6	5
Lower Roadbed	Light, Moderate, or Heavy Traffic	0.3~0.8	5	4	3
	Very, Extremely Heavy Traffic	0.3~1.2	5	4	—

Subgrade should be constructed layer by layer and compacted accordingly. The maximum grain size of fill materials should be less than 100mm and the cross slope of roadbed should be the same as the road cross slope. The degree of compaction for subgrade roadbed should meet the requirements as listed in Table 7-3. It should be noted that:

- The compaction degree is calculated with the maximum dry density which is measured through the heavy compaction moisture-density test based on the current testing specification.
- When the asphalt or concrete pavement structure is used in Class-III or Class-IV highway, the compaction requirement of Class-II highway should be employed.

Table 7-3 Requirements of Degree of Compaction for Subgrade Roadbed

Roadbed Components	Depth from Roadbed Surface	Roadbed Compaction Degree (%)		
		Expressway or Class-I Highway	Class-II Highway	Class-III or Class-IV Highway
Upper Roadbed	0~0.3	≥96	≥95	≥94

continue

Roadbed Components		Depth from Roadbed Surface	Roadbed Compaction Degree (%)		
			Expressway or Class-I Highway	Class-II Highway	Class-III or Class-IV Highway
Lower Roadbed	Light, Moderate, or Heavy Traffic	0.3~0.8	≥96	≥95	≥49
	Very, Extremely Heavy Traffic	0.3~1.2	≥96	≥95	—

7.3.3 Subgrade Design Criteria

The major criterion of subgrade design is the overall resilient modulus on the roadbed surface and the verification criterion is the vertical compressive strain on the roadbed surface. The design requirements are as follows:

- The resilient modulus of the roadbed surface under equilibrium moisture conditions shouldn't meet the corresponding requirements in asphalt pavement or cement concrete pavement design specifications[2,3].

- The vertical compressive strain on the roadbed surface for asphalt pavements should meet the asphalt pavement permanent deformation control requirements, whereas the vertical compressive strain on the roadbed surface requirement isn't necessary for cement concrete pavement.

For newly-built highways, the design value of subgrade resilient modulus E_0 can be determined by the following equation:

$$E_0 = K_s K_\eta M_R \geq [E_0] \tag{7-1}$$

In the Equation, E_0 is the design value of subgrade resilient modulus under equilibrium moisture conditions while $[E_0]$ is the required value of subgrade resilient modulus for pavement structural design.

The determination of is $[E_0]$ dependent on the asphalt pavement structural design requirements and the methods can be found in the corresponding specifications. In this textbook, the Chapters 8 and 9 will introduce the subgrade requirements.

In order to determine the design value of subgrade resilient modulus (E_0), M_R, K_s, and K_η should be determined by the methods as discussed below:

Methods for Determining M_R: M_R is the dynamic resilient modulus of subgrade under standard conditions (the standard moisture condition is a moisture condition when the soil is at its optimum moisture content and maximum dry density). There are three methods for determining M_R:

- The 1st approach for determining M_R is through the dynamic triaxial testing with the testing procedure presented in the appendix A of the national subgrade design specification[13].

- The 2nd approach for determining is through the reference values as listed in Table 7-4 and Table 7-5 according to the national subgrade design specification[13]. This approach is suitable when the laboratory testing is not available or difficult.
- The 3rd approach for determining M_R is through the roadbed soil CBR value with Equations 7-2 and 7-3.

$$M_R = 17.6 \text{CBR}^{0.54} \quad (7\text{-}2)$$

$$M_R = 22.1 \text{CBR}^{0.55} \quad (7\text{-}3)$$

Table 7-4 Reference Value of Resilient Modulus for Subgrade Soil under the Standard Conditions

Soil Groups	M_R values (MPa)
Gravels (G)	110 ~ 135
Gravels with fine-grained soils (GF)	100 ~ 130
Gravels with silty soils (GM)	100 ~ 125
Gravels with clayey soils (GC)	95 ~ 120
Sands (S)	95 ~ 125
Sands with fine-grained soils (SF)	80 ~ 115
Sands with silty soils (SM)	65 ~ 95
Sands with clayey soils (SC)	60 ~ 90
Silty soils with the lower liquid limit (ML)	50 ~ 90
Clayey soils with the lower liquid limit (CL)	50 ~ 85
Silty soils with the higher liquid limit (MH)	30 ~ 70
Clayey soils with the higher liquid limit (CH)	20 ~ 50

Notes: 1. For gravels or sands with the larger value of D60 (particle size whose passing percentage is larger than 60%), the higher M_R value is recommended.
2. For soils with fine-grained particles, the lower M_R value is recommended if it contains the larger percentage of particles passing 0.075mm or has the higher plastic index value.
3. The smaller M_R value is recommended if the traffic loading level is light, moderate, or heavy, while the larger M_R value is recommended if the traffic loading level is very or extremely heavy.

Table 7-5 Reference Value of Resilient Modulus for Granular Materials under the Standard Condition

Soil Groups	M_R values (MPa)
Graded Crushed Stones	180 ~ 400
Unscreened Crushed Stones	180 ~ 220
Graded Gravels	150 ~ 300
Natural Sand Gravels	100 ~ 140

Methods for determining (*Reduction coefficient*): is reduction coefficient of subgrade modulus under the dry-wet cycling or freeze-thaw cycling, which can be determined through experiments. The typical value of is ranging from 0.7 to 0.95. In the preliminary design, the designer can select a value from 0.7 to 0.95 according to the local climatic conditions, subgrade soil types, and drainage conditions.

Methods for determining k_s (*Moisture content adjustment coefficient*): k_s is the moisture content adjustment coefficient for subgrade resilient modulus, which can be defined as the ratio of the resilient modulus under equilibrium moisture condition to the resilient modulus under the standard condition.

According to the national subgrade design specification[13], there are two steps for determining:

- The 1st step is to determine the moisture conditions with the method presented in the appendix C in the specification[13]. Readers may refer to the specification[13] or the Chapter 3 of this textbook. The subgrade moisture condition may be one of three conditions of dry, moist, and wet.
- The 2nd step is to determine the coefficient with the method presented in the appendix D in the specification[13]. When the subgrade is under a wet condition, Table 7-6 may be used to determine the coefficient. When the subgrade is under a dry condition, Table 7-7 may be used to determine the coefficient. When the subgrade is under a moist condition, it can be considered as the combination of a dry condition and a wet condition. With the Table 7-6 and Table 7-2, the coefficients in wet and dry conditions can be determined respectively, and the linear interpolation may be used to determine the coefficient of the moist condition.

Table 7-6 The moisture content adjustment coefficient for wet subgrade

Soil Type	Sands	Sands with fine-grained soils	Silty Soils	Clayey Soils
Top of subgrade work area	0.8~0.9	0.5~0.6	0.5~0.7	0.6~1.0
Bottom of subgrade work area	0.5~0.6	0.4~0.5	0.4~0.6	0.5~0.9

Notes: 1. For sands, the larger coefficient value is recommended for the higher value of D60.
2. For sands with fine-grained soils, the lower coefficient value is recommended if it contains a larger percentage of fine particles or has the higher plastic index value.
3. For silty and clayey soils, the lower coefficient value is recommended for the lower value of the subgrade height.

Table 7-7 The moisture content adjustment coefficient for dry subgrade

Soil Type	TMI					
S	-50	-30	-10	10	30	50
SM	1.3~1.84	1.14~1.80	1.02~1.77	0.93~1.73	1.3~1.84	0.8~1.64
SC	1.59~1.65	1.10~1.26	0.83~0.97	0.73~0.83	0.7~0.76	0.7~0.76

continue

Soil Type	TMI					
ML	1.35~1.55	1.01~1.23	0.76~0.96	0.58~0.77	0.51~0.65	0.42~0.62
CL	1.22~1.71	0.73~1.52	0.57~1.24	0.51~1.02	0.49~0.88	0.48~0.81

Notes: 1. For sands, the larger coefficient value is recommended for the higher value of D_{60};

2. For the other soil types, the adjustment coefficient is dependent on percentage of fine-grained soils; increasing the percentage results in decreasing of the coefficient.

7.4 Subgrade Cross-section Design

The subgrade design elevation is generally different from the ground elevation. Based on the subgrade cross section types, the subgrade can be classified into embankment/fill, cut, and cut and fill. In an embankment/fill section, the subgrade design elevation is higher than the ground elevation and the subgrade surface is at the top surface of the embankment/fill. In a cut section, the subgrade design elevation is lower than the ground elevation and the subgrade surface is at the bottom of the cut. If the ground slope is relatively steeper and wide, one side of the subgrade needs to be filled and the other side needs to be cut. This type of subgrade is often referred to as "cut and fill". Cut and fill type subgrade is often used on highways in rolling terrain and mountainous areas. The subgrade supports the subbase and/or the pavement section. To ensure a stable, long-lasting, and maintenance free roadway, the subgrade is required to be constructed using certain proven procedures that provide satisfactory results.

7.4.1 Three Key Elements of a Subgrade Cross-section

According to the Chinese engineering practice, the subgrade cross-section is composed of the subgrade width, subgrade height, and subgrade side slope. Followed are the definitions of the three key elements:

Subgrade Width: The subgrade width is mainly composed of travel lanes, central reserve, and road shoulders as well as the emergency stop area, climbing lane and so on. The width of a travel lane is from 3.5 to 3.75m, the shoulder width is from 1.0 to 3.0m, and the central reserve is about 3.0m. For a four-lane expressway as shown in Fig. 7-2, the subgrade width may be equal to $4 \times 3.75 + 2 \times 3 + 3 = 24(m)$.

Subgrade Height: The subgrade height is referred to the height of filling materials or the depth of excavation. Since the original ground may have a slope, the height at the road center is different from that at the road edges, the center height and edge height should be distinguished. The center height is referred to the distance between the design elevation of subgrade center line and the original ground, while the edge height is referred to the distance between the design elevation of subgrade edge line and the fill slope toe or the cut slope top. In Chinese practice, the edge height is commonly used as the subgrade height as shown in Fig. 7-3.

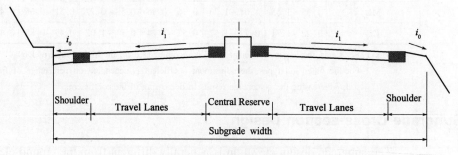

Fig. 7-2 Subgrade width

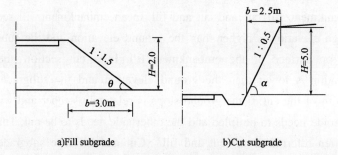

a)Fill subgrade   b)Cut subgrade

Fig. 7-3 Subgrade height and slope

Subgrade Side Slope: The subgrade side slope is defined as the ratio of the subgrade height to the slope width and denoted by $1:m$ for the fill subgrade and $1:n$ for the cut subgrade. As shown in Fig. 7-3a), the subgrade height $H = 2.0$m and the slope width $b = 3.0$m, therefore, the slope is $2:3 = 1:1.5$. As shown in Fig. 7-3b), the subgrade height $H = 5.0$m and the slope width $b = 2.5$m, therefore, the slope is $5:2.5 = 1:0.5$.

7.4.2 Fill Subgrade Design

Fill Subgrade Composition: Fig. 7-4 shows a typical structure of a fill subgrade with pavement structure. It is obvious that a fill subgrade is composed of the upper roadbed, the lower roadbed, the upper embankment, and the lower embankment. It should be noted that the height of a fill subgrade (H) is a sum of subgrade and pavement and the subgrade width (W) is the width of the pavement surface plus the shoulders instead of that of the subgrade top surface. The three key elements of a fill subgrade geometry are width, height, and slopes (including the left slope and the right slope).

Fill Types and Typical Cross-sections: Based on the fill height, fill subgrade can be divided into low fill, high fill and average or ordinary fill. When a fill height is less than subgrade work area depth, it can be defined as the low embankment. For the fill height of more than 20m, it can be defined as the high fill. For the embankment with slope steeper than 1 : 2.5, it can be defined as the steep slope fill. In addition, there are some other types of fills, including soaked fills, fills with protected slope toes, embankment with fill materials from the excavated irrigation channel. Fig. 7-5 shows the typical cross-sections of fill subgrades.

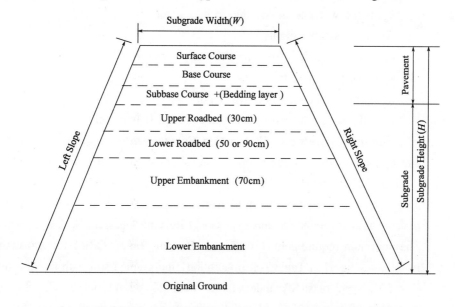

Fig. 7-4 Illustration of Fill Subgrade with Pavement Structure

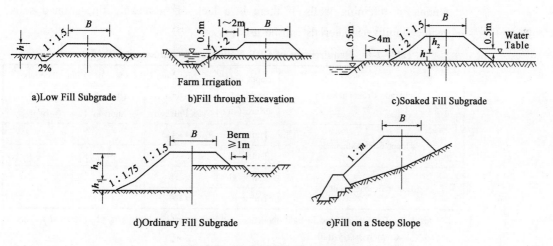

Fig. 7-5 Typical Fill Cross-sections

Fill Height: There are various factors which may significantly impact the fill height. In the national design specification[13], the optimum embankment height of a fill subgrade should satisfy the Equation 7-4:

$$H_{op} = \max\{(h_{sw} - h_0) + h_w + h_{bw} + \Delta h_1 + h_p, h_{wd} + h_p, h_f + h_p\} \quad (7\text{-}4)$$

Where:

H_{op} is the optimum embankment height;

h_{sw} is the design water level due to flooding;

h_0 is the ground elevation;

h_w is the water level rise due to waves;

h_{bw} is the water level rise due to backwater;

Δh is the safety height;

h_1 is the subgrade critical height under a medium wet condition;

h_p is the pavement thickness;

h_{wd} is the subgrade work area depth;

h_f is the subgrade frozen depth in seasonal freezing areas.

Filling Materials and Compaction Requirements: It should be noted that the embankment in this section refers to the subgrade part which is below the roadbed. Well graded coarse soils like gravel and sand are preferred as the fill material for embankment and the maximum grain size should be less than 150mm. Silt cannot be directly used for embankments in seasonal freezing areas and soaked embankments. The minimum requirement of California Bearing Ratio (CBR) for embankment fill materials is listed in Table 7-8. In addition, fine-grained soil with liquid limit higher than 50% and plasticity index larger than 26 should not be directly used for embankment construction. Materials with good permeability should be used for soaked embankment, back of abutment for bridges and culverts, and back of abutment for retaining walls. If there is a lack of permeable fine-grained soils, inorganic stabilized materials can be used.

Table 7-8 Requirement of CBR Value for Embankment Fill Materials

Subgrade Components	Depth from Roadbed surface (m)	Minimum CBR (%) of Filling Materials		
		Expressway or Class-I highway	Class-II highway	Class-III or IV highway
Upper Embankment	Traffic #1	0.8~1.5	4	3
	Traffic #2	1.2~1.9	4	3
Lower Embankment	Traffic #1	>1.5	3	2
	Traffic #2	>1.9		

Notes: 1. Traffic#1 is referred to light, moderate, and heavy traffic, while traffic#2 is referred to very or extremely heavy traffic.

2. When filling materials cannot meet CBR requirements, treatments should be performed through adding lime, cement, fly-ash, etc.

3. When asphalt or cement pavement is used in a class-III or IV highway, the CBR requirement of Class II highway should be employed.

The embankment should be constructed layer by layer and uniformly compacted. The degree of compaction should meet the requirements as presented in Table 7-9.

7. Highway Subgrade Design

Table 7-9   Degree of compaction requirements for embankment

Subgrade Components		Depth from Roadbed Surface (m)	Compaction Degree (%)		
			Expressway or Class-I Highway	Class-II Highway	Class-III or IV Highway
Upper Embankment	Traffic #1	0.8~1.5	≥94	≥94	≥93
	Traffic #2	1.2~1.9	≥94	≥94	—
Lower Embankment	Traffic #1	>1.5	≥93	≥92	≥90
	Traffic #2	>1.9			

Notes: 1. Traffic #1 is referred to light, moderate, and heavy traffic, while traffic #2 is referred to very or extremely heavy traffic.
2. When asphalt or cement pavement is used in a class-III or IV highway, the compaction requirement of Class II highway should be employed.
3. When fly-ash and industrial residues are used as embankment filling materials, or when the project is located in very dry or wet regions, the compaction degree may be 1%~2% lower than the required value in the table.

Fill Slope Design: The following three conditions should be considered when one designs the fill slope.

- First of all, slope ratio depends on the properties of slope soils and slope rocks, hydrological conditions, and slope height. For the embankment with good geological conditions and less than 20m height, the slope ratio should not be steeper than those presented in Table 7-10.
- Secondly, for fills higher than 20m, step-shaped slopes should be constructed and the stability should be verified by simplified Bishop Method.
- Thirdly, for submerged slope section of the soaked embankment, the slope ratio should not be steeper than 1:1.75.

Table 7-10   Fill Slope When $H \leqslant 20m$

Filling Material Types	Fill Slope	
	Upper Slope ($H \leqslant 8m$)	Lower Slope ($H \leqslant 12m$)
Fine-grained	1:1.5	1:1.75
Coarse-grained	1:1.5	1:1.75
Over coarse-grained	1:1.3	1:1.5

Original Ground beneath Embankment: The filling materials are paved on the ground. It is necessary to consider the features of the original ground beneath the embankment. The following three aspects should be considered:

- When the embankment is built on an *inclined original ground*, the following three considerations should be paid:
    (1) If the inclined slope is less than 1:5, the embankment should

be built after removing turfs humus;

(2) If the inclined slope is bewteen 1 : 5 and 1 : 2.5, the original ground should be benched and the bench width should be more than 2m;

(3) When the inclined slope is more than 1 : 2.5, the stability analysis should be performed.

- When the embankment is *impacted by the ground water*, there are two solutions: The first is to consider the measures of intercepting, draining, or leading water out of the embankment; the second is to use permeable materials under the embankment.
- Compactness of the *original ground* should not be less than 90% for expressway, class-I highway, and class-II highway and 85% for class-III and class-IV highways. When the fill is a low embankment, the original ground should be excavated. The treatment thickness should be deeper than the roadbed depth.

Bridge and Culvert Approach Embankment: When an embankment is approaching to a bridge or culvert, measures should be provided to smoothly transfer the two types of deformations. The length of transition embankment can be estimated with the following Equation:

$$L = (2 \sim 3)H + (3 \sim 5) \tag{7-5}$$

The filling materials in the transition embankment should be specially considered. Additionally, the compactness should not be less than 96%.

High Embankment and Inclined Embankment: When the fill subgrade is a high embankment or an inclined embankment, the slope stability analysis should be performed with considering the following three engineering conditions:

- The first condition is a normal condition which is the most popular condition during the subgrade service life;
- The second is the special condition I where subgrade experiences large rainfalls;
- The third is the special condition II where subgrade may experience earthquakes.

According to the national subgrade design specification[13], the simplified Bishop method (as shown in Fig. 7-6) should be used to analyze the stability of a high embankment with Equation 7-6. The Residual thrust method should be used to analyze the inclined embankment as demonstrated in the section 5.3.4 of the Chapter 5.

$$F_s = \frac{\sum [c_i b_i + (W_i + Q_i)\tan\varphi_i]/(W + Q_i)}{(W_i + Q_i)\sin\alpha_i} \tag{7-6}$$

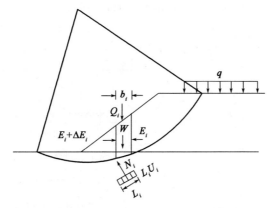

Fig. 7-6 Illustration of a high embankment stability analysis with the simplified Bishop method

$$m_{\alpha i} = \cos\alpha_i + \frac{\sin\alpha_i}{F_s} \qquad (7\text{-}7)$$

The minimum requirements on the stability coefficients are shown in Table 7-11 for the high embankments or inclined embankments.

Table 7-11 Stability coefficients for high embankments or inclined embankments

Analysis Tasks	Strength Criterion	Engineering Conditions	Stability Coefficients	
			Expressway, Class-I or II Highway	Class-III or IV Highway
Embankment stability or overall stability of subgrade structure	Consolidated quick shear strength or tri-axial consolidated undrained shear strength	Normal	1.45	1.35
		Special I	1.35	1.25
	Quick shear strength	Normal	1.35	1.30
		Special I	1.25	1.15
Sliding stability along a weak slope surface	—	Normal	1.30	1.25
		Special I	1.20	1.15

Note: When a class-III or IV highway plays a significant role in the local road network, the Class-II highway requirements should be taken for the embankment stability analysis.

7.4.3 Cut Subgrade Design

Cut Subgrade Composition: Fig. 7-7 shows a typical structure of a cut subgrade. It is obvious that a cut subgrade is composed of the upper roadbed, the lower roadbed and the original soils or rock beneath the roadbed. The height of a cut subgrade (H) is from the slope top to pavement surface and the subgrade width

(W) is the width of the pavement surface plus the shoulders.

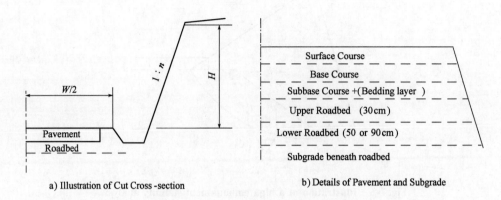

a) Illustration of Cut Cross-section

b) Details of Pavement and Subgrade

Fig. 7-7 Illustration of Cut Subgrade with Pavement Structure

Cut Types and Typical Cross-sections: Based on the cut height, cut subgrade can be divided into ordinary cuts and deep cuts. When a cut subgrade height is less than 20m for the soil slope (or 30m for the rock slope), it can be defined as the ordinary cut subgrade while it is defined as the deep cut subgrade when the height is more than 20cm for the soil slope (or 30m for the rock slope). According to the cut cross-section, cut subgrades may be divided into the full-cut subgrade, benched-cut subgrade, and half-tunnel subgrade as shown in Fig. 7-8.

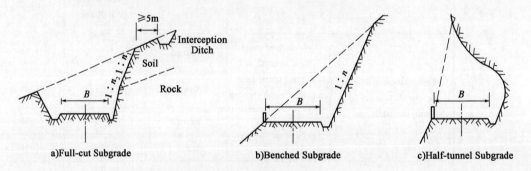

a) Full-cut Subgrade

b) Benched Subgrade

c) Half-tunnel Subgrade

Fig. 7-8 Typical Cut Subgrade Cross-section

Cut Height Design: The cut height is mainly dependent on the road geometric design with considering effects of environmental conditions and drainage design. In the subgrade and pavement engineering, the height is the distance from the cut slope top to the pavement surface. In the vertical alignment design, the height is the excavation depth at the road center.

Cut Slope Design: Cut slopes are dependent on hydrology, geology, slope height, drainage, protection measures, construction methods, etc. The cut slope design may be divided into two types, namely the ordinary cut and the deep cut. The ordinary cut slopes can be determined through the recommended values as listed in Table 7-12 and Table 7-13.

Table 7-12 Soil Cut Slope When $H \leqslant 20 \mathrm{m}$

Soil Types		Slope Ratio
Clayey soils, silty clay, silt with plasticity index larger than 3		1 : 1
Middle-size, coarse, and gravels over dedium density		1 : 1.5
Boulders, crushed stones, round gravels, angular gravels	Glued and dense	1 : 0.75
	With medium density	1 : 1

Table 7-13 Rock Cut Slope When $H \leqslant 30 \mathrm{m}$

Rock Types	Weathering Degree	Slope Ratio	
		$H < 15 \mathrm{m}$	$15 \mathrm{m} \leqslant H \leqslant 30 \mathrm{mm}$
Type I	Unweathered or micro-weathered	1 : 0.1 ~ 1 : 0.3	1 : 0.1 ~ 1 : 0.3
	Lightly weathered	1 : 0.1 ~ 1 : 0.3	1 : 0.3 ~ 1 : 0.5
Type II	Unweathered or micro-weathered	1 : 0.1 ~ 1 : 0.3	1 : 0.3 ~ 1 : 0.5
	Lightly weathered	1 : 0.3 ~ 1 : 0.5	1 : 0.5 ~ 1 : 0.75
Type III	Unweathered or micro-weathered	1 : 0.3 ~ 1 : 0.5	—
	Lightly weathered	1 : 0.5 ~ 1 : 0.75	—
Type IV	Lightly weathered	1 : 0.5 ~ 1 : 1	—
	Highly weathered	1 : 0.75 ~ 1 : 1	—

Notes: 1. When reliable data or experience is available, the cut slope is not restricted by this table.
2. Requirements of highly-weathered type IV rock are suitable for soft rocks.

Deep-cut Slope Design: For the deep cut slopes, the independent design should be performed based on the national subgrade design specification[13]. Followed are a few key points:

- In terms of the slope shapes, a deep cut slope cross-section may be a broken line or a step-shape line. If the shape is a step-shape line, a platform is usually constructed at the transition between the two slopes.
- Engineering exploration works should be performed before designing a deep cut slope for obtaining the essential data (details are presented in the specification[13]).
- The stability analysis methods may include Bishop method, residual thrust method, curve-line sliding slope analysis methods, and so on.
- The stability coefficient requirements are shown in Table 7-14 and the stability analysis under the earthquake condition should be performed according to the design specification[13] on the anti-earthquake design of highway engineering.

Table 7-14 Stability Coefficients Requirements

Engineering Conditions	Stability Coefficient	
	Expressway, Class- I Highway	Class- II, III, or IV Highway
Normal	1.20 ~ 1.30	1.15 ~ 1.25
Special I	1.10 ~ 1.20	1.05 ~ 1.15

Notes: 1. The larger value should be selected for the cut slope with a complex geological condition or a severe consequence.

2. The larger value should be selected when the slope failure may impact some important buildings (such as bridge, tunnel, high voltage towers, oil or gas pipelines, etc.), villages, and schools.

3. The temporary slope during construction should be no less than 1.05.

Over-excavation: when the original soil or rock beneath the roadbed does not meet the specification[13] requirements. It is necessary to over-excavate the roadbed and treat the underlying soils through engineering measures.

7.4.4 Fill-cut Subgrade Design

Fill-Cut Subgrade Composition: A typical structure of a fill-cut subgrade consists of the fill part and the cut part. In the fill part, the layers may include the upper roadbed, lower roadbed, the upper embankment, the lower embankment, and the underlying subgrade; while in the cut part, the layers may include the upper roadbed, the lower roadbed, and the underlying subgrade. The height of a fill-cut subgrade has two values which are the fill height and the cut height. The subgrade width (W) is the width of the pavement surface plus the shoulders.

Fill-cut Types and Typical Cross-sections: Fig. 7-9 shows typical fill-cut cross-sections.

Design Factors: Detailed requirements on the fill-cut subgrade design are presented in the design specification[13]. Since the fill-cut has the features of both the embankment and the cut, therefore, the requirements of fill and cut should be employed for the fill section and the cut section of a fill-cut subgrade, respectively. The roadbed should meet the following requirements:

- When the cut section cannot meet the roadbed requirements, overall excavation and treatment should be performed;
- When the fill section cannot meet the roadbed requirements, the engineering measures also should be provided;
- In the fill section, the permeable filling material is preferred;
- Sometimes, geogrid or the other engineering reinforcement measures may be provided to improve the capability of the fill-cut subgrade;
- When the cut section is rock soils, the fill section should be paved with rock soils.

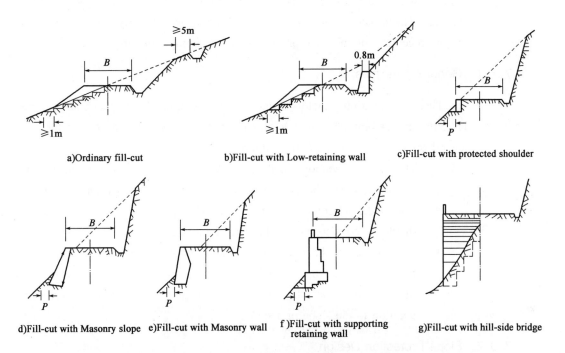

a) Ordinary fill-cut b) Fill-cut with Low-retaining wall c) Fill-cut with protected shoulder

d) Fill-cut with Masonry slope e) Fill-cut with Masonry wall f) Fill-cut with supporting retaining wall g) Fill-cut with hill-side bridge

Fig. 7-9 Typical Fill-cut Subgrade Cross-section

7.5 Subgrade Drainage Requirements

Highway drainage design has been introduced in Chapter 4. In this section, a brief introduction will be given to the subgrade drainage requirements according to the national subgrade design specification. Followed are the key points:

- Surface water is not allowed to drain onto bridge surface or into tunnels, or into their drainage system.
- Drainage facilities should be functional, safe, reliable, and easy to construct and maintain. The construction materials should meet the requirements in the appendix D of the design specification[16].
- Reinforced concrete covers or side fences (guardrail) should be provided for rectangular ditches in expressway or class-I highway. The bearing capability should be validated.
- Protection should be given to subdrains under ditches when they are under the frozen level.
- The catchwater drains should be no less than 5 meters from the top of the cut slope and no less than 2 meters from the fill foot.

7.6 Subgrade Slope Protection and Retaining Structures

In addition to the geometric and structural design of subgrade, protection and retaining structures are also significant for improving the durability and stability of subgrade. The target of this chapter is to discuss the popularly-used measures and design procedures of subgrade protection and retaining structures.

7.6.1 General principles

There are various factors which may significantly impact the subgrade durability and stability. In order to minimize their effects, the following three key general principles should be kept in mind:

- The slope protection should be built on a stable slope and the retaining structures should be used when the slope may be in an instable condition.
- During the subgrade construction, if temporary structures are needed, they should be consistent with the permanent structures.
- In rainy areas, the intercepting drains should be carefully considered in addition to the slope protection measures. In the road sections with the higher water tables, the subsurface drainage system should be designed in addition to the slope protection.

7.6.2 Slope Protection Design

There are two slope protection types, namely the slope surface protection and the water-erosion slope protection. The purpose of the slope surface protection design is to minimize effects of environment-related factors, such as weathering, rainfalls, and so on. The purpose of the water-erosion slope protection is to minimize the effects of water erosion for the subgrade along the rivers.

Slope Surface Protection Methods: In order to protect the subgrade slope from various environment-related factors, there are three types of methods, namely the plant slope surface protection methods, the framework plant slope surface protection methods, and the engineering slope surface protection methods. For the plant slope surface protection methods, the plants, such as turf, bushes, or both of them, are cultivated on the slope surface for protecting the slope from effects of environment-related erosion. When the slope is less than 1 : 1, it is recommended to cultivate turfs. Otherwise, it is recommended to cultivate bushes or bushes and turfs. The framework plant slope surface protection methods may include different types according to the framework shapes and plant types. The engineering slope protection methods may include the gunite slope surface protection, the net-suspended gunite slope surface protection, the dry-laid rubble slope surface protection, bounded rubble slope surface protection, and so on. Readers may refer to the design specification[13] for detailed requirements of those slope protection methods.

Water-erosion Slope Protection Methods: When the subgrade is built along the river, water-erosion should be seriously considered. The slope protection methods may include the direct protection methods and indirect protection methods. The direct protection methods may include the plant slope protection, the gabion slope protection, the retaining wall protection, the rubble protection, the pile protection, and so on. The indirect protection may include the spur dam, the longitudinal dam, and cellular dam.

- *Example* #1: ***Gabion Slope Protection***: Gabion is a box filled with stones, sands and soils for use in civil engineering, road building, military application and so on as shown in Fig. 7-10. Gabions slope protection method are mainly used to protect slopes of subgrade along the rivers.

Fig. 7-10 Gabion Slope Protection

- *Example* #2: ***Indirect Slope Protection Methods***: As shown in Fig. 7-11 the spur dams, the longitudinal dams, and cellular dam are used to lead and slow down the water for minimizing the water-erosion.

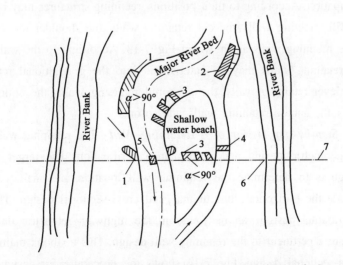

Fig. 7-11 An example of indirect slope protection method

1-Longitudinal dam; 2-Cellular dam; 3-Spur dam; 4-Retaining dam; 5-Division dam; 6-Bridge pier; 7-Road centerline

7.6.3 Design of Retaining Structures

Retaining structures may include retaining walls, slide-resistant piles, soil nailing walls, and so on. In this section, the retaining structures are referred to the retaining walls and the other types of retaining structures are detailed in the national design specification[13].

Configuration of a Retaining Structure: Fig. 7-12 shows the components of a typical retaining wall, which include top of the wall, front of the wall, back of the wall, body of the wall, toe of the wall, heel of the wall, foundation, and bottom of the foundation. The major target of the retaining wall design is to determine its geometry and verify its mechanics.

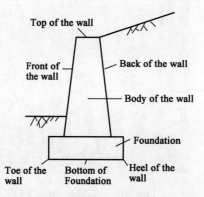

Fig. 7-12 Configuration of a Typical Retaining Wall

Retaining Structure Types: Retaining structures are highly used in highway engineering in order to improve the subgrade stability and reduce the land occupation. According to their positions, retaining structures may be categorized into the fill retaining walls, the cut retaining walls, the shoulder retaining wall, and the slope retaining walls as shown in Fig. 7-13. According to the wall structure types, the retaining walls may be categorized into the gravitational retaining walls, the cantilever retaining walls, the anchored retaining walls, the counter fort retaining walls, the gabion retaining walls, and so on.

Step-by-step Design of a Retaining Wall: The retaining wall design involves the geometric design and performance verification. The target of the geometric design is to determine the retaining wall location and main components which include the horizontal, longitudinal, and cross-sectional design. The horizontal and longitudinal design can be found in the highway geometric design and specific literature pertinent to the retaining wall design. This textbook mainly focused on the cross-sectional design. Fig. 7-14 shows the procedure for design a retaining wall based on the national subgrade design specification[13]. In the procedure, the stability and strength analysis will be briefly discussed in this section and readers may find details of the other three steps in the design specification[13].

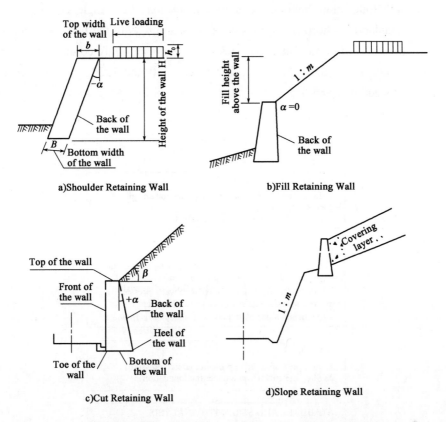

Fig. 7-13 Retaining walls categorized according to the supporting positions

As shown in Fig. 7-14, there are three key tasks for retaining wall stability and strength analysis, namely stability analysis, foundation stress analysis, and strength analysis. Stability analysis may include the sliding stability and the overturning stability.

The *sliding stability* should satisfy the sliding stability Equation (Equation 7-8) and the sliding stability coefficient can be determined with the Equation 7-9.

$$[1.1G + \gamma_{Q1}(E_y + E_x \tan\alpha_0) - \gamma_{Q2} E_p \tan\alpha_0]\mu + (1.1G + \gamma_{Q1} E_y)\tan\alpha_0 - \gamma_{Q1} E_x + \gamma_{Q2} E_p > 0$$

(7-8)

$$K_0 = \frac{[N + (E_x - E'_p)\tan\alpha_0]\mu + E'_p}{E_x - N\tan\alpha_0}$$

(7-9)

In the two Equations, G is the gravitational force (kN). For the soaked part of the retaining wall, the buoyancy force should be considered. E_x and E_y are the horizontal and vertical components of the active earth pressure, while E_p is the horizontal component of the passive earth pressure ($E_p = 0$) for the soaked retaining wall. $E'_p = 0.3E_p$. N is the vertical component of the resultant force on the retaining wall foundation bottom. α_0 is the foundation slant angle and $\alpha_0 = 0$ when the foundation is horizontally positioned. γ_{Q1} and γ_{Q2} are the two coefficients which are presented in the national design specification. According to various load combinations, the value of γ_{Q1} is between 1.0 and 1.30, while the value of γ_{Q2} is between 0.3 and 0.5.

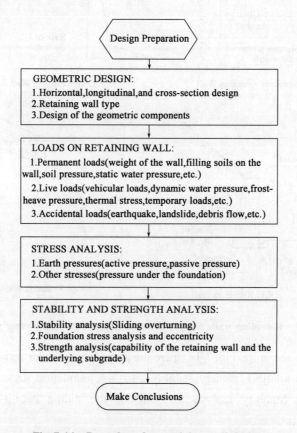

Fig. 7-14 Procedure for retaining wall design

The ***over-turning stability*** should satisfy the overturning stability Equation (Equation 7-10) and the overturning stability coefficient can be determined by the Equation 7-11.

$$0.8G + \gamma_{Q1}(E_y Z_x - E_x Z_y) + \gamma_{Q2} E_p Z_p > 0 \qquad (7\text{-}10)$$

$$K_0 = \frac{G Z_G + E_y Z_x + E'_p Z_p}{E_x Z_y} \qquad (7\text{-}11)$$

In the two Equations, Z_G is the distance between the foundation toe and the resultant force of wall weight, foundation weight, weight of filling soil on the foundation, and the other vertical force on the wall. Z_x is the distance between the foundation toe and E_y; Z_y is the distance between the foundation toe and E_x; Z_p is the distance between the foundation toe and E_p.

The **vertical stresses on the underlying subgrade** should not exceed the allowable value which is specified in the highway bridge and culvert subgrade and foundation design specification[13]. The vertical stresses may include the stress at toe of the wall (σ_1) and the stress at heel of the wall (σ_2). Those two vertical stresses are dependent on the eccentricity of the resultant force (e_0). Followed are equations for calculating the eccentricity and two stresses:

$$e_0 = \frac{M_d}{N_d} \tag{7-12}$$

Where M_d is the moment at the foundation center (MPa) and N_d is vertical force acted on the bottom of foundation (kN/m). Readers may find details on the determination of M_d, N_d in Chapter 5 and the national subgrade design specification[13].

When $e_0 \leqslant \dfrac{B}{6}$,

$$\sigma_{1,2} = \frac{N_d}{A}\left(1 \pm \frac{6e_0}{B}\right) \tag{7-13}$$

When $e_0 > \dfrac{B}{6} = \dfrac{2N_d}{3(0.5B - e_0)}$,

$$\sigma_2 = 0 \tag{7-14}$$

In those two Equations, B is the foundation width and A is the foundation bottom area per meter. When the foundation is rectangular, $A = B \times 1 = B$. It should be noted that the eccentricity should be no larger than $B/4$ for rock subgrade and $B/6$ for soil subgrade.

In addition to the retaining wall stability analysis and foundation stress analysis, the bearing capability of the retaining wall and its components should also be verified. Readers may find more details in the national subgrade design specification[13].

7.7 Subsidiary Facility Design

In addition to the major subgrade components, there are subsidiary facilities which are also very important in subgrade design. They are the borrow earth area and the spoil area.

Borrow Earth Area Design: a borrow earth area is also called borrow pit or borrowing-pit. When design the borrow pit, the following requirements should be met according to the subgrade design specification[13]:

- The first consideration is to keep the borrow pit off the embankment with

a reasonable distance for minimizing effects on the embankment stability.
- The second consideration is to keep the borrow pit far away from the bridge approaching sections.
- The third consideration is the borrow pit should not be deeper than the water table and the longitudinal slope should be more than 0.2% if the pit is also used for draining water purposes.

Spoil area design: a spoil area is built when the redundant soils from the cut sections should be treated. The designer should consider the following requirements:
- The first consideration is not to impact the subgrade or inclined slope stability;
- The second consideration is not to alter the water flow direction due to the construction of spoil areas.

7.8 Summary of Chapter 7

This chapter has discussed on subgrade design based on the current subgrade design specification[13]. Followed are key points:

1. First of all, the design methodology and design principles are introduced;

2. Secondly, the roadbed design is introduced, which include the roadbed definition, thickness, CBR requirements, design criteria, and field verification method.

3. Thirdly, the major target of a cross-section design is to determine the subgrade width, the subgrade height, and the subgrade slope. The three typical cross-sections are fill, cut, and fill-cut. In each of the typical cross-section may be further categorized into different types.

4. The last major task discussed is the design of protection and retaining structures. In the textbook, the design procedures are presented and the readers may refer to the national design specification[13] for more details.

Problems and Questions

1. Assuming an expressway is planned in your hometown, estimate the minimum requirements of the roadbed in a dry condition. (Hints: *the first is to find the roadbed material; the second is to determine minimum CBR; the third is to estimate MR through the empirical equation; The fourth is to find the national zone and determine TMI; determine the coefficients and the design resilient modulus*)

2. Draft the structural composition of a fill subgrade, a cut subgrade, and a fill-cut subgrade.

3. Discuss the design considerations of a low embankment, a high embankment, and a soaked subgrade.

4. In order to determine the fill height, which factors should be considered?

5. List a few subgrade slope protection methods and explain their advantages.

6. Design of a retaining structure may involve the sliding stability analysis, the overturning stability analysis, the underlying subgrade capability analysis, and the retaining wall strength analysis. Your task is to design a gravitational retaining wall with information below:

- The length of wall is 20m and the other parameters are shown in Fig. p7-1.
- Properties of soils behind the wall: unit weight, $\gamma = 20 \text{kN/m}^3$, internal frictional angle $\varphi = 35°$, the frictional angle between the wall and the filling soil $\delta = 17.5°$.
- Properties of soils underlying the wall: the bearing capability $[\sigma] = 500\text{kPa}$ and the frictional coefficient is 0.5.
- Material of the wall: unit weight $\gamma_w = 20 \text{kN/m}^3$, the allowable compressive stress is 500kPa and the allowable shear stress is 80kPa.

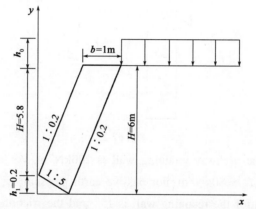

Fig. p7-1 **Illustration of a gravitational wall of problem 6**

7. Please define the following concepts:

Roadbed; Subgrade workzone; Low embankment; High embankment; Steep slope embankment; Deep cut; Degree of compaction.

8. Can a soil with 6% CBR be used as the filling material of roadbed for an expressway?

9. For a subgrade under dry moisture condition with the following other conditions, please determine the design value of subgrade resilient modulus.

Located in seasonal frozen area; subgrade soil is sand; TMI = 10; CBR value of subgrade filling material = 18% ; degree of compaction = 96%.

10. For a subgrade embankment in seasonal frozen area, the design flood level = 20m, ground elevation = 17.5m, backwater height = 1.0m, wave height = 0.3m, safety height = 0.5m. The subgrade critical height at moist condition = 2.5m, subgrade workzone depth = 3.5m, seasonal frozen depth = 3.0m, pavement thickness =

0.5m. Please determine the appropriate subgrade embankment height.

11. For an embankment slope with a circular failure surface, the ith slice has a width of 2m. The bottom inclination angle is 30°. The slice has a height of 7m in the embankment and 3m underneath the ground surface. Embankment soil is $\gamma = 18\text{kN/m}^3$, $c = 15\text{kPa}$, $\varphi = 15°$; ground soil, $\gamma = 20\text{kN/m}^3$, $c = 18\text{kPa}$, $\varphi = 20°$. Please determine the slope stability coefficient F_s of this slice using simplified Bishop method.

12. For a subgrade with 8m height retaining wall, the pavement width is 8m. The retaining wall has a vertical back surface and the ground surface is flat. The unit weight of fill materials is 20kN/m^3, $f = 30°$, $c = 0$, $d = 15°$, as shown in Fig. p7-2. Please calculate the active earth pressure applied on the back of the retaining wall while considering the vehicle loading. Note: Refer to Subgrade specification H.0.1 on Page 119.

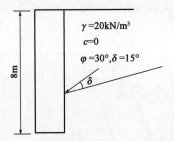

Fig. p7-2

13. The highway retaining wall is 200kN/m. For active earth pressure, $E_x = 200\text{kN/m}$, $E_y = 80\text{kN/m}$; For passive earth pressure, $E_p = 100\text{kN/m}$. The angle of the bottom for the retaining wall is 15° and the friction coefficient is 0.65. Please determine the sliding stability.

14. For a highway retaining wall with the following geometry as shown in Fig. p7-3, its self-weight is 180kN/m. For active earth pressure, $E_x = 175\text{kN/m}$, $E_y = 55\text{kN/m}$; for passive earth pressure, $E_p = 100\text{kN/m}$, $Z_p = 0.3$. Please determine the overturning stability.

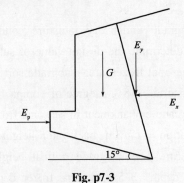

Fig. p7-3

15. Regarding the failure of soil behind retaining wall, answer the following questions:

(1) What are the FIVE possible types of failure?

(2) For the following example, as shown in Fig. p7-4, please check where is the possible failure surface with the assumption of active earth pressure? Height of retaining wall $H = 5.0$m; γ for filler material = 17kN/m^3; $\varphi = 35°$; $\delta = 2/3\varphi$. For additional information, refer to the APPENDIX.

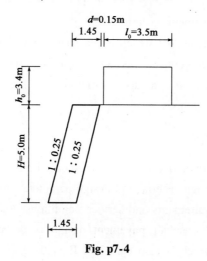

Fig. p7-4

8. Asphalt Pavement Design

Asphalt pavement design is the process to create and evaluate an asphalt pavement structure model which is the basis for pavement construction. The model may be altered according to the construction requirements. The focus of this chapter is to discuss how to design such a structure model and the Chapter 10 will introduce the construction methods.

8.1 Design Methodology

When talking about a design method, there are three key aspects, namely design theory, design criteria, and design parameters which are directly related to the serviceability requirements and service conditions. According to the national design specifications[2,14], asphalt pavement design is based on a mechanistic-empirical design method which is also called M-E method. 'M' represents the mechanical model which is built based on the theory of the multi-layered elastic system and 'E' represents the empirical model which is a set of transfer functions for linking the mechanical computational results to pavement distresses. Fig. 8-1 shows the general design methodology which includes not only the key subjects in each design step but also the chapters covering the corressponding subjects.

Followed are explanations of Fig. 8-1:

(1) Asphalt pavement design starts from the design preparation which includes design data from design assignment, key requirements from specification[2,8], and other relevant information.

(2) Traffic analysis serves two purposes, namely calculation of equivalent single axle loads and determination of traffic loading levels. This step should be performed after the design preparation and will be used in the pavement configuration initialization and pavement response analysis.

(3) Environmental conditions include temperature and moisture which impact both paving materials and pavement structural responses. Even though the national design specification[8] do not emphasize developments of climatic models, it is recommended to use the existing climatic models in your design. They include the heat transfer model for determining temperature distribution with respect to space and time, moisture equilibrium model for determining final moisture distribution in

the subgrade, and infiltration and drainage models for predicting the degree of saturation of granular bases. The environmental analysis should also be performed before the structure configuration.

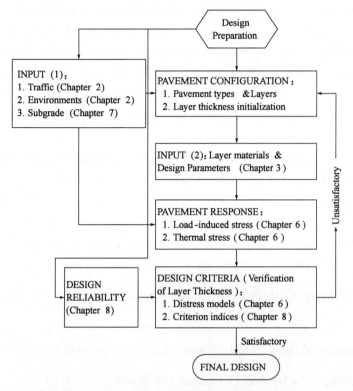

Fig. 8-1 Methodology for asphalt pavement design

(4) Pavement configuration includes number of layers, thickness of each layer, type of materials, and interlayer bonding. The process to initialize the pavement configuration is referred as "pavement combination design" which should be performed under the national design specifications[2,8] of design and construction.

(5) Layer materials mainly include asphalt-bounded mixes, hydraulic binder-bounded mixes, and unbounded mixtures. The basic material properties for the structural models are modulus, Poisson's ratio, and strength. Since temperature and moisture are various acrocss the year, it is unreasonable to use the same modulus for each layer. Therefore, one year is divided into a number of periods and different modulus values are used for different periods, based on the corresponding environmental conditions.

(6) Resilient modulus of subgrade is another key input for the structural models. Similar to the pavement layer materials, environments may impact the resilient modulus of subgrade values throughout the year. It is necessary to divide each year into a number of periods and set different values based on the specific

conditions.

(7) Pavement responses may be represented by the internal stresses, strains, and deflections which are computed through the mechanical analysis based on the multi-layered elastic system theory. It should be noted that the load-induced stresses are considered as the major responses and the environment-induced stresses are not considered as the key responses for asphalt pavement design according to the current asphalt pavement design specification[2]. For some special projects, however, the environment-induced stresses may become the major considerations. Therefore, it is necessary to consider all potential factors carefully before one starts a pavement design.

(8) If possible, distress model including fatigue cracking model, rutting model, and thermal cracking models should be used to predict distresses of the proposed pavement structure. Under certain reliability, if the predicted distresses are satisfactory compared with the actual distresses, the design is acceptable. Otherwise, the pavement configuration will be subjected to design iterations until the satisfactory result achieves.

8.2 Design Theory, Criterion, and Parameters

This section briefly introduces three key aspects of the asphalt pavement design method and details will be discussed in the subsequent sections.

8.2.1 Design Theory and Computational Model

As mentioned above, the asphalt pavement design is based on the multi-layered elastic system theory and the computational model is shown in Fig. 8-2. At the positions of A, B, C, and D as illustrated in the figure, stress, strain, or deflection are computed as the critical mechanical responses of a proposed pavement structure. Those mechanical responses will be used to determine whether the proposed design meets the design criteria or not.

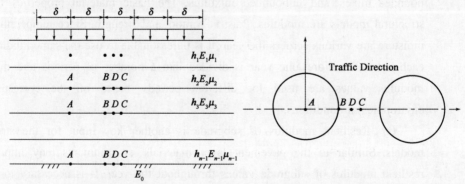

Fig. 8-2 Computational model for asphalt pavement design

8.2.2 Design Criteria and Controlling Parameters

In the previous version of design specification (JTG D50—2006)[14], the surface resilient deflection is employed as the controlling parameter to evaluate the overall stiffness of the pavement structure and the tensile stresses at the bottom of bonnded layers are employed as the controlling parameter to evaluate fatigue resistance of pavement layers.

In the current design specification (JTG D50—2017)[2], the surface resilient deflection is no longer used and a few new criteria and controlling parameters are added. Followed is a brief introduction according to the current specification[2]:

(1) *Reliability Criterion*: Engineering reliability means the ability of a system or component to perform its required functions under stated conditions for a specified time period. In the asphalt pavement design, the reliability is referred to the probability that a trial pavement structure can survive environmental and traffic loading conditions through a specific design period. Table 8-1 shows the minimum values of the target reliability and reliability index.

Table 8-1 Reliability criteria in the national asphalt pavement design specification[2]

Highway class	Expressway	Class-I	Class-II	Class-III	Class-IV
Target Reliability (%)	95	90	85	80	70
Reliability Index	1.65	1.28	1.04	0.84	0.52

(2) *Design Life Criterion*: For a newly-built highway, the pavement design life should be no less than the value listed in Table 8-2. For the re-built roads, this table can be used as the reference value instead of the compulsory value.

Table 8-2 Minimum value of asphalt pavement service life

Highway Class	Expressway	Class-I	Class-II	Class-III	Class-IV
Design Life	15	15	12	10	8

(3) *Axle Loading Criterion*: The standard axle load is the single axle on dual tires. The total weight of the axle is 100kN, the tire imprint pressure is 0.7MPa, the loading area diameter is 213mm, and the distance between the two loading areas is 319.5mm as listed in the Table 2-5. The traffic analysis should be performed based on the appendix A of the specification[2] for computing the accumulative ESAL (Equivalent Single Axle Loads). Readers may review Chapter 2 for details and the subsequent sections of this chapter will continue to discuss this topic.

(4) *Traffic Loading Classification Criterion*: Instead of using the cumulative ESAL as the design criterion, the current design specification employs the traffic

volume of large buses and trucks as the design criterion as shown in Table 8-3. In the table, the large buses or trucks are referred to the vehicles of type 2 ~ 11.

Table 8-3 Traffic loading classification criterion for asphalt pavement design

Traffic Loading Class	Extremely Heavy	Very Heavy	Heavy	Moderate	Light
Number of large buses and trucks in the design life ($\times 10^6$)	$\geqslant 50.0$	50.0 ~ 19.0	19.0 ~ 8.0	8.0 ~ 4.0	< 4.0

(5) **Structural Performance Criteria**: As discussed in Chapter 6, the major serviceability of asphalt pavement may include the high-temperature stability, the low-temperature stability, the fatigue resistance, the water-stability, aging, permeability, and skidding resistance. In other words, the proposed pavement structure should meet the above serviceability requirements. The structural performance criteria are the minimum requirements which should be satisfied. According to the national design specification[2], the criteria include fatigue cracking, permanent deformation, and thermal cracking as listed below:

- For asphalt layers, fatigue cracking, permanent deformation, and low-temperature cracking should be controlled. When the *fatigue cracking* is considered as the design criterion, the fatigue life from Appendix B.1 of the specification should be no less than the corresponding accumulative ESAL from Appendix A of the specification[2]. Then, the tensile strain at the bottom of asphalt layers shall be chosen as the controlling parameter. When *the permanent deformation* is employed as the design criterion, the accumulative permanent deformation of asphalt layers shall be calculated with Appendix B.3 as the controlling parameter and its minimum value is shown in Table 8-4. When *the low-temperature cracking* is employed as the design criterion, the low-temperature cracking index (CI) can be calculated with Appendix B.5 as the controlling parameter and its maximum value is shown in Table 8-5.

Table 8-4 Allowable maximum permanent deformation of asphalt layer

Base Type	Asphalt Permanent Deformation	
	Expressway, Class-I highway	Class-II, Class-III Highway
HBM base; cement concrete base; asphalt base + HBM subbase	15	20
Others	10	15

Table 8-5 Allowable maximum low-temperature cracking index (CI)

Base Type	Asphalt Permanent Deformation	
	Expressway, Class-I highway	Class-II, Class-III Highway
HBM base; cement concrete base; asphalt base + HBM subbase	15	20
Others	10	15

- For HBM layer, fatigue cracking is considered as the design criterion, the fatigue life from Appendix B.2 of the specification[2] should be no less than the corresponding accumulative ESAL from Appendix A of the specification[2]. The controlling parameters are the tensile stress at the bottom of HBM base layers.
- For subgrade, the permanent deformation is considered as the design criterion. The vertical compressive strain at the top of subgrade can be calculated through stress analysis and its maximum value is calculated by the method in Appendix B.4.
- After the performance criteria checking, frost-thaw effects should be evaluated with the method presented in Appendix B.6 to check whether the overall thickness of the proposed pavement structure meets the design criteria.

(6) *Handover inspection criteria*: After subgrade and pavement construction, field tests should be taken to check asphalt surface skidding with the criteria shown in Table 8-6, the subgrade surface deflection presented in Appendix B.7 of the specification[2], and the pavement surface deflection presented in Appendix B.7 of the specification[2].

Table 8-6 Handover inspection criteria in terms of skidding resistance

Annual Rainfall (mm)	Handover Inspection Criteria	
	Sideway force coefficient (SFC60)	Texture depth (TD) (mm)
>1000	≥54	≥0.55
500~1000	≥50	≥0.50
250~500	≥45	≥0.45

8.3 Design Data Collection and Analysis

8.3.1 Design Data Collection

For asphalt pavement design, there are various data which should be collected and analyzed. They can be categorized into environment-related data, paving materials, traffic data, and subgrade conditions. Since some of them have been discussed in the previous chapters, the target of this section is to review them and add some new information from the design specification[2].

(1) **Environment-related Data** is used to determine temperature and water which may impact pavement design. Readers may refer to the climatic zoning specification, surveying, reports of the existing projects, and so on. Details about the environmental data and analysis methods have been discussed in Chapter 2.

(2) **Paving Materials** are referred to the source materials for making mixtures and they play significant roles in pavement design. In the data collection stage, the designer should collect and analyze the following information: The first is the availability of material sources. When the local material sources cannot meet the project requirements, the construction cost and period will increase. Therefore, it is recommended to use the local materials if possible. The second is the material quality which directly impacts the pavement short-term and long-term performance. The third is construction and service conditions which may impact selection of materials.

(3) **Traffic Data** may include vehicle types, axle types, axle load, traffic volume, annual increasing rate, and so on (discussed in Chapter 2). It should be noted that vehicles of type 1 are not considered in determining the accumulative ESAL.

(4) **Subgrade** is the underlying structure beneath the pavement. It is necessary to obtain the basic information of subgrade, which may include soil types, moisture conditions, resilient modulus, and so on.

(5) **The other data** may include hydrology, construction equipment, geology, and so on.

8.3.2 Determination of Accumulative ESAL

In order to determine the accumulative ESAL, two methods are presented in Chapter 2. They are the 'TF_i' method and the 'ATF' method. In the national asphalt pavement design, the 'ATF' method is employed to calculate the accumulative ESAL for each type vehicles as demonstrated in Fig. 8-3. The design ESAL is sum of the ESAL of vehicle types of 2 ~ 11. Followed is a brief introduction of the analysis procedure:

In the step #1, in order to determine ATF_m, there are four key variables: the number of vehicles, the number of axles, and percentage of axles are from the traffic data, while equivalent axle load factor for each type of vehicles ($EALF_m$) can be determined with Equation 8-1.

$$EALF_i = c_1 c_2 \left(\frac{P_i}{P_s}\right)^n \tag{8-1}$$

In the Equation, c_1 is the axle coefficient as listed in Table 8-7; c_2 is the wheel coefficient which may be 4.5 for single ties and 1.0 for dual tires; the exponent of n is listed in Table 8-7; P_i and P_s are the actual axle load and the standard axle load (100kN), respectively.

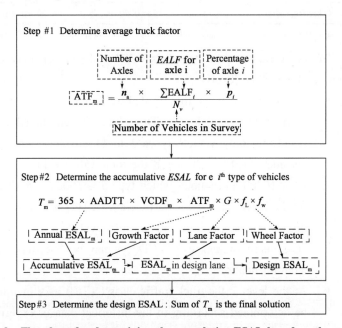

Fig. 8-3 Flowchart for determining the cumulative ESAL based on the current asphalt pavement design specification[2]

Table 8-7 Recommended values of axle coefficient and exponent of n

Design Criterion	Axle Type	c_1	n
Tensile strain and permanent deformation of asphalt mixes	Tandem axle	2.1	4
	Tripe axle	3.2	
Vertical compressive strain at the subgrade surface	Tandem axle	4.2	5
	Tripe axle	8.7	
Tensile stress of HBM mixes	Tandem axle	2.6	13
	Tripe axle	3.8	

In the step #2, in order to determine the accumulative ESAL for the mth type of vehicles (T_m), there are six variables: AADTT is the annual average daily truck traffic from the traffic data; the growth factor (G) can be easily determined with the annual increasing rate and design period; the wheel factor is equal to 1.0; the lane factor (f_L) can be determined by the following three methods (or three levels):

- Directly calculate the lane factor when the survey data is available;
- Use the local empirical value;
- Use the empirical value from the national design specification[2] as listed in Table 8-8.

Table 8-8 Lane factor from the national design specification[2]

One-way Travel Lanes	1	2	3	≥4
Expressway	—	0.70~0.85	0.45~0.60	0.40~0.50
Other Highways	1.00	0.50~0.75	0.50~0.75	—

Note: The lower value for the larger effects of the non-motor traffic flow, and vice versa.

The last variable of the step #2 is $VCDF_m$ (the vehicle class distribution factor) which can be at three levels:

- At the level 1, when the detailed traffic data is available, the percentage of each type of vehicle ($VCDF_m$) can be determined easliy. It should be noted that only vehicle types 2 to 11 are considered (the type 1 is not considered). For instance, if the total traffic volume of vehicles from 2 to 11 is 10000 and among which type 5 is 1500, then $VCDF_5 = 15\%$.

- At the level 2, the truck traffic class (TTC) as shown in Table 8-9 should be determined according to the historical data or experience. The vehicle class distribution factor ($VCDF_m$) may be determined based on the local recommendation.

- At the level 3, the truck traffic class (TTC) as shown in Table 8-9 should be determined according to the historical data or experience. $VCDF_m$ may be determined using the reference value from the design specification[2] as listed in the Table 8-10.

Table 8-9 Standard for highway TTC classification(%)

TTC	Percentage of Integrated Trucks (Vehicle type 3~6)	Percentage of Semi-trailer Trucks (Vehicle type 7~10)
TTC1	<40~	>50
TTC2	<40	<50
TTC3	40~70	>20
TTC4	40~70	<20
TTC5	>70	—

Table 8-10 $VCDF_m$ for different truck traffic classes(%)

TTC	VCDFm for truck types (T2~T11)									
	T2	T3	T4	T5	T6	T7	T8	T9	T10	T11
TTC1	6.4	15.3	1.4	0.0	11.9	3.1	16.3	20.4	25.2	0.0
TTC2	22.0	23.3	2.7	0.0	8.3	7.5	17.1	8.5	10.6	0.0
TTC3	17.8	33.1	3.4	0.0	12.5	4.4	9.1	10.6	8.5	0.7
TTC4	28.9	43.9	5.5	0.0	9.4	2.0	4.6	3.4	2.3	0.1
TTC5	9.9	42.3	14.8	0.0	22.7	2.0	2.3	3.2	2.5	0.2

Once the first two steps are completed, the final design ESAL can be easily calculated through summarizing T_m in the step#3.

8.3.3 Allowable Subgrade Resilient Modulus

Details on determination of the subgrade resilient modulus on a specific project have been discussed in the Chapter 7. Table 8-11 shows the allowable subgrade resilient modulus ($[E_0]$) which is dependent on the traffic loading classification.

Table 8-11 The allowable subgrade resilient modulus($[E_0]$)(MPa)

Traffic Loading Class	Extremely Heavy	Very Heavy	Heavy	Moderate& Light
Minimum value of allowable resilient modulus	70	60	50	40

8.4 Pavement Combination Design

The combination design is to initialize a layered structure through selecting proper layer materials and corresponding layer thicknesses with considering traffic, subgrade, pavement types, mechanics, functions, and so on. The pavement layers may include the surface course which may consist of the upper, middle, and bottom surface layers, the base course which may consist of 1~3 layers, the subbase course which may consist of 1~2 layers, functional layers which may be drainage layers, water-resistance layer, antifouling layer, and frost-protection layers, and the interlayer bonding which may be prime coats, tack coats, and seal coats as shown in Fig. 8-4.

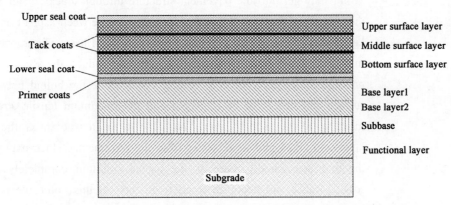

Fig. 8-4 Illustration of a typical asphalt pavement structural configuration

8.4.1 Asphalt Pavement Classification

According to the base layer materials, asphalt pavement can be classified into the following four types in the national design specification[2] of China, namely the asphalt pavement with HBM base, asphalt pavement with asphalt base, asphalt pavement with unbound granular base, and asphalt pavement with concrete base.

Asphalt pavement with HBM base is also called the semi-rigid base asphalt pavement in the previous version of the design specification[2]. When adjacent layers are completely bounded, the maximum tensile stress is usually located at the bottom of the HBM base. When the adjacent layers are not fully bounded, the maximum tensile stress may be located at asphalt layers. Therefore, it is important to employ engineering measures for improving the bounds between layers. The most commonly used approach is to use the prime coat between the asphalt layer and the HBM layer.

In terms of pavement serviceability and distresses, this type pavement may have the typical distresses as follows:

- At high temperature, the instability rutting is the most popular distress. Therefore, asphalt mixtures with the better high-temperature stability should be carefully designed.
- At low temperature, the thermal transverse cracking is another popular distress. Especially under the conditions where the temperature is low and the temperature keeps changing from time to time, the thermal cracking may become the primary distress.
- When temperature and moisture condition vary from time to time, the HBM base may have cracks which may be reflected onto the asphalt surface course. As a result, reflective cracking appear. This type of cracks is usually from the bottom to up and significantly impacts pavement serviceability.
- Water may get into the pavement structure through cracks or air voids of the asphalt mixes, it is trapped at the interface between asphalt and HBM layers due to inadequate permeability of the HBM base. The trapped water may reduce the bound material strength and induce the dynamic water pressure under the vehicular loading. As a result, the bound between the surface and base will be damaged and the maximum tensile stress may move up to the asphalt layer. Then, due to the tensile stress, the asphalt layer will crack and more water from the pavement surface may get into the interface. Finally, part of the asphalt mixture completely fails to service traffic and becomes small fragments. At this point, the pavement has potholes of different sizes.
- In terms of layer stiffness, the HBM mixes have the largest stiffness, the asphalt mixtures have larger stiffness, and the unbound mixes have smaller stiffness. The overall stiffness of the whole pavement structure is between the asphalt base pavement and the concrete base pavement.

Asphalt Pavement with Asphalt Base is also called the full-depth asphalt pavement in most countries. When adjacent layers are completely bounded, the maximum tensile stress is usually located at the bottom of the asphalt base. When the adjacent layers are not fully bounded, the maximum tensile stress may be located at any layer of asphalt surface course. Therefore, it is important to employ engineering measures for improving the bounds between layers. The most popular measure is to use the tack coats between the asphalt layers.

In terms of pavement serviceability and distresses, this type pavement may have the typical distresses as follows:

- At high temperatures, both the structural rutting and the instability rutting should be carefully considered. When the asphalt base has the higher modulus, the asphalt surface may have instability rutting. Otherwise, when the asphalt base is weak, the whole asphalt pavement structure may have the structural rutting. Therefore, if this type of pavement is designed, both the high-temperature stability of asphalt mixtures and structural mechanical responses should be carefully considered.
- At low temperatures, the thermal transverse cracking is another popular distress. Especially under the conditions where the temperature is low and the temperature keeps changing from time to time, the thermal cracking may become the primary distress. This type of cracking is from up to bottom and also called top-down cracking. It should be noted that this type of pavement seldom has bottom-up cracking.
- Water may get into the pavement structure through cracks or air voids of the asphalt mixes, it can be infiltrated through the pavement structure since asphalt base has air voids. As a result, water is seldom trapped at the interface between asphalt surface and base layers due to adequate permeability of the asphalt base. Therefore, the water stability is mainly referred to the decreasing of asphalt mixture strength. Potholes may also exist on this type of pavement, but the mechanism is due to the top-down cracking and the dynamic pressure of water trapped in the top-down cracking.
- In terms of layer stiffness, since asphalt mixtures have similar stiffness values, the whole pavement structure is much more homogenous than the HBM base asphalt pavement.

Asphalt Pavement with Granular Base is also one of the flexible pavements. When adjacent layers are completely bounded, the maximum tensile stress is usually located at the bottom of the asphalt surface. When the adjacent layers are not fully bounded, the maximum tensile stress may be located at any layer of asphalt surface course. Therefore, it is important to employ engineering measures for improving the bounds between layers. The most popular measure is to use the tack coats between the asphalt layers.

In terms of pavement serviceability and distresses, this type pavement may have the typical distresses as follows:

- At high temperature, the structural rutting should be carefully considered. Therefore, if this type of pavement is designed, structural mechanical responses should be carefully considered.
- At low temperature, the thermal transverse cracking is another popular distress. Especially under the conditions where the temperature is low and the temperature keeps changing from time to time, the thermal cracking may become the primary distress. This type of cracking is from top to bottom and also called top-down cracking.
- Under repetitions of traffic loads, fatigue cracking becomes much more common compared with other pavement types due to the weak supporting of the underlying layers.
- Water may get into the pavement structure through cracks or air voids of the asphalt mixes, it can be infiltrated through the pavement structure since the granular base has large air voids. As a result, water is seldom trapped at the interface between asphalt surface and base layers due to adequate permeability of the granular base. Therefore, the water stability is mainly referred to the decreasing of asphalt mixture strength. Potholes may also exist on this type of pavement, but the mechanism is due to the top-down cracking and bottom-up cracking.
- In terms of layer stiffness, since asphalt mixtures have much higher stiffness than the granular base layers, the majority of loading is on the asphalt layer. Therefore, this type of pavement is mainly used in the moderate or light traffic roads.

Asphalt Pavement with Concrete Base is also called the rigid base asphalt pavement. Since cement concrete has much higher stiffness than asphalt layers, the asphalt layer is usually in a compressive condition when the bounds between layers are perfect. Since the design of this type of pavement is based on the national rigid pavement design specification[3], it is not main focus of this chapter.

In terms of pavement serviceability and distresses, this type pavement may have the typical distresses as follows:

- At high temperature, the major distress is the instability rutting of the asphalt surface. When this type of pavement is designed, the asphalt mixture high-temperature stability should be carefully considered.
- At low temperature, the thermal transverse cracking is another popular

distress. Especially under the conditions where the temperature is low and the temperature keeps changing from time to time, the thermal cracking may become the primary distress. This type of cracking is from top to bottom and also called top-down cracking.
- Under repetitions of traffic loads, fatigue cracking may become an issue, but the bending stress of the asphalt layer is not a major contribution.
- Water may get into the pavement structure through cracks or air voids of the asphalt mixes and trapped onto the interface between asphalt and cement concrete layer. As a result, bound between asphalt and concrete layers may be damaged and the asphalt layer may be in tensile stress condition. Then, cracks are induced due to tensile stress.
- In terms of layer stiffness, both concrete and asphalt layers have high stiffness and this type of pavement has the largest stiffness.

Based on the serviceability and distresses, the four pavement types are suitable to different traffic loading conditions as shown in Table 8-12.

Table 8-12 Pavement types and their applications to different loading conditions

Traffic Loading Class	Extremely Heavy	Very Heavy	Heavy	Moderate&Light
Pavement Types	Asphalt pavement with HBM base			
	Asphalt pavement with asphalt base			
	Asphalt pavement with concrete base			—
	—		Asphalt pavement with granular base	

8.4.2 Pavement Requirements on Subgrade

According to the national pavement design specification[2], a pavement subgrade should meet the following requirements:
- The subgrade should be stable, dense, and in the horizontal direction. This is the basic requirement for providing a long-term and uniform supporting.
- Drainage facilities should be carefully designed in rainy regions, especially at junctions between fill and cut or the cut section.
- When the subgrade soils are rocky materials, the leveling layers of 200 ~ 300mm should be provided for uniform supporting to the pavement structure.
- For a newly-built highway, the roadbed should be in a dry or most condition and sufficient drainage facilities should be designed to present the surface or undersurface water from impacting the pavement structure.

8.4.3 Pavement Base and Subbase Courses

According to the national pavement design specification[2], base and subbase should have enough bearing capability, fatigue cracking-resistance, durability, and water stability. If the base materials are asphalt or granular materials, they should have adequate resistance to permanent deformation.

Materials of the asphalt pavement base or subbase can be categorized into four types, namely the HBM mixes, granular mixes, asphalt mixes, and cement concrete. Followed is a brief introduction to how to design a pavement base or subbase with those materials:

HBM Mixes can be further classified into three classes, namely HBM-1, HBM-2 and HBM-3. The HBM-1 mixes can be the cement-stabilized graded crushed stones or gravels, the cement-fly-ash-stabilized graded crushed stones or gravels, and the lime-fly-ash-stabilized graded crushed stones or gravel. This type of HBM mixes can be used as base or subbase materials in any classes of traffic loading conditions. The HBM-2 mixes can be the cement-stability unscreened crushed stones or gravels, the cement-fly-ash-stabilized unscreened crushed stones or gravels, and the lime-fly-ash-stabilized unscreened crushed stones or gravel, the cement-stabilized soils, the lime-stabilized soils, and the lime-fly-ash-stabilized soils. This type of HBM mixes is mainly used as the base materials in light traffic loading conditions or the subbase materials in any traffic loading conditions. The HBM-3 is the reclaimed mixes from the older roads, which can be used as base or subbase materials in different traffic classes according to its original material quality.

Asphalt Mixes are also called asphalt treated base (ATB) mixtures which are classified into three classes, namely ATB-1, ATB-2, and ATB-3. The ATB-1 mixtures can be dense-graded asphalt macadam, semi-open-graded asphalt macadam, and open-graded asphalt macadam which is recommended as the base materials of heavy, very heavy, and extremely heavy traffic loading. The ATB-2 is referred to asphalt penetration macadams which are recommend as base materials of light, moderate, and heavy traffic loading. The ATB-3 is the reclaimed asphalt pavement (RAP) mixtures which are further categorized into the field mixed RAP mixtures and the plant mixed RAP mixtures. The plant mixed RAP mixtures have a better quality and are recommended as base materials of heavy, very heavy, and extremely heavy traffic loading, while the field mixed RAP mixtures have a relatively low quality and can be used as the base or subbase materials of different traffic loading conditions.

Granular Mixes are also called unbound base materials which be classified into three classes, namely G-1 and G-2. The G-1 mixtures are referred to graded crushed stones which can be used as base materials of heavy, moderate, and light traffic loading conditions or subbase materials of different traffic conditions. The G-2 mixes are referred to the graded gravels, unscreened crushed stones, natural gravels, and dry bound mixtures (single-size coarse aggregate + chips as filling materials), which can be used as base materials of the light or moderate traffic loading and subbase materials of any traffic loading.

Concrete Materials are also called rigid base materials which is usually used as base materials of very or extremely heavy traffic loading conditions. As shown in Table 8-13.

Table 8-13 Minimum thicknesses of base and subbase layers

Mixture Types	Normal Maximum Aggregate Size (mm)	Minimum Layer Thickness (mm)
Dense-graded/Semi-open-graded/ open-graded asphalt macadam	19.0	50
	26.5	80
	31.5	100
	37.5	120
Asphalt penetration macadam	—	40
Lean concrete	31.5	120
Hydraulically-bound mixtures	19.0,26.5,31.5,37.5	150
	53.0	180
Graded crushed stones/Graded Gravels/ Unscreened gravels/Natural sands	26.5,31.5,37.5	100
	53.0	120
Dry bound macadam	37.5	75
	53.0	100
	63.0	120

8.4.4 Pavement Surface Courses

According to the national pavement design specification[2], the asphalt surface course should meet requirements of smoothness, rutting-resistance, fatigue-resistance, low-temperature stability, and water-stability. The wearing layer should also meet the requirements of skidding-resistance and polishing-resistance. When the dense-graded mixtures are used as the upper surface layer, they should be with low permeability for minimizing effects of water getting into the pavement structure.

Materials of the asphalt pavement surface course can be categorized into three classes, namely SC-1, SC-2, and SC-3. The materials of SC-1 include continuously-graded asphalt mixtures and plant-mixed RAP mixtures, which can be used in the surface course of any type of traffic loading conditions. The materials of SC-2 are referred to the stone-mastic asphalt (SMA) mixtures, which are usually used in the wearing surface of heavy, very heavy, and extremely heavy traffic loading conditions. The materials of SC-3 include penetration macadam with coated chips and asphalt surface treatment which are mainly used as surface materials in light or moderate traffic loading.

The minimum thickness of the surface course materials are shown in Table 8-14. It should be noted that the construction thicknesses of different types of materials are dependent on the construction equipment. Therefore, when one initializes the pavement layer thickness should consider the construction requirements. For instance, when considering the construction equipment, the maximum thickness of the asphalt layer is 10cm and the minimum thickness is 6.0cm when considering maximum particle size. If thickness in the design is 12cm, the asphalt surface layer can be constructed in two sub-layers. If the design is 11cm, it is hard to make construction.

Table 8-14 Minimum thicknesses of base and subbase layers

Asphalt Mixture Types	Minimum Layer Thickness of Different Normal Maximum Aggregate Sizes (mm)					
	4.75	9.5	13.2	16.0	19.0	26.5
Continuously-graded Asphalt Mixtures	15	25	35	40	50	75
Sand Mastic Asphalt (SMA)	—	30	40	50	60	—
Open-graded Asphalt Mixture	—	20	25	30	—	—

8.4.5 Pavement Functional Layers

Surface, base, and subbase are the major components of an asphalt pavement structure, which takes the majority of the traffic loading. Functional layers, such as the cushion layer, seal coats, tack coats, and primer coat, are also designed for protecting the major structural layers and linking adjacent layers.

Cushion Layer is also called bedding layer or capping layer, which can be categorized into water-resisting layer, drainage layer, antifouling layer, and frost protection layer.

The function of a water-resisting layer is to protect the pavement structure from effects of capillary water. The water-resisting layers may be used in the following three conditions:
- When the subgrade is in a wet condition, the water-resisting layer should be considered;
- When the subgrade is built with materials with a high percentage of silty soils, the water-resisting layer should be considered;

- When the capillary water is moving from bottom to top and gives adverse effects on the pavement structure, the water-resisting layer should be considered.

The function of a drainage layer is to protect subgrade and pavement from effects of surface or undersurface water which gets into subgrade or pavement structure and cannot be timely drained into the drainage system.

The function of a frost-protection layer is to protect subgrade and pavement from the frost-thaw effects. When the pavement structure thickness is not enough, the frost-protection layer should be added beneath the subbase for protecting subgrade from the frost effects. Section 8.6 will introduce how to design the minimum pavement thickness when considering frost-thaw effects. If the proposed pavement thickness is smaller than the minimum thickness requirements, a frost-protection layer should be designed.

Seal coats may be applied to the top of the pavement surface or on the top of the HBM base for protecting the surface and base from effects of environmental conditions.

The tack coats are usually used for linking two asphalt layers and primer coats are used at the top of HBM base as shown in Fig. 8-4.

8.4.6 Pavement Shoulders

Pavement shoulders may have different structures from the travel lanes. When designing pavement shoulders, it should be kept in mind, that water drainage and the shoulder performance should be consistent with the travel lanes.

8.4.7 Pavement Drainage

In the combination design, pavement internal drainage should be considered. Details about pavement drainage have been discussed in Chapter 4.

8.5 Mix Proportion Design and Material Parameters

Fundamentals of pavement materials have been discussed in Chapter 3 of this textbook and the textbook of *Road Construction Materials*. Therefore, this section herein will introduce the basic material requirements and design parameters instead of details on mix proportion design.

8.5.1 General Requirements

First of all, pavement material proportion design should consider highway class, traffic loading classes, climatic conditions, functional requirements of each layer, local material properties, economic benefits, and so on.

Secondly, in addition to meet the requirements of the national design specification of asphalt pavements, the source material properties, the mixture properties, and the mixture proportion requirements should also meet the requirements of the national *asphalt pavement construction specification*[8] and the national *pavement base construction specification*[27]. It should be noted that designers may find the minimum requirements in the specification and they should also consider the local experience and the project requirements for making a better design.

Thirdly, there are three levels for determining the pavement material design parameters:
- Level 1: laboratory tests are employed to measure the pavement materials;
- Level 2: the design parameters are determined through the empirical equations;
- Level 3: the design parameters are the typical values which are presented in the design specification.

The level 1 should be employed in the construction documentation design of the expressway or class-Ⅰ highway pavement design. The level 2 or the level 3 may be used for other conditions.

8.5.2 Proportion and Parameters of Granular Materials

In the national asphalt pavement design specification[2], the proportion and performance requirements include particle sizes, California bearing ratio (CBR), and resilient modulus as discussed below:

In terms of *particle sizes*, the normal maximum particle size should meet the requirements as listed in Table 8-15. For graded stones or gravels, the percentage of the particles less than 0.075mm should be less than 5%. If this requirement cannot be met, part of the fine aggregates can be replaced by natural sands.

Table 8-15 Requirements on the normal maximum particle sizes of granular mixes

Materials and Application Conditions	Normal Maximum Particle Size
Granular base layer of expressway or class-Ⅰ highway	No larger than 26.5mm
Subbase with graded stones or graded sand gravels of expressway or class Ⅰ highway	No larger than 31.5mm
Subbase with natural gravels of expressway or class Ⅰ highway	No larger than 53mm
Base or subbase materials of class-Ⅱ, Ⅲ, & Ⅳ	No larger than 53mm
Dry bound mixtures	1/2 ~ 1/3 of the layer thickness
Frost-protection cushion layer with sand gravels or crushed stones	No larger than 53mm

In terms of **CBR values**, the CBR values are recommended as shown in Table 8-16 for graded stones of base or subbase layers.

Table 8-16 CBR values of graded stones of base or subbase layers

Pavement Layers	Highway Classes	Extremely-heavy/ Very-heavy Traffic	Heavy Traffic	Moderate/ Light Traffic
Base Layer	Expressway, class- I highway	≥200	≥180	≥160
	Other classes of highways	≥160	≥140	≥120
Subbase Layer	Expressway, class- I highway	≥120	≥100	≥80
	Other classes of highways	≥1000	≥80	≥60

When graded gravels or natural sand gravels are used in the base layer, their CBR values should be no less than 80. When they are used in the subbase layer, their CBR values should be no less than 80 for extreme heavy, very heavy, and heavy traffic loading conditions, no less than 60 for moderate traffic loading conditions, and 40 for light traffic loading conditions.

The granular material *resilient modulus* is dependent on the moisture condition and the compactness. The requirements on compactness of granular materials are presented in the *construction specification of highway pavement base*. The standard value of resilient modulus (E_0) is defined as the resilient modulus (M_R) under the optimum water content and the required compactness, which may be determined with one of the two levels as follows:

- Level 1: Tri-axial tests under repeated loading should be performed and the average value is the resilient modulus of granular material.
- Level 3: The resilient modulus may be determined with the recommendation as listed in Table 8-17.

Table 8-17 Reference resilient modulus of granular base or subbase materials

Material Types and Position	MR under Optimum Water Contents and the Required Compaction	Moisture-adjusted MR
Graded Macadam Base	200~400	300~700
Graded Macadam Subbase	180~250	190~440
Graded Gravel Base	150~300	250~600
Graded Gravel Subbase	150~220	160~380
Unscreened macadam layer	180~220	200~400
Natural gravels	105~135	130~240

Note: The higher values should be selected for materials with the better performance, the better gradation, or the larger compactness.

The design parameter used in the pavement structural mechanical analysis is the standard resilient modulus multiplying by the moisture coefficient which is ranging from 1.6 to 2.0.

8.5.3 Proportion and Parameters of Hydraulic Bound Mixtures

In the national asphalt pavement design specification[2], the proportion and performance requirements of hydraulic bound material (HBM) mixes include particle sizes, binder contents, unconfined compressive strength, bending strength, and Young's modulus.

In terms of *particle sizes*, the normal maximum particle size of a HBM mix should meet the requirements as listed in Table 8-18.

Table 8-18 Requirements on the normal maximum particle sizes of HBM mixes

Materials and Application Conditions	Normal Maximum Particle Size
Base layer of expressway or class-I highway	No larger than 31.5mm
Subbase layer of expressway or class-I highway Base layer of the other classes of highways	No larger than 37.5mm
Subbase layer of class-II or lower classes of highways	No larger than 53mm

Under vehicular loads, the HBM mixes should have enough *compressive strength* which is measured with the unconfined compressive loading tests. In the national design specification, the unconfined compressive strength is recommended as shown in Table 8-19.

Table 8-19 HBM mixes' unconfined compressive strength of 7 days

Materials	Pavement Layer	Highway Classes	Extremely-heavy/Very-heavy Traffic	Heavy Traffic	Moderate/Light Traffic
Cement Stabilized Mixtures	Base Layer	Expressway, Class-I Highway	5.0–7.0	4.0–6.0	3.0–5.0
		Class-II, III, and IV Highway	4.0–6.0	3.0–5.0	2.0–4.0
	Subbase Layer	Expressway, Class-I Highway	3.0–5.0	2.5–4.5	2.0–4.0
		Class-II, III, and IV Highway	2.5–4.5	2.0–4.0	1.0–3.0

continue

Materials	Pavement Layer	Highway Classes	Extremely-heavy/ Very-heavy Traffic	Heavy Traffic	Moderate/ Light Traffic
Cement Fly-ash Stabilized Mixtures	Base Layer	Expressway, Class-I Highway	4.0-5.0	3.5-4.5	3.0-4.0
		Class-II, III, and IV Highway	3.5-4.5	3.0-4.0	2.5-3.5
	Subbase Layer	Expressway, Class-I Highway	2.5-3.5	2.0-3.0	1.5-2.5
		Class-II, III, and IV Highway	2.0-3.0	1.5-2.5	1.0-2.0
Lime Fly-ash Stabilized Mixtures	Base Layer	Expressway, Class-I Highway	≥1.1	≥1.0	≥0.9
		Class-II, III, and IV Highway	≥0.9	≥0.8	≥0.7
	Subbase Layer	Expressway, Class-I Highway	≥0.8	≥0.7	≥0.6
		Class-II, III, and IV	≥0.7	≥0.6	≥0.5
Lime Stabilized Mixtures	Base Layer	Class-II, III, and IV Highway	—	—	≥0.8[a]
	Subbase Layer	Expressway, Class-I Highway	—	—	≥0.8
		Class-II, III, and IV Highway	—	—	0.5-0.7[b]

Note: [a] the compressive strength should be larger than 0.5 MPa for soils with the low plastic index (less than 7).

[b] the lower limit value is used for soils with the plastic index less than 7, while the upper limit value is used for soils with the plastic index no less than 7.

In terms of ***the flexural strength and the Young's modulus*** of HBM mixes, there are two levels for determining the two parameters:

- Level 1: The lab tests may be performed according to the appendix E of the design specification and meet the requirements of *the testing specification of highway engineering HBM mixes*[28]. When conducting the lab tests with the method above, the curing periods are 90 days for cement stabilized mixes or cement-fly-ash stabilized mixes and 180 days for the lime-stabilized mixes or lime-fly-ash stabilized mixes. The average value of the testing results is the standard value of the bending strength or Young's modulus.
- Level 3: the flexural strength and Young's modulus can be determined through looking up Table 8-20.

Table 8-20 Recommendation on flexural strength and Young's modulus of HBM mixes

Materials	Flexural Strength	Young's Modulus
Cement stabilized/cement fly-ash stabilized/ lime cement fly-ash stabilized granular mixtures	1.5 ~ 2.0	18000 ~ 28000
	0.9 ~ 1.5	14000 ~ 20000
Cement stabilized/cement fly-ash stabilized/ lime cement fly-ash stabilized Soils	0.6 ~ 1.0	5000 ~ 7000
Lime stabilized soils	0.3 ~ 0.7	3000 ~ 5000

Note: The higher limit value should be selected for materials with the better performance, the higher binder content, the better gradation, or the higher compactness, vice versa.

It should be noted that the flexural strength and Young's modulus as determined above should be corrected when they are used for the pavement structural analysis. Followed are the two methods of correction:

- The measured or recommended Young's modulus should be corrected through multiplying by a coefficient of 0.5;
- When the lime-stabilized materials are used for expressway or class-I highway, the design bending tensile strength should meet the requirements as shown in Table 8-21.

Table 8-21 Lime-fly-ash stabilized mixes

Climatic Zones	Severely Frozen	Moderately Frozen
Residual compressive strength ratio(%)	≤65	≤70

8.5.4 Proportion and Parameters of Asphalt Mixes

In the national asphalt pavement design specification[2], the proportion and performance requirements of asphalt mixture mixes include particle sizes, low temperature stability, high temperature stability, penetration strength, water stability, unconfined compressive strength, bending strength, and dynamic compressive modulus, and Poisson's ratio. Followed are explanations:

In terms of ***particle sizes***, the normal maximum particle size should be no larger than 16.0mm for the upper surface layer, no less than 16.0mm for the middle and bottom layers, and no less than 26.5mm for asphalt treated base (ATB).

In terms of ***low temperature stability***, for class-II highway, class-I highway, and expressway the bending beam tests of asphalt mixtures should be performed to measure their damage strain values when the mixture's normal maximum particle sizes are equal to or smaller than 19.0mm. The testing temperature is about -10℃ and loading frequency is 50mm/min. Table 8-22 shows the minimum requirements on the low temperature bending strains.

Table 8-22 Technical requirements on the low-temperature bending strains of asphalt mixtures

Climate and Technical Indices	Failure Strains for the Following Climatic Zones(μ_ε)								Lab Testing Method
The Lowest Annual Temperature(℃)	< -37.0		<37.0 - 21.5			-21.5 - 9.0		>9.0	
	1. Severely frozen zones		2. Winter frozen zones			3. Winter cold zones		4. Winter warm zones	
	1-1	2-1	1-2	2-2	3-2	1-3	2-3	1-4 2-4	
Minimum Strain for Ordinary Asphalt Mixtures	2600		2300			2000			T 0715
Minimum Strain for Modified Asphalt Mixtures	3000		2800			2500			

Note: The climatic zone is determined based on the current specification of highway asphalt pavement construction (JTB F40)[8].

In terms of ***high-temperature stability***, for class-I highway and expressway the rutting tests under certain loading conditions should be performed. Table 8-23 shows the testing conditions and the rutting requirements.

Table 8-23 Dynamic stability through the rutting tests of asphalt mixture (repetitions/mm)

The Average Highest Temperature of July and Climatic Zone (℃)	>30				20~30				<20	Lab Testing Method
	1. Scorching summer zone				2. Hot summer zone				3. Warm summer zone	
	1-1	1-2	1-3	1-4	2-1	2-2	2-3	2-4	3-2	
Minimum DS for ordinary asphalt mixtures	800	1000	600	800	600					T 0719
Minimum DS for modified asphalt mixture	2800	3200	2000	2400	1800					
Minimum DS for Ordinary SMA	1500									
Minimum DS for Modified SMA	3000									
Minimum DS for OGFC	1500 for the moderate and light traffic and 3000 for the other traffic classes									

Note: 1. The climatic zone is determined based on the current specification of highway asphalt pavement construction (JTB F40)[8].
2. If July is not the hottest month, the hottest month should be considered to calculate the average highest temperature.
3. The higher DS is recommended for some special engineering conditions, such as bridge deck pavement, long slope pavement, pavements of factories or mines, etc.
4. For the Scorching weather, very heavy traffic, or extremely heavy traffic, users may select the testing temperature or loading conditions.

In terms of ***penetration strength***, the uniaxial penetration testing method as demonstrated in Appendix F of the design specification[2] is employed and the two empirical models are presented for different types of asphalt pavements as shown in Equations 8-2 and 8-6.

The Equation 8-2 can be used to evaluate asphalt mixtures of the asphalt pavement with HBM base, the asphalt pavement with asphalt base and HBM subbase, and the asphalt pavement with concrete base.

$$R_{\tau s} \geqslant \left(\frac{0.31 \lg N_{e5} - 0.68}{\lg[R_a] - 13.11 \lg T_d - \lg \psi_s + 2.50} \right)^{1.86} \qquad (8-2)$$

where:

$[R_a]$ is allowable permanent deformation of asphalt mixtures (mm) as specified in Table 8-4;

N_{e5} is ESAL in the design period or in a period from the open traffic to the first rutting maintenance (monthly average temperature should be larger than 0℃), which is calculated according to Appendix A;

T_d is design temperature (℃), which is the average local temperature of the months whose average monthly temperature higher than 0℃;

ψ_s is pavement structure coefficient which is calculated in the following Equation:

$$\psi_s = (0.52h_a^{-0.003} - 317.59h_b^{-1.32})E_b^{0.1} \tag{8-3}$$

h_a is asphalt mixture thickness (mm);

h_b is HBM or cement concrete thickness (mm);

E_b is HBM or Concrete modulus (MPa);

$R_{\tau s}$ is asphalt mixture penetration strength which is calculated in the following Equation:

$$R_{\tau s} = \sum_{i=1}^{n} \omega_{is} R_{\tau i} \tag{8-4}$$

$R_{\tau i}$ is the asphalt mixture penetration strength of the ith layer (MPa), which is determined based on the Appendix F, 0.4 ~ 0.7MPa for ordinary asphalt mixtures, 0.7 ~ 1.2MPa for modified asphalt mixtures;

n is number of Asphalt mixture layers;

ω_{is} is the weight factor of the ith layered asphalt mixture, which is the ratio of shear stress at the ith layer center to the sum of shear stresses at the centers of the other layers, which is calculated as follows:

$$\omega_{is} = \frac{\tau_i}{\sum_{i=1}^{n} \tau_i} \tag{8-5}$$

When $n = 1, \omega = 1$; when $n = 2, \omega_1 = 0.48, \omega_2 = 0.52$; when $n = 3, \omega_1 = 0.35, \omega_2 = 0.23$.

The Equation 8-6 can be used to evaluate asphalt mixtures of the asphalt pavement with granular base and the asphalt pavement with asphalt base.

$$R_{\tau s} \geq \left(\frac{0.35\lg N_{e5} - 1.16}{\lg[R_a] - 1.62\lg T_d - \lg\psi_s + 2.76}\right)^{1.38} \tag{8-6}$$

where:

ψ_s is pavement structural coefficient which can be determined with Equation 8-7:

$$\psi_s = 20.16h_a^{-0.642} + 820916h_b^{-2.84} \tag{8-7}$$

$R_{\tau g}$ is overall penetration strength of asphalt layers as computed in Equation 8-8:

$$R_{\tau g} = \sum_{i=1}^{n} \omega_{ig} R_{\tau i} \tag{8-8}$$

ω_{ig} is the weight factor of the ith layered asphalt mixture, which is the ratio of shear stress at the ith layer center to the sum of shear stresses at the centers of the other layers, which is calculated as follows:

$$\omega_{is} = \frac{\tau_i}{\sum_{i=1}^{n} \tau_i} \tag{8-9}$$

When $n = 1, \omega_1 = 1$; when $n = 2, \omega_1 = 0.44, \omega_2 = 0.56$; when $n = 3, \omega_1 = 0.27$, $\omega_2 = 0.36; \omega_2 = 0.37$.

In terms of *water stability*, the immersion Marshall testing method and the frost-thaw indirect tension testing method are used to evaluate asphalt mixtures. The minimum requirements are shown in Table 8-24.

Table 8-24　Technical requirements on asphalt mixture water-stability

Asphalt Mixture Types	Technical Indices(%) under the Following Annual Rainfall(mm)		Testing Methods
	≥500	<500	
Residual Immersion Marshall Stability(%)			
Minimum value for ordinary asphalt mixtures	80	75	T 0709
Minimum value for modified asphalt mixtures	85	80	
Minimum value for ordinary SMA mixtures	75		
Minimum value for modified SMA mixtures	80		
Residual rupture strength ratio of frost-thaw tests(%)			
Minimum value for ordinary asphalt mixtures	75	70	T 0729
Minimum value for modified asphalt mixtures	80	75	
Minimum value for ordinary SMA mixtures	75		
Minimum value for modified SMA mixtures	80		

In terms of *dynamic modulus*, there are three levels of determination methods:
- Level 1: the dynamic compressive modulus testing method may be employed according to the testing specifcation of asphalt and asphalt mixtures in Highway Engineering[29]. The average result of replicate samples is the dynamic modulus which can be used in the design. The lab testing temperature is 20℃, while the loading frequency is 10Hz for asphalt mixtures of the surface course and 5Hz for those of the base course.
- Level 2: the dynamic modulus may be determined through an empirical model as shown in Eqaution 8-10. It should be noted that the model is

suitable for petroleum asphalt mixtures with regular graduations.

$$\lg E_a = 4.59 - 0.02f + 2.58G^* - 0.14P_a - 0.041V - 0.03\text{VCA}_{\text{DRC}} - 2.65 \times 1.1^{\lg G^*} \cdot f^{-0.06} - 0.05 \times 1.52^{\lg \text{VCA}_{\text{DRC}}} \cdot f^{-0.21} + 0.0031f \cdot P_a + 0.0024V \tag{8-10}$$

where:

E_a is asphalt mixture resilient modulus (MPa);

f is testing frequency (Hz);

G^* is dynamic shear modulus of asphalt under temperature of 60℃ and rotation speed of 10rad/s;

P_a is asphalt-aggregate ratio of asphalt mixture (%);

V is aid void content of the compacted asphalt mixture (%);

VCA_{DRC} is voids of coarse aggregates of dry tamping mixture (%).

- Level 3: the dynamic modulus may be determined according to the recommendation of the specification[2] as shown in Table 8-25.

Table 8-25 Dynamic compressive modulus of asphalt mixes at 20℃ from the design specification[2]

Asphalt Mixture Types	Asphalt Types			
	#70	#90	#110	SBS-modified
SMA10, SMA13, SMA16	—	—	—	7500 ~ 12000
AC10, AC13	8000 ~ 12000	7500 ~ 11500	7000 ~ 10500	8500 ~ 12500
AC16, AC20, AC25	9000 ~ 13000	8500 ~ 13000	7500 ~ 12000	9000 ~ 13500
ATB25	7000 ~ 11000	—	—	—

Notes: 1. For ATB25, dynamic compressive modulus is measured at frequency of 5Hz, while for other types of asphalt mixtures, dynamic compressive modulus is measured at a frequency of 10Hz.

2. The higher values are recommended for mixtures with the higher asphalt viscosity, the better gradation, and the lower voids.

8.5.5 Poisson's Ratios of Layer Materials

According to the national asphalt pavement design specification[2], the Poisson's ratios of commonly-used layer materials are shown in Table 8-26.

Table 8-26 Poisson's ratio of commonly-used layer materials

	Subgrade Soils	Granular Mixtures	HBM Mixtures	Dense-graded Asphalt Mixtures	Open or Semi-open Graded Asphalt Mixtures
Poisson's Ratio	0.40	0.35	0.25	0.25	0.40

8.6 Verification of Layer Thickness

In order to verify the proposed layer thickness, the design criteria discussed in section 8.2 should be checked. Appendix G of the design specification[2] presents an approach for determining temperature adjustment coefficient and Appendix B of the specification[2] presents approaches for checking the main design criteria. This section herein introduces those methods as follows.

8.6.1 Determination of Temperature Adjustment Coefficient and Effective Temperature

Temperature is one of the most important factors which may significantly impact asphalt pavement performance. In the national design specification[2], however, the constant resilient modulus or dynamic modulus of the pavement layers is used as the inputs for pavement stress analysis. For instance, the moduli of asphalt layers are the moduli measured under 20℃ even though asphalt layer moduli are dependent on temperatures.

In order to consider effects of different temperatures, temperature adjustment coefficient and effective temperature are proposed in the national design specification[2]. Followed are the three steps for determining those two parameters:

Step #1 Benchmark Structure of Asphalt Pavement: The pavement structure is equivalent into a two-layered structure which is composed of the equivalent asphalt layer and the equivalent base layer as shown in Fig. 8-5. The two-layered structure is called the benchmark structure in this textbook. The layer thicknesses and moduli of the benchmark structure are determined by the following two Equations:

$$h_i^* = h_{i1} + h_{i2} \tag{8-11}$$

$$E_i^* = \frac{E_{i1}h_{i1}^3 + E_{i2}h_{i2}^3}{(h_{i1} + h_{i2})^3} + \frac{3}{h_{i1} + h_{i2}}\left(\frac{1}{E_{i1}h_{i1}} + \frac{1}{E_{i2}h_{i2}}\right)^{-1} \tag{8-12}$$

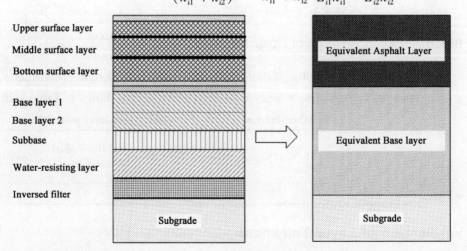

Fig. 8-5 Illustration of asphalt pavement structure equivalency

In the above equations, h_i^* and E_i^* are thickness and modulus of the benchmark structure; h_{i1} and h_{i2} are thicknesses of the adjacent layers; E_{i1} and E_{i2} are moduli of the adjacent layers. For asphalt layers $i = a$ and for base layers $i = b$. When asphalt layers or base layers are more than two layers, the equivalent thickness and moduli can be determined by iteratively using the two equations above.

Example 8-1:

An asphalt pavement combination is shown in the following table, Determine its benchmark structure.

Structural Layers	Material Types	Thickness (mm)	Modulus(MPa)
Surface Layer	AC13 (SBS modified)	40	11000
	AC20(pen# 90)	60	10000
	AC25(pen# 90)	80	10000
Base Layer	Cement stabilized crushed stone	360	12000
Subbase Layer	Graded crushed stone	180	300

Solution:

There are three asphalt layers in the asphalt pavement structure. The equivalent thickness and equivalent modulus of the first two asphalt layers are calculated as follows:

$$h_{a1}^* = h_{a1} + h_{a2} = 40\text{mm} + 60\text{mm} = 100\text{mm} = 0.1\text{m}$$

$$E_{a1}^* = \frac{E_{a1}h_{a1}^3 + E_{a2}h_{a2}^3}{(h_{a1} + h_{a2})^3} + \frac{3}{h_{a1} + h_{a2}} \left(\frac{1}{E_{a1}h_{a1}} + \frac{1}{E_{a2}h_{a2}} \right)^{-1}$$

$$= \frac{11 \times 0.04^3 + 10 \times 0.06^3}{0.1^3} + \frac{3}{0.1} \left(\frac{1}{11 \times 0.04} + \frac{1}{10 \times 0.06} \right)^{-1}$$

$$= 10.48(\text{GPa})$$

The equivalent layer of the first two asphalt layers is considered as an integrated layer to determine the final thickness and modulus of the equivalent asphalt layer:

$$h_a^* = h_{a1}^* + h_{a3} = 100\text{mm} + 80\text{mm} = 180\text{mm} = 0.18\text{m}$$

$$E_a^* = \frac{E_{a1}^* h_{a1}^{*3} + E_{a2}h_{a2}^3}{(h_{a1}^* + h_{a2})^3} + \frac{3}{h_{a1}^* + h_{a2}} \left(\frac{1}{E_{a1}^* h_{a1}^*} + \frac{1}{E_{a2}h_{a2}} \right)^{-1}$$

$$= \frac{10.48 \times 0.1^3 + 10 \times 0.08^3}{0.18^3} + \frac{3}{0.18} \left(\frac{1}{10.48 \times 0.1} + \frac{1}{10 \times 0.08} \right)^{-1}$$

$$= 10.24(\text{GPa})$$

The base and subbase can be equivalent into one layer. Therefore, the equivalent thickness and the equivalent modulus of the benchmark structure base layer are calculated as follows:

$$h_{b1}^* = h_{b1} + h_{b2} = 360\text{mm} + 180\text{mm} = 540\text{mm} = 0.54\text{m}$$

$$E_{b1}^* = \frac{E_{b1}h_{b1}^3 + E_{b2}h_{b2}^3}{(h_{b1} + h_{b2})^3} + \frac{3}{h_{b1} + h_{b2}}\left(\frac{1}{E_{b1}h_{b1}} + \frac{1}{E_{b2}h_{b2}}\right)^{-1}$$

$$= \frac{12 \times 0.36^3 + 0.3 \times 0.06^3}{0.54^3} + \frac{3}{0.54}\left(\frac{1}{12 \times 0.36} + \frac{1}{0.3 \times 0.18}\right)^{-1}$$

$$= 3.86(\text{GPa})$$

In summary, the benchmark structure is determined as shown in the figure below:

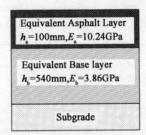

Step #2 Temperature Adjustment Coefficient and Equivalent Temperature of Benchmark Pavement Structure: Those two parameters are dependent on the local environmental condition. In the national design specifications, they are presented in the appendix G.1.2 as shown in Table 8-27.

Table 8-27 Temperature Adjustment Coefficient and Equivalent Temperature of Benchmark Pavement Structure in Different Locations

(Appendix G.1.2 of the national design specification[2])

Location	Monthly average temperature (upper value)	Monthly average temperature (lower value)	Annual average temperature	Temperature adjustment coefficient		Equivalent temperature
				Tensile stress of asphalt or HBM mixes as criterion	Subgrade compressive strain as criterion	
Beijing	26.9	-2.7	13.1	1.23	1.09	20.1
Jinan	28.0	0.2	15.1	1.32	1.17	21.8
Taiyuan	23.9	-5.2	10.5	1.12	0.98	17.3
Xi'an	27.5	0.1	14.3	1.28	1.13	20.9
Shanghai	28.0	4.7	16.7	1.38	1.23	22.5
Chongqing	28.3	7.8	18.4	1.46	1.31	23.6
Hangzhou	28.4	4.5	16.9	1.40	1.25	22.8
Fuzhou	28.9	11.3	20.2	1.55	1.40	24.9
Lanzhou	22.9	-4.7	10.5	1.12	0.98	17.0
Guangzhou	28.7	14.0	22.4	1.66	1.52	26.5
Zhengzhou	27.4	0.6	14.7	1.30	1.15	21.2

Step #3 Temperature Adjustment Coefficient of the Proposed Asphalt Pavement Structure: According to the national design specification[2], the final values of temperature adjustment coefficient and equivalent temperature are determined by the following Equation:

$$k_{Ti} = A_h A_E \tilde{k}_{Ti}^{1+B_h+B_E} \qquad (8\text{-}13)$$

Where $\tilde{k}_{Ti}$ is the temperature adjustment coefficient of the benchmark structure as listed in the Table 8-27; k_{Ti} is the temperature adjustment coefficient of the asphalt pavement structure; A_h, A_E, B_h, B_E are closely related to the thickness ratio (λ_h) and the layer modulus ratio (λ_E) of the benchmark structure.

$$\lambda_h = \frac{h_a^*}{h_b^*} \qquad (8\text{-}14)$$

$$\lambda_E = \frac{E_a^*}{E_b^*} \qquad (8\text{-}15)$$

When the design criterion is the fatigue cracking of asphalt layers, A_h, A_E, B_h are determined as follows:

$$A_E = 0.76\lambda_E^{0.09} \qquad (8\text{-}16)$$

$$A_h = 1.14\lambda_h^{0.17} \qquad (8\text{-}17)$$

$$B_E = 0.14\ln(\lambda_E/20) \qquad (8\text{-}18)$$

$$B_h = 0.23\ln(\lambda_h/0.45) \qquad (8\text{-}19)$$

When the design criterion is the fatigue cracking of HBM base layers, A_h, A_E, B_h, B_E are determined as follows:

$$A_E = 0.10\lambda_E + 0.89 \qquad (8\text{-}20)$$

$$A_h = 10.73\lambda_h + 0.67 \qquad (8\text{-}21)$$

$$B_E = 0.15\ln(\lambda_E/1.14) \qquad (8\text{-}22)$$

$$B_h = 0.44\ln(\lambda_h/0.45) \qquad (8\text{-}23)$$

When the design criterion is the compressive strain at the subgrade top surface, A_h, A_E, B_h, B_E are determined as follows:

$$A_E = 0.006\lambda_E + 0.89 \qquad (8\text{-}24)$$

$$A_h = 0.67\lambda_h + 0.70 \qquad (8\text{-}25)$$

$$B_E = 0.12\ln(\lambda_E/1.14) \qquad (8\text{-}26)$$

$$B_h = 0.38\ln(\lambda_h/0.45) \qquad (8\text{-}27)$$

Example 8-2:

Determine temperature adjustment coefficient for the asphalt pavement combination of Example 8-1 if the road is constructed in Beijing and the design

criterion is asphalt layer fatigue cracking.
Solution:

From Example 8-1, $\lambda_h = \dfrac{180}{540} = 0.33$; $\lambda_E = \dfrac{10.240}{3.86} = 2.65$. From Table 8-27, $\tilde{k}_{Ti} = 1.23$. With the information above, A_E, B_E, B_E, B_h can be determined with Equations 8-10, 8-11, 8-12, and 9-13. The temperature adjustment coefficient of asphalt pavement can be determined with Equation 8-7:

$$k_{Ti} = 0.897$$

Step #4 Equivalent Temperature of the Proposed Asphalt Pavement Structure:
When the asphalt layer permanent deformation is taken as the design criterion, the equivalent temperature should be calculated with the following Equation:

$$T_{pef} = T_\varepsilon + 0.016 h_a \tag{8-28}$$

In the Equation, T_ε is the equivalent temperature of the benchmark structure.

Example 8-3:
Determine effective temperature for the asphalt pavement combination of Example 8-1 if the road is constructed in Beijing.

Solution:
From Example 8-1, $h_a = 180$ mm. From Table 8-27, $T_\varepsilon = 20.1$. The effective temperature of asphalt pavement can be determined with Equation 8-22: $k_{Ti} = 22.98$.

8.6.2 Fatigue Cracking of Asphalt Layer as Design Criterion

There are various factors which impact asphalt mixture fatigue behaviors. In the national design specification[2], seven key factors are considered:

- The first factor is voids filled by asphalt (VFA) which is ranging from 68 to 83 for asphalt concrete mixture and 75~85 for stone mastic asphalt (SMA) mixtures. Increasing VFA results in a longer fatigue life. The unit of VFA is %.
- The second factor is the dynamic modulus of asphalt mixture (E_a) at the temperature of 20℃. Increasing of E_a may result in a shorter fatigue life. The unit of E_a is MPa.
- The third factor is tensile strain at the bottom of the asphalt layer (ε_a), which is determined through pavement stress analysis based on the multi-layered elastic system theory. Increasing the tensile strain may result in decreasing of fatigue life. The unit of tensile strain is μ_ε or 10^{-6}.
- The fourth factor is the temperature adjustment coefficient (k_{Tl}) which has been discussed in the previous section. Increasing of k_{Tl} may result in decreasing of the fatigue life.
- The fifth factor is the fatigue loading mode coefficient (k_b) which can be

determined with the Equation below:

$$k_b = \left[\frac{1 + 0.3E_a^{0.43}(VFA)^{-0.85}e^{(0.024h_a-5.41)}}{1 + e^{0.024h_a-5.41}}\right]^{3.33} \quad (8-29)$$

- The sixth factor is the seasonal frost adjustment coefficient (k_a), which is dependent on the frost severity as shown in Table 8-28.
- The seventh factor is the target reliability index (β), which is presented in section 8.2.

Table 8-28 Seasonal frost adjustment coefficient (k_a)

Frost Area	Severe Frost	Moderate Frost	Light Frost	Other
Frost index F (℃·d)	≥2000	2000 – 800	800 – 50	≤50
k_a	0.60 – 0.70	0.70 – 0.80	0.80 – 1.00	1.00

With the seven factors above considered, the fatigue life of the proposed asphalt pavement structure (N_{fl}) can be predicted with the Equation 8-30. In order to meet the design requirements, N_{fl} should be larger than the accumulative ESAL which has been discussed in section 8.3.

$$N_{fl} = 6.32 \times 10^{(15.96-0.29\beta)} k_a k_b k_{Tl}^{-1} \left(\frac{1}{\varepsilon_a}\right)^{3.97} \left(\frac{1}{E_a}\right)^{1.58} (VFA)^{2.72} \quad (8-30)$$

In the Equation above, temperature adjustment coefficient (k_{Tl}) and the seasonal frost adjustment coefficient (k_a) are the two environment-related parameters which are dependent on the project location. The dynamic modulus of asphalt mixture (E_a) and voids filled by asphalt (VFA) are material properties, which should meet the material design requirements as discussed in section 8.5. Once the material properties are determined, the key design task is to adjust the layer thickness which directly impacts the values of the fatigue loading mode coefficient (k_b) and tensile strain at the bottom of the asphalt layer (ε_a).

8.6.3 Fatigue Cracking of HBM Base Layer as Design Criterion

There are various factors which impact HBM mixture fatigue behaviors. In the national design specification, eight key factors are considered:
- The first factor is the target reliability index (β), which is presented in section 8.2.
- The second factor is the field correction coefficient (k_c) which is calculated in Equation 8-31. Parameters of c_1, c_2 and c_3 in the Equation are listed in Table 8-29.

$$k_c = c_1 e^{c_2(h_a+h_b)} + c_3 \quad (8-31)$$

Table 8-29 Parameters of c_1, c_2 and c_3 for determining
the field correction coefficient (k_c)

	Newly-built or Rebuilt Pavement Layers		Pavement Overlayers	
	Hydraulically-bound granular mixtures	Hydraulically-bound soils	Hydraulically-bound granular mixtures	Hydraulically-bound soils
c_1	14.0	35.0	18.5	21.0
c_2	-0.0076	-0.0156	-0.01	-0.0125
c_3	-1.47	-0.83	-1.32	-0.82

- The third factor is the tensile stress at the bottom of HBM layer (σ_t), which is determined through the pavement stress analysis based on the multi-layered elastic system theory. Increasing the tensile strain may result in decreasing of fatigue life. The unit of tensile stress is MPa.
- The fourth factor is the flexural strength (R_s) which is the key mechanical properties of HBM mixtures and usually measured through the lab testing. The unit of R_s is MPa.
- The fifth factor is fatigue parameters (a and b) which are dependent on the fatigue curve. Table 8-30 shows the typical values of a and b.
- The sixth factor is temperature adjustment coefficient (k_{T2}) which has been discussed in the previous section. Increasing of this coefficient may result in decreasing of the fatigue life.
- The seventh factor is the seasonal frost adjustment coefficient (k_a), which is dependent on the frost severity as shown in Table 8-28.

Table 8-30 Fatigue curve-related parameters of a and b

	a	b
Hydraulically-bound granular mixtures	13.24	12.52
Hydraulically-bound soils	12.18	12.79

With the seven factors above considered, the fatigue life of the proposed asphalt pavement structure (N_{f2}) can be predicted with the Equation 8-32. In order to meet the design requirements, N_{f2} should be larger than the accumulative ESAL which has been discussed in section 8.3.

$$N_{f2} = k_a k_{T2}^{-1} 10^{\left(a - b\frac{\sigma_1}{R_s} + k_e - 0.57\beta\right)} \tag{8-32}$$

8.6.4 Permanent Deformation of Asphalt Layer as Design Criterion

The national design specification presents a four-step approach to evaluate permanent deformation resistance of an asphalt pavement structure:

Step #1 Division of Asphalt Layers into Smaller Sub-layers: The original asphalt layers are further divided into smaller sub-layers with the following

principles:
- For the first asphalt layer, each of its sub-layer thickness should be between 10mm and 20mm;
- For the second asphalt layer, each of its sub-layer thickness should be no more than 25mm;
- For the third asphalt layer, each of its sub-layer thickness should be no more than 100mm;
- For the fourth asphalt layer, sub-division is not necessary.

Step #2 Determination of Sub-layers' Permanent Deformation: With the approach presented in step#1, the original asphalt layers are divided into n sub-layers. This step is to determine the permanent deformation of the ith sub-layer (R_{ai}).

$$R_{ai} = 2.31 \times 10^{-8} k_{Ri} T_{pef}^{2.93} p_i^{1.80} N_{e3}^{0.48} \left(\frac{h_i}{h_0}\right) R_{0i} \qquad (8-33)$$

In the Equation, h_i is the thickness of the ith sub-layer with the unit of mm; h_0 is the thickness of rutting testing samples with the unit of mm; N_{e3} is the accumulative ESAL which is determined through the approach presented in section 8.3; p_i is the compressive stress at the top of the ith sub-layer with the unit of MPa; T_{pef} is the effective temperature which has been discussed in the previous section; k_{Ri} is the integrated correction coefficient of the ith sub-layer which may be determined in Equation 8-34.

$$k_{Ri} = (d_1 + d_2 \cdot z_i) \times 0.9731^{z_i} \qquad (8-34)$$
$$d_1 = -1.35 \times 10^{-4} h_a^2 + 9.798.18 \times 10^{-2} h_a - 14.50 \qquad (8-35)$$
$$d_2 = 8.78 \times 10^{-7} h_a^2 - 1.50 \times 10^{-3} h_a + 0.90 \qquad (8-36)$$

In Equation 8-34, z_i is the depth of the ith sub-layer with the unit of mm. According to the national design specification[2], $z_1 = 15$mm and z_i (when $i > 1$) is equal to the distance between the top surface and the middle point of the ith sub-layer. The asphalt layer thickness (h_a) is equal to 200mm when it is larger than 200mm for calculating d_1 and d_2 with the Equations 8-35 and 8-36.

R_{oi} is the rutting depth (mm) of the ith sub-layer which is usually measured through the standard rutting test at the temperature of 60℃, with a pressure of 0.7MPa, and the loading cycles are 2520. Since R_{oi} is the high-temperature property of asphalt mixture, the design requirement of paving materials presented in section 8.5 should be considered.

In the national design specification[2], the dynamic stability (DS) is used to evaluate the asphalt mixture high-temperature performance as demonstrated in Table 8-23. Therefore, it is necessary to convert the rutting depth into DS through

Equation 8-37. It should be noted that this converting can be applied to the rutting testing sample thickness of 50mm.

$$DS = 9365 R_0^{-1.48} \qquad (8\text{-}37)$$

When DS is determined in the mix proportion design, R_0 may be predicted through Equation 8-37. When the requirement on R_0 is presented, the predicted DS through Equation 8-37 should meet the requirement in Table 8-23.

Step #3 Determination of Asphalt Layer Permanent Deformation: The total permanent deformation of asphalt layers (R_a) is a sum of the sub-layer deformations (R_{ai}). When R_a is less than the allowable maximum permanent deformation in Table 8-4, the design is acceptable.

8.6.5 Subgrade Surface Compressive Strainas Design Criterion

The vertical subgrade surface compressive strain is a commonly-used controlling parameter for verifying the pavement permanent deformation resistance in flexible pavement design. AASHTO road testing data was analyzed to build the relationship between the vertical compressive strain at the subgrade top surface and the accumulative ESAL of 100kN-axles. As a result, Equation 8-38 is used to calculate the allowable compressive strain in the current design specification[2]:

$$[\varepsilon_z] = 1.25 \times 10^{4-0.1\beta}(k_{T3} N_{e4})^{-0.21} \qquad (8\text{-}38)$$

In the Equation, $[\varepsilon_z]$ is the vertical compressive strain at the subgrade top surface; β is the target reliability index; k_{T3} is the temperature adjustment coefficient; and N_{e4} is the accumulative ESAL.

Based on the pavement stress analysis with the multi-layered elastic theory, the vertical compressive strain at the subgrade top surface may be calculated for the proposed pavement structure. If the calculated strain (ε_z) is smaller than the allowable strain $[\varepsilon_z]$, the design meets this criterion. Otherwise, the proposed pavement structure should be modified until it meets this criterion.

8.6.6 Asphalt Layer Low-temperature Cracking as Design Criterion

For roads in seasonal frost areas, low-temperature cracking is one of the most popular distresses. In the current specification[2], the crack index (CI) model was developed based on the Hass model through analyzing more than 10 asphalt pavement sections. The CI model is expressed in Equation 8-39:

$$CI = 1.95 \times 10^{-3} S_t \lg b - 0.075(T + 0.07 h_a) \lg S_t + 0.15 \qquad (8\text{-}39)$$

In the Equation, T is the low-temperature (℃) which is the average value of the lowest temperature for 10 consecutive years; S_t is the creep stiffness of the asphalt binder measured through the bending beam rheometer (BBR) tests under the loading time of 180s and at the temperature of $T + 10$℃ (Unit is MPa); h_a is the asphalt layer thickness (mm); b is the subgrade type parameter which is equal to 5 for the sand subgrade, 3 for the silty clay subgrade, and 2 for clay subgrade.

The calculated CI from Equation 8-39 should meet the design criterion in Table 8-5. If the criterion cannot be met, re-design should be taken on the selection of asphalt binders until the criterion is met.

8.6.7 Anti-freezing Thickness as Design Criterion

In seasonal frozen areas, when the subgrade moisture condition is moist or wet, the pavement thickness should be large enough for protecting the subgrade from frost-thaw effects. Followed is the method for determining the minimum asphalt pavement thickness according to the current design specification[2]:

The first step of this method is to determine the maximum perennial frost depth (mm) with Equation 8-40:

$$Z_{max} = abcZ_d \qquad (8\text{-}40)$$

In the Equation, Z_{max} is the road maximum perennial frost depth (mm); Z_d is the land perennial frost depth (mm) which is determined through looking up the local database; a, b, and c are the three key parameters which can be found in Table 8-31 ~ Table 8-33.

Table 8-31　Thermal physical parameter (a) of subgrade and pavement

Subgrade Materials	Clayey Soils	Silty Soils	Silty Sands	Fine grained sand, clayey sands	Sands or gravels with fine-graded soils
Thermal-physical coefficient	1.05	1.10	1.20	1.30	1.35
Pavement materials	Cement concrete	Asphalt concrete	Graded Macadam	Lime-fly-ash or cement bounded granular mixtures	Lime-fly-ash or cement bounded soils
Thermal-physical coefficient	1.40	1.35	1.45	1.40	1.35

Table 8-32　Humidity parameter of subgrade, b

Type	Dry	Moist	Wet
Humidity parameter	1.0	0.95	0.90

Table 8-33　Parameter of subgrade cross-section, c

Type	Filling Height (m)					Cutting Height (m)			
	0	2	4	6	>6	2	4	6	>6
Section parameter	1.0	1.02	1.05	1.08	1.10	0.98	0.95	0.92	0.90

For the moist and wet conditions of subgrade in seasonal frost areas, the anti-frost layer should be set when the pavement thickness is less than the minimum anti-frost thickness listed in Table 8-34.

Table 8-34 The minimum anti-frost thickness of asphalt pavement (mm)

Humidity Type of Subgrade	Soil Type	Historical Maximum Frost Thickness (mm)			
		500-1000	1000-1500	1500-2000	>2000
Moist	Clayed soil	300-450	350-500	400-600	500-700
	Silty soil	300-450	400-600	450-700	500-750
Wet	Clayed soil	350-550	450-600	500-700	550-800
	Silty soil	400-600	500-700	600-800	650-1000

8.7 Drawings of Pavement Design

Engineering drawings of asphalt pavement design may include the plan view, typical cross-sections, design calculation, and detailed drawings. Readers may referred to the engineering drawing specifications or books for details.

8.8 Summary of Chapter 8

This chapter has presents methodology, procedure, and examples of the asphalt pavement design. Followed are key points:

1. The asphalt pavement design is a mechanistic-empirical design method or M-E design method. The multi-layered elastic system theory is commonly used to calculate the mechanical responses of the pavement structure, while empirical equations are developed through experimental testing or field observations. Since both the mechanical theories and empirical equations are improving from time to time, the asphalt pavement design methods are also kept improving from time to time. The current design speicification which took effect in 2017 was developed from the previous version which took effect in 2006. After a few years, a new version will appear for including more advanced research findings of recent years.

2. The basic steps of asphalt pavement design process include data collection and analysis, pavement layer combination, mix proportion and material properties, pavement thickness verifications, and engineering drawings. It should be noted herein that both layer materials and thicknesses should be considered simultaneously in the design step of pavement layer combination.

Problems and Questions

1. One alternative of the pavement structure is to use asphalt pavement. An asphalt pavement combination is proposed as shown in the following table. Answer

the following questions:

Structural Layers	Material Types	Thickness (mm)	Modulus (MPa)
Surface Layer	AC13 (SBS modified)	40	11000
	AC20 (pen# 90)	60	10000
	AC25 (pen# 90)	80	10000
Base Layer	Cement stabilized crushed stone	360	12000
Subbase Layer	Graded crushed stone	180	300

(1) Assuming the maximum compaction thickness of asphalt-treated base (ATB-25) is 12cm and the minimum thickness is 8cm, could you make two new combination designs considering ATB-25 as part of base course?

(2) Please list the design criteria/design index for verifying the pavement thicknesses of the proposed pavement structure.

(3) If the base layer is replaced with asphalt stabilized crushed stone, what are the design criteria?

2. For the tensile stress in both x and y direction can be calculated by using Multilayer Elastic Layer Analysis program for the given pavement structure. Please identify the stress that should be used for the fatigue life determination of BASE layer, as shown in Fig. P8-1.

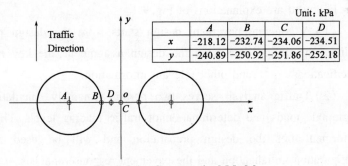

Fig. P 8-1 Computatinal Model

9. Concrete Pavement Design

Similar to asphalt pavement design, concrete pavement design is the process to create and evaluate a concrete pavement structure model, which is the basis for construction. The model may be altered according to the construction requirements. The focus of this chapter is to discuss how to design such a concrete pavement structure model, and the construction methods will be introduced in Chapter 10 which will be included in the second edition of this textbook.

9.1 Design Methodology

According to the national design specification[3], concrete pavement design is based on a mechanistic-empirical design method in which structural models are employed to analyze the pavement responses and experience-based criteria is utilized to evaluate the proposed pavement configuration. Fig. 9-1 shows the general design methodology which includes not only the key subjects in each design step but also the chapters covering the appropriate subjects.

Followed are explanations of Fig. 9-1:

(1) A concrete pavement design starts from the design preparation which includes the design data from the design assignment, the key requirements from specifications[3,7,18], and other relevant information.

(2) Traffic analysis serves two purposes, namely calculation of equivalent single axle loads and determination of traffic loading levels. This step should be performed after the design preparation and will be used in the pavement configuration initialization and the pavement response analysis.

(3) Environmental conditions include temperature and moisture which impact both paving materials and pavement structural responses. Even though the national design specification does not emphasize developments of climatic models, it is recommended to use the existing climatic models. They include the heat transfer model for determining the temperature distribution with respect to space and time, the moisture equilibrium model for determining the final moisture distribution in the subgrade, and the infiltration and drainage model for predicting the degree of saturation of granular bases. The environmental analysis should also be performed

before the structure configuration and its parameters are the key inputs in the structural response analysis.

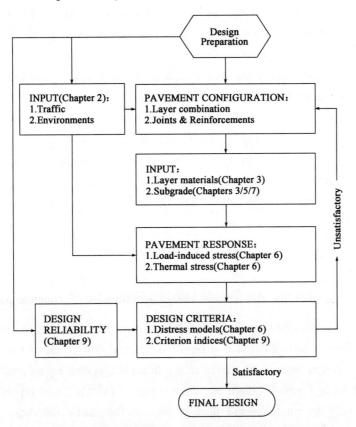

Fig. 9-1 Methodology for concrete pavement design

(4) Pavement configuration includes the number of layers, the thickness of each layer, and type of materials as well as the joint spacing, dowel bars, tie bars, and reinforcement.

(5) Layer materials include cement concrete, bounded or unbounded mixtures of base layers, and bedding layer materials. The basic material properties for the structural models are Young's modulus and Possion's ratio of concrete and resilient moduli of the other materials. If temperature and moisture at different times of the year vary significantly, it is unreasonable to use the same modulus for each layer throughout the entire year. When that is the case, each year should be divided into a number of periods, each with a different set of moduli based on the specific environmental conditions.

(6) Resilient modulus of subgrade is another key input for the structural models. Similar to the layer materials, environment may impact the resilient modulus values throughout the year. It is necessary to divide each year into a number of periods and set different values based on the specific conditions.

(7) Pavement structural models include the single-layered plate system on elastic foundation, the two-layered plate system on elastic foundation, and composite models according to the national design specification[3]. Even though it is not specified in the specification[3], it is recommended to perform the finite element analysis for important projects. The pavement responses may include stresses, strains, and deflections. For concrete pavements, the load-induced and thermal stresses are critical.

(8) If possible, distress models including fatigue cracking model, faulting model, and joint deterioration model should be used to predict distresses of the proposed pavement structure. Under certain reliability, if the predicted distresses are satisfactory compared with the actual distresses, the design is acceptable. Otherwise, the pavement configuration will be subjected to design iterations until the satisfactory result achieves.

9.2 Design Theory, Criteria, and Parameters

9.2.1 Design Theory and Critical Loading Position

As discussed in Chapter 6, the focus of a concrete pavement mechanical analysis is to calculate the stresses, strains, and deflections of the concrete surface. The design basis is the theory of the thin plate system on an elastic foundation. As shown in Fig. 6-16, there are three types of models based on this design theory, namely the single-layered plate system on the elastic foundation, the two-layered plate system on the elastic foundation, and the composite plate system on the elastic foundation.

As discussed in Chapter 6, the critical loading position is located at the center of the longitudinal joints and the critical stress is located at the bottom of the concrete slab. The base layer has the identical critical loading position to that of the concrete surface.

9.2.2 Design Criteria and Parameters

1) Design Reliability, Variance, and Parameters

Engineering reliability means the ability of a system or component to perform its required functions under stated conditions for a specified time period. In the concrete pavement design, the reliability is referred to the probability that a trial pavement structure can survive environmental and traffic loading conditions through the specific design period.

The key parameter which reflects the design reliability is the reliability coefficient which is used in the performance criteria and a procedure is presented in the national design specification[3]:

The first step is to determine the target reliability which is dependent on highway class as shown Table 9-1. For instance, the target reliability is 95% for expressway and 90% for class- I highway.

Table 9-1 Design reliability criteria in the national design specification[3]

Highway Class	Expressway	Class- I	Class- II	Class- III	Class- IV
Safety	Level- I		Level- II	Level- III	
Design Period (year)	30		20	15	10
Target Reliability (%)	95	90	85	80	70
Reliability Index	1.64	1.28	1.04	0.84	0.52

The second step is to determine the coefficient of variation (CV) of materials and layer thickness: Dependent on highway classification, construction quality, and project management level, and materials pavement layer thickness may have some discrepancy from the original design. In the national design specification[3], material and thickness discrepancy is classified into three variance levels, namely *low, moderate, and high*. For the expressway and class- I highway, the variance level should be low, while for class- II highway, the variance level should no higher than moderate.

CV is also known as relative standard deviation (RSD) as computed in Equations below:

$$CV = \frac{\sigma}{\mu} \quad (9\text{-}1)$$

$$\mu = \frac{\sum_{i=1}^{n} x_i}{n} \quad (9\text{-}2)$$

$$\sigma = \sqrt{\frac{\sum_{i=1}^{n}(\mu - x_i)^2}{n-1}} \quad (9\text{-}3)$$

According to the national design specification[3], cement concrete bending strength, the equivalent modulus on the top surface of base, and the thickness of concrete slabs should be measured and their corresponding CV values are determined in the above equations. When it is difficult to determine CVs through experimental tests, Table 9-2 may be used to determine CVs of material performance and slab thickness.

Table 9-2 Criteria for the coefficient of variance

Variance Levels	High	Moderate	Low
Cement Concrete Bending Strength	$0.05 \leq CV \leq 0.10$	$0.10 < CV \leq 0.15$	$0.15 < CV \leq 0.20$

continue

Variance Levels	High	Moderate	Low
Equivalent modulus at the top surface of pavement base	$0.15 \leqslant CV \leqslant 0.25$	$0.25 < CV \leqslant 0.35$	$0.35 < CV \leqslant 0.55$
Concrete slab thickness	$0.02 \leqslant CV \leqslant 0.04$	$0.04 < CV \leqslant 0.06$	$0.06 < CV \leqslant 0.08$

The third step is to determine the reliability coefficient through the Table 9-3 with the specific target reliability and variance level.

Table 9-3 Reliability Coefficient

Variance Levels	Target reliability			
	95	90	85	80~70
Low	1.2~1.33	1.09~1.16	1.04~1.08	—
Moderate	1.33~1.5	1.16~1.23	1.08~1.13	1.04~1.07
High	—	1.23~1.33	1.13~1.18	1.07~1.11

Example 9-1:
Determine the reliability coefficient of an expressway according to the national design specification[2] assuming materials, construction quality, and project management level can meet all the requirements.

Solution:
For an expressway design, the target reliability is 95% from Table 9-1, and the variance level is low. Therefore, the reliability coefficient is 1.2~1.33.

2) Performance Criteria and Parameters

In order to evaluate the proposed pavement structure serviceability, the first criterion is to combine effects of the load-induced fatigue stress and the thermal fatigue stress as shown in Equation 9-4.

$$\gamma_r(\sigma_{pr} + \sigma_{tr}) \leqslant f_r \tag{9-4}$$

In the Equation, γ_r is the reliability coefficient and f_r is the concrete flexural strength.

Another criterion is the combine effects of the maximum load-induced stress and the maximum thermal stress as expressed in Equation 9-5.

$$\gamma_r(\sigma_{p,max} + \sigma_{t,max}) \leqslant f_r \tag{9-5}$$

The third criterion is the effects of the load-induced fatigue stress on the lean concrete or rolled concrete base as expressed in Equation 9-6.

$$\gamma_r \sigma_{bpr} \leqslant f_{br} \tag{9-6}$$

3) Traffic Loading Criteria and Parameters

According to the national design specification[3], the equivalent axial load factor (EALF) can be calculated with Equation 9-7.

$$\text{EALFm}_x = \left(\frac{P_x}{P_s}\right)^{16} \tag{9-7}$$

Where P_x, P_s are the magnitude of the axle load x and the standard axle load.

Based on the accumulative ESAL which may be determined with the method presented in the appendix A of the design specification[3], the traffic loading is divided into five levels as shown in Table 9-4, namely extreme heavy traffic, very heavy traffic, heavy traffic, moderate traffic, and light traffic.

Table 9-4 Traffic loading classification for concrete pavement design

Traffic Class	Extremely Heavy	Very Heavy	Heavy	Moderate	Light
Accumulative equivalent axle loads of 100kN on the design lane within the analysis period (10^4)	$> 1 \times 10^6$	$1 \times 10^6 - 2000$	$2000 - 100$	$100 - 3$	< 3

4) Criteria for Concrete Bending Strength

Concrete materials may include the cement concrete and fiber concrete materials, whose flexural strength with the curing period of 28 days should be larger than the values shown in Table 9-5.

Table 9-5 Standard values of cement concrete bending strength

Traffic Loading Class	Extremely Heavy, Very Heavy, and Heavy	Moderate	Light
Cement Concrete Flexural Strength (MPa)	No less than 5.0	4.5	4.0
Fiber Concrete Flexural Strength (MPa)	No less than 6.0	5.5	5.0

5) Criteria for Frost-protection Layer

For seasonal frozen areas, the minimum pavement thickness should meet the requirements as shown in Table 9-6.

Table 9-6 Minimum thickness of concrete pavement structure with considering frost-thaw effects (cm)

Subgrade Moisture Types	Subgrade Soil Types	Maximum Frozen Depth (cm)			
		50 – 100	100 – 150	150 – 200	> 200
Moist Subgrade	Soils sensitive to frost effects	30 – 50	40 – 60	50 – 70	60 – 95
	Soils very sensitive to frost effects	40 – 60	50 – 70	60 – 85	70 – 110
Wet Subgrade	Soils sensitive to frost effects	40 – 60	50 – 70	60 – 90	75 – 120
	Soils very sensitive to frost effects	45 – 70	55 – 80	70 – 100	80 – 130

6) Temperature Gradient Criterion

According to the specification[3], the maximum thermal gradients of different climatic zoning is shown in Table 9-7.

Table 9-7 Maximum thermal gradient T_g

Climatic Zoning	II / V	III	IV, VI	VII
Maximum Thermal Gradient (℃/m)	83 – 88	95 – 90	86 – 92	93 – 98

9.3 Design Preparation and Data Analysis

As mentioned above, design data preparation should be completed before a concrete pavement design: First of all, the climatic zoning should be identified according to the project location. For instance, if the project is located at Yulin of Shaanxi province, the climatic zoning is Ⅲ2a and the corresponding environment-related parameters may be obtained: the moisture coefficient is 0.5 ~ 0.75, the annual rainfall is 400 ~ 600mm, the max frozen depth is 100 ~ 120cm, and etc. The second is traffic data which includes traffic volume, vehicle types, axle load spectrum, growth factor, and etc. Another important data is pavement and subgrade material sources. Attentions should be paid to the availability, quality, variance, and cost of the existing material sources.

In addition, hydrology, construction equipments, and construction variance should also be investigated if possible.

9.3.1 Traffic Data Collection and Analysis

According to the appendix A of the national design specification[3], the traffic analysis may be performed with the "ATF" method which has been discussed in Chapter 2. Followed is the step-by-step procedure:

Step 1: Traffic Data Collection: The designer may collect the two-way traffic volume in terms of the annual average daily traffic (AADT) and vehicle types through the local traffic investigation stations. The annual average daily truck traffic (ADTT) data is determined by removing passenger vehicles or trucks with no more than two axles and four wheels.

It should be noted that the ADTT data is the two-way traffic volume. Therefore, directional coefficient (f_d) should be determined by surveying. When it is difficult to conduct survey, the designer may use the reference value which is from 0.5 to 0.6.

According to the highway class, functional requirements, development of economy and transportation, the traffic increasing rate should be determined.

The WIM data of truck axles should be collected through statistically analysis on 3000 trucks which at least have two axles and 6 wheels. The data includes numbers, weights, and percentages of single axles (if the axles are tandem and tridem axles, they may be multiplied by double and tripe times, respectively).

Step 2: Calculation of "ATF": With the method described in Figure 2-13, the number of vehicles in survey (N_v) is 3000 and through the collected data in the step 1 it is easy to determine the number of axles and the corresponding percentages of axles. The equivalent axle load factor ($EALF_i$) can be determined with Equation 9-7. Evidently, all the four independent variables are determined, and the ATF can be easily computed.

Step 3: Calculation of accumulative ESAL: With the information from the above two steps, ADTT and ATF are determined. With the traffic increasing rate, the growth factor (G) can also be easily determined. The remaining independent variables for computing the accumulative ESAL are the lane factor which can be determined through multiplying the value of Table 9-8. The directional coefficient which is around 0.5, and the wheel factor which is the transverse distribution coefficient as shown Table 9-9.

Table 9-8 Lane factor of truck traffic flow

One-way Traffic Lane		1	2	3	≥4
Lane Factor	Expressway	—	0.70~0.85	0.45~0.60	0.40~0.50
	The other classes of highways*	1.00	0.50~0.75	0.50~0.75	—

Note: The lower value for Higher effects of non-motor traffic.

Table 9-9 Transverse distribution coefficient of wheel traffic for rigid pavements

Highway Class		Longitudinal Joint Edge
Expressway, class-I highway, and toll station		0.17~0.22
Class-II and lower classes of highways	Traffic lane width >7m	0.34~0.39
	Traffic lane width ≤7m	0.54~0.62

Note: Lower value for higher effects of non-motor traffic.

9.3.2 Subgrade Supporting

According to the national cement concrete pavement design specification[3], subgrade should be stable, dense, homogenous, and to provide uniform supporting to the rigid pavement structure. Before design of a rigid pavement structure, the subgrade supporting conditions should be analyzed and the resilient modulus at the roadbed surface should meet the requirements in Table 9-10.

Table 9-10 Minimum resilient modulus at the roadbed surface for rigid pavements

Traffic Loading Classes	Extremely/Very Heavy Traffic	Heavy/Moderate Traffic	Light Traffic
Minimum Resilient Modulus (MPa)	80	60	40

In the Appendix E of national cement concrete pavement design specification[3], a subgrade resilient modulus determination method is provided: The first step is to select a reference value based on the soil types as shown in Table 9-11; The second step is to determine the moisture adjustment coefficient which is dependent on the water table and soil types as shown in Table 9-12; The last step is to determine the design resilient modulus through multiplying the reference value with the moisture adjustment coefficient.

Table 9-11 Reference value of subgrade resilient modulus

Soil Groups	Value Range (MPa)	Representative Value (MPa)
Well-graded Gravels (GW)	240~290	250
Poorly-graded Gravels (GP)	170~240	190
Gravels with Fine-grained Soils (GF)	120~240	180
Silty Gravels (GM)	160~270	220
Clayey Gravels (GC)	120~190	150
Well-graded Sands (SW)	120~190	150
Poorly-graded Sands (SP)	100~160	130
Sands with Fine-grained Soils (SF)	80~160	120
Silty Sands (SM)	120~190	150
Clayey Sands (SC)	80~120	100
Silty Soils with Low Liquid Limit (ML)	70~110	90
Clay Soils with Low Liquid Limit (CL)	50~100	70
Silty Soils with High Liquid Limit (MH)	30~70	50
Clay Soils With Low Liquid Limit (CH)	20~50	30

Note: 1. For gravels and sands, the lower modulus value is recommended for the larger value of D_{60} (sieve size passing 60%).
2. For the other soils with fine particles, the lower modulus value is recommended for the larger contents of particles less than 0.075 and the higher plastic index.

Table 9-12 Moisture adjustment coefficient of subgrade resilient modulus

Soil Groups	Distance from Water Table to Top of Roadbed (m)					
	1.0	1.5	2.0	2.5	3.0	4.0
Gravels with Fine-grained Soils (GF) Earthy Gravels (GM/GC)	0.81~0.88	0.86~1.00	0.91~1.00	0.96~1.00	—	—
Sands with Fine-grained Soils (SF), Earthy Sands (SM/SC)	0.80~0.86	0.83~0.97	0.87~1.00	0.90~1.00	0.94~1.00	—
Silty Soils with Low Liquid Limit (ML)	0.71~0.74	0.75~0.81	0.78~0.89	0.82~0.97	0.86~1.00	0.94~1.00

continue

Soil Groups	Distance from Water Table to Top of Roadbed (m)					
	1.0	1.5	2.0	2.5	3.0	4.0
Clay Soils with Low Liquid Limit (CL)	0.70~0.73	0.72~0.80	0.74~0.88	0.75~0.95	0.77~1.00	0.81~1.00
Silty Soils with High Liquid Limit (MH)	0.70~0.71	0.71~0.75	0.72~0.78	0.73~0.82	0.73~0.86	0.74~0.94

Note: The lower value is recommended for material with more particles passing 0.075mm-sieve and larger plastic index.

9.4 Concrete Pavement Combination Design

As shown in Fig. 9-2, a concrete pavement cross-section is a layered structure containing concrete surface, base, subbase, and bedding layer. In horizontal directions, a concrete pavement may have longitudinal joints and transverse joints. The dowel bars and tie bars are commonly utilized to connect the joints. The surface textures are made to improve the ride quality. Additionally, reinforcements are also used in some projects to improve the structure capability.

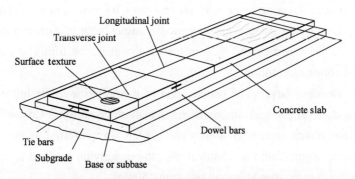

Fig. 9-2 Typical concrete pavement configuration

9.4.1 Layer Combination

The target of layer combination design is to determine the number of layers, the thickness of each layer, and type of materials based on the design requirements as specified in the design specification. Followed are key points for layer combination design:

General Requirements: First of all, highway classes and traffic loading classifications should be considered. For the high class of highway with the heavy traffic loading, it is necessary to increase the number of layers, thickness of layer, and material quality. Secondly, the subgrade conditions should be analyzed: for the weak subgrade, treatments should be given and additional requirements should be given to both layer materials and thickness. If the subgrade is in a excellent condition, the layer thickness may be reduced for saving engineering cost. The third factors is the layer material properties and the corresponding roles in the structure. In a good design, each layer has a specified function that contribute to the whole pavement structure; In the contrast, a bad design may leads to premature chistresses of pavement structure. The fourth factor which should be carefully considered is the interfaces features between adjacent layers. The stiffness ratio, permeability, and binding conditions of adjacent layers should be specially designed. The last factor is the environment effects: when temperature sensitive materials are selected, the pavement may have the thermal stress related distresses. When the moisture sensitive materials are selected, frozen-thaw effects need to be considered.

Subgrade: In the design specification, the resilient modulus on the roadbed surface is used for the subsequent pavement response analysis. Determination of the resilient modulus has been discussed in the previous chapters. Table 9-10 shows the resilient modulus value requirement under different traffic loading conditions.

For the roadbed in rocky cutting sections or the roadbed with rocky filling materials, a leveling layer with no less than 100mm is needed. The layer materials may be crushed stones, cement bound mixtures with low cement contents.

In the specification[13], there are requirements on filling materials, water table, frost conditions, and etc.

Bedding Layer: The major target of a bedding layer design is to minimize the frost-thaw effect and improve the moisture conditions. Coarse grained granular mixtures, such as crushed stones and gravels, are preferred as paving materials. The bedding layer should be identical with the underlying roadbed in terms of width and the thicknesses should be no less than 150mm.

Base or Subbase Layer: The major target of a base or subbase layer is to provide a uniform supporting to the concrete surface even though it takes part of traffic loads. Therefore, the two key requirements are the erosion resistance and the stiffness value, respectively.

In terms of erosion resistance, lean concrete and asphalt concrete are better than cement bound mixtures and asphalt stabilized macadam, which are better than lime-fly-ash bound mixtures, and unbound granular mixtures. In terms of stiffness values, the higher the layer stiffness, the better the load transfer behaviors, but increasing stiffness may result in larger curling stresses at the same time.

Based on traffic classification, the corresponding layer materials are recommended as listed in Table 9-13.

9. Concrete Pavement Design

Table 9-13　Recommendation of base and subbase layer materials

Traffic Class	Extreme Heavy	Very Heavy	Heavy	Moderate	Light
Base Materials	Lean Concrete, Rolled Concrete, Asphalt concrete		Dense graded asphalt macadam, Cement stabilized macadam	Graded crushed stones, Cement-stabilized mixes, lime-fly-ash stabilized mixes	
Subbase Materials	Cement-stabilized mixes, Lime-fly-ash stabilized mixes, Graded crushed stones			Unscreened crushed stones, graded crushed stones, or no subbase	

When concrete is used in the hard shoulder, the structure and thickness of the shoulder base should be identical to that of the travel lanes. The width of base should be 300mm or 650mm larger than that of the travel lanes.

In a base or subbase design, the thickness should meet both the performance and construction requirements. Table 9-14 shows the recommended construction thickness from the national construction specification.

Table 9-14　Recommended construction thickness

Materials	Layer Thickness (mm)
Lean concrete/ Rolled concrete	120~200
HBM	150~200
AC10	25~40
AC13	35~65
AC16	40~70
AC20	50~75
AM20	50~75
AM25	75~100
Porous CBM	100~150
Graded crushed stones/ Unscreened crushed stones or gravels	100~200

Concrete Surface Layers: The concrete surface is directly exposed to traffic and environmental conditions. It should be strong and durable to support the majority of the traffic loads and functional to serve traffic flow. A concrete surface should have high stiffness, high strength, high durability, good skidding and polishing resistance.

According to different types of concrete surface, concrete pavements are divided into jointed plain concrete pavements (JPCP), jointed reinforced concrete pavements (JRCP), continuously-reinforced concrete pavements (CRCP), and composite pavements. Table 9-15 shows the recommendations of concrete surface materials which are dependent on classification of highways and traffic loading.

Table 9-15 Recommendation of concrete surface materials

Types		Application Conditions
JPCP/JRCP		All types of highway
CRCP		Expressway
Composite pavement	Dense-graded asphalt concrete Upper Surface	Expressway under extremely or very heavy traffic
	CRCP/JPCP	
Roller-compacted concrete surface		Class two or lower highways
Fiber-reinforced concrete pavement		Pavements with restrained elevation or concrete overlays
Precast concrete blocks as surface		Bridge approaching of class-two or lower highways Parking lots in service area

The concrete surface thickness is dependent on traffic, highway class, and variance levels as shown in Table 9-16. Once the three factors are determined, the surface thickness may be initialized.

Table 9-16 Recommendation of concrete surface thickness

Traffic Class	Highway Class	Variance Levels	Surface Thickness (mm)
Extremely heavy	—	Low	≥320
Very heavy	Expressway	Low	320~280
	Class I	Moderate	300~260
		Low	280~240
	Class II	Moderate	
Heavy	Expressway	Low	
	Class I	Moderate	270~230
		Low	260~220
	Class II	Moderate	
Moderate	Class II	High	250~220
		Moderate	240~210
	Class III	High	
	Class IV	Moderate	230~200
Light	Class III	High	220~190
	Class IV	Moderate	210~180

In addition to materials and thickness, the surface texture and dimension should also be considered. According to the specification[3], the surface texture should be made on concrete slab for providing enough frictional force and the texture depth should meet the corresponding requirements. The dimension of concrete surface should be 0.6m wider than the travel lanes to avoid placing the longitudinal joints on the wheel tracks.

Road Shoulder: The shoulder is usually slightly narrower than a full traffic lane. For expressway or class- I highway, the shoulder structure is identical to that of driveway even though fewer vehicles pass through the shoulder. For other classes of highways, shoulders should have the identical base and subbase with the driveway.

If asphalt concrete is used for paving shoulders, hot mix asphalt mixtures are recommended for traffic volume higher than the moderate level. Shoulders should connect with the driveway through tie bars if concrete shoulder is used. If the driveway pavement surface is the jointed concrete slabs, the transverse joints should be consistent between the driveway and the shoulder.

Drainage: The cross slope of the driveway should be 1% ~ 2% and that of the shoulder may be 2% ~ 3%. For permeable base, collecting ditches or pipes should be built. At the same time, drainage pipes should lay out in every 50 ~ 100m in transverse direction.

9.4.2 Joint Design

Joints may be divided into longitudinal joints, transverse joints, and intersection joints according to joint directions. They can also be divided into contraction joints, expansion joints, and construction joints based on the jointing mechanism. The longitudinal joints are parallel to the traffic direction while the transverse joints are perpendicular to the traffic direction. The intersection joints are located in the road intersections. The target of the joint design is to select joint types, joint spacing, joint configuration, and joint layout. Followed are key points in joint design:

General Principles: For jointed plain concrete pavements, jointed reinforced concrete pavements, roller-compacted concrete pavements, and steel fiber reinforced concrete pavements, the rectangular slabs are preferred. The transverse and longitudinal joints should be perpendicular and transverse joints along longitudinal joints should not be malposed to minimize effects of cracking reflection as shown in Fig. 9-3.

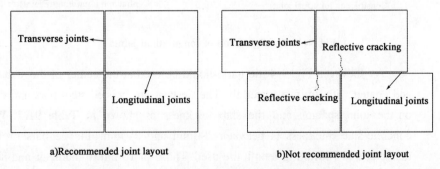

Fig. 9-3 Transverse joints along a longitudinal joint

The spacing of 3 ~ 4.5m is recommend for the longitudinal joints. The transverse joint spacing depends on pavement types and the slab thickness:

- For jointed plain concrete pavements, the spacing of transverse joints should be about 4 ~ 6m. The ratio of the slab length to the width should be no more than 1.35 and the slab area should be less than 25 square meters.
- For roller-compacted or fiber-reinforced concrete pavements, the transverse joint spacing should be 6 ~ 10m.
- For jointed reinforced concrete pavements, the spacing of transverse joints should be about 6 ~ 15m. The ratio of the slab length to the width should be no more than 2.5 and the slab area should be less than 45 square meters.

Configuration and Layout of Longitudinal Joints. Dependent on the pavement width, the travel lanes, the hard shoulders, and the paver, the concrete pavement may have the longitudinal contraction joints and the longitudinal construction joints. When the paver width is not enough for the full-width construction, the two adjacent concrete slabs cannot be paved at the same time. As a result, the construction joint as shown in Fig. 9-4a) is formed between the two slabs. For the jointed plain concrete pavement wider than 4.5m and the roller-compacted concrete pavement wider than 7.5m, the longitudinal contraction joint as shown in Fig. 9-4b) is needed when the paver is wide enough for the full-width construction.

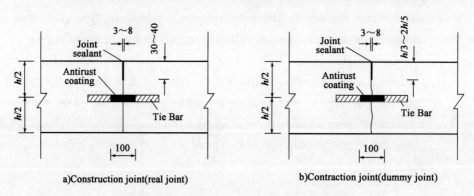

a) Construction joint (real joint) b) Contraction joint (dummy joint)

Fig. 9-4 Configuration of longitudinal joints

As shown in Fig. 9-4, tie bars should be used at the center of the slab thickness and coated with antirust materials. The tie bars are twisted steel bars and dependent on the joint spacing and the slab thickness as shown in Table 9-17. When the concrete slab thickness is between 200mm and 250mm, the tie bars of 14mm in diameter and 700mm in length are used. Those of 16mm in diameter and 800mm in length are used when the slab thickness is larger than 260mm.

Table 9-17 Diameter, length, and spacing of tie bars

Slab Thickness (mm)	Bar Diameter (mm)	Bar Length (mm)	Bar Spacing (mm) of Different Slab Width (m)					
			3	3.5	3.75	4.5	6	7.5
200~250	14	700	900	800	700	600	500	400
≥260	16	800	800	700	600	500	400	300

Configuration and Layout of Transverse Joints. Transverse joints are used to relieve tensile stress, relieve compressive stress, and transfer the traffic loading from one slab to another. According to their functions, there are three types of transverse joints, namely the contraction joints shown in Fig. 9-5, the expansion joints shown in Fig. 9-6, and the construction joints shown in Fig. 9-7. When temperature decreaes, the concrete slabs tend to contract and the tensile stress may be induced. At this situation, contraction joints are used to relieve the tensile stress through transferring the thermal energy down to the underlying base layer. When temperature increases, the concrete slabs tend to expand and the compressive stress may be induced. Large compressive stress may result in the blowups of concrete pavements. In order to minimize these effects, expansion joints are used to relieve of the compressive stress. When the construction work must stop due to emergency, machine breakdown, or any other needs, construction joints should be placed. If possible, the transverse construction joints should be placed at the location of the contraction joints.

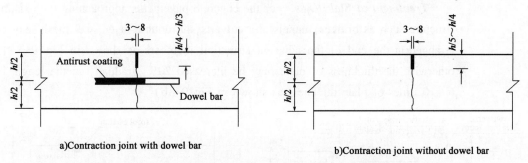

a) Contraction joint with dowel bar   b) Contraction joint without dowel bar

Fig. 9-5 Configuration of Transverse Contraction Joints

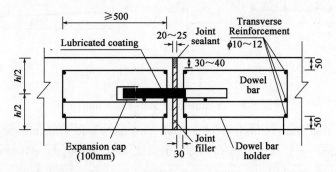

ig. 9-6 Configuration of Transverse Expansion Joints (unit: mm)

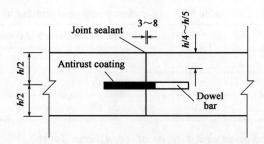

Fig. 9-7 Configuration of Transverse Construction Joints

Layout of Intersection Joints. When the two roads are orthogonally intersected, the longitudinal joints of the two intersecting roads should be consistent by changing their transverse joint spacings. When the two roads are skewly intersected, the main road should have its longitudinal joints consistent and its transverse joints changing according to the minor road's longitudinal joints. For the joint arrangement of curving section of intersecting roads, there should be no or less staggered joints or sharp gussets. When the staggered joints and sharp gussets exist, the anti-cracking steel bars and corner reinforced should be added.

The transverse joints at the end of widened section of the secondary road curve should be in the form of expansion joints. There should be 2 ~ 3 expansion joints in a straight line segment for large expansion.

Treatment at Slab Ends. For the concrete pavements approaching the existing structure such as bridges, tunnels and culverts, the double-layer steel mesh may be arranged at the end of the adjacent structural members as shown in Fig. 9-8a); otherwise the thickness of plate may be increased 20% gradually in the length of 6 ~ 10 times of plate thickness as shown in Fig. 9-8b).

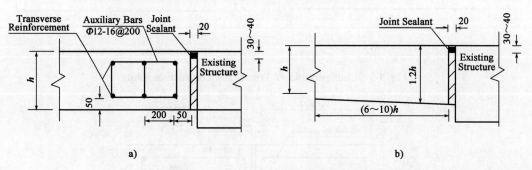

Fig. 9-8 Treatment at Slab Ends (unit: mm)

For the connection of asphalt pavement and concrete pavement, a transition section of 3 meters should be provided. In addition, the pavement of the transition section should be arranged in a stepped manner on two types of pavements.

End of the connection of continuous reinforcement concrete pavement and other types of pavement or structure should be provided with an anchoring structure.

Filling Materials. The materials of the expansion joints should adapt to the expansion and contraction of concrete slabs, not be easily deformed during construction, and will have high recovery rate and as well as durability. Foam rubber sheets and asphalt fiber boards should be used for expressway and Grade-I highways; wood or fiber boards are also available for highways of other grades.

9.4.3 Concrete Pavement Reinforcements

In the following situations, reinforcements are needed and the corresponding design methods are briefly described:

Reinforcement Design of Jointed Reinforced Concrete Pavements: The reinforcement is dependent on the slab thickness (h), joint spacing (L_s), the interface friction coefficient (μ), and steel bar strength (f_{sy}). The area of steel bar per unit length or width is expressed in Equation 9-8.

$$A_s = \frac{15 L_s h \mu}{f_{sy}} \qquad (9\text{-}8)$$

Both the longitudinal and transverse reinforcements should be calculated with Equation 9-4. The diameters of steel bars in the both directions should be identical or similar to each other. The minimum spacing between two adjacent steel bars should be no less than two times of the maximum aggregate size. The other requirements may be found in the design specification[3].

Reinforcement Design of Continuously-reinforced Concrete Pavements: The reinforcement is mainly dependent on traffic loading classification: the reinforcement percentage should be 0.6% ~ 0.7% for the moderate traffic, 0.7% ~ 0.8% for the heavy traffic, 0.8% ~ 0.9% for the very heavy traffic, and 0.9% ~ 1.0% for the extremely heavy traffic.

Other Reinforcement Design: In addition to the two types of reinforcements above, reinforcements are also given at concrete slab edge, joint, and free boundaries:

- The reinforcements at the bottom of the concrete slab edge are needed for plain concrete pavement with the weak foundation, for joints without dowel bars, and for junctions between the main line and the ramp.
- Under the very heavy or extremely heavy traffic loading conditions, corner steel bars are needed at the expansion joints, construction joints, and the other free boundaries (edges).

- Under extremely heavy traffic loading conditions, the corner steel bars are also needed at the contraction joints.
- When the concrete surface over pass through a structure (such as box or circular culverts), the reinforcement should be provided.

The detailed design procedure and requirements are provided in the national design specification.

9.5 Mix Proportion and Pavement Thickness Verification

9.5.1 Mix Proportion and Parameters for Stress Analysis

The key parameters for pavement stress analysis include geometric parameters, mechanical parameters, and the reliability coefficient. Since these contents have been discussed in the previous sections, only mechanical parameters are presented herein:

Soils and Granular Materials. Resilient modulus is used to characterize soils and granular materials. It can be measured through repeated triaxial compressive tests. The testing sample of soils should be 100mm in diameter and 200mm in height, while the sample of granular mixtures should be 150mm in diameter and 300mm in height.

Hydraulically-bounded Mixtures. Resilient modulus is also used to characterize hydraulically-bound mixtures. It can be measured through uniaxial compressive tests. The sample dimension should be 100mm in diameter and 200mm in height or 150mm in diameter and 300mm in height. The curing periods are 90 days for the cement-bound mixtures and 180 days for the lime fly ash bound mixtures. The samples should be soaked in water for one day before testing.

Asphalt Mixtures. Dynamic modulus is used to characterize asphalt mixtures. It is measured through the uniaxial compressive tests under cyclic loading. The sample dimension is 100mm in diameter and 150mm in height.

Cement Concrete. Resilient modulus and flexural strength are two key parameters which are measured through the uniaxial compressive tests.

In addition to the lab testing methods, these key parameters can also be empirically determined and could be found in the appendices of the national specification[3].

9.5.2 Determination of Pavement Responses

In the national design specification[3], the load-induced fatigue and the maximum stresses should be calculated to evaluate effects of traffic loading, while the thermal fatigue stress and the maximum thermal curling stress are computed to evaluate effects from temperature changing. In Chapter 6, the solutions to those stresses have been provided under normal conditions. In this section, a series of coefficients are employed to transfer the stress values of the normal conditions into those of the practical conditions.

Transfer Coefficients : This first coefficient is the fatigue coefficient which is dependent on the accumulative equivalent single axle loads as expressed in Equation 9-9.

$$k_f = N_e^\lambda \tag{9-9}$$

Where N_e^λ is the accumulative equivalent single axle loads and λ is the fatigue index which is dependent on material properties $\lambda = 0.057$ for plain concrete, reinforced concrete, and continuously-reinforced concrete; $\lambda = 0.065$ for rolled concrete and lean concrete; and $\lambda = 0.053 - 0.017\rho_f \dfrac{l_f}{d_f}$ for steel fiber-reinforced concrete; p_f, l_f and d_f are the volumetric percentage, length, and diameter of the steel fibers.

The second coefficient is the stress reduction coefficient, denoted with k_r. When the road shoulder is built with concrete materials, $k_r = 0.87 \sim 0.92$. The lower value is recommended when the shoulder and driveway have the identical thickness. The higher value should be selected when the shoulder surface is thinner than the driveway surface. When the flexible shoulders are used, $k_r = 1$.

The third coefficient is the correction coefficient, denoted by k_c. This coefficient is employed to consider the difference between theoretical and actual solutions. Based on the highway classification, the coefficient is listed in the Table 9-18.

Table 9-18   Correction Coefficient k_c

Highway Class	Expressway	Class I	Class II	Class III and IV
k_c	1.15	1.10	1.05	1.00

The fourth coefficient is the thermal fatigue stress coefficient, denoted by k_t. This coefficient is dependent on the climatic zoning and concrete bending strength and expressed in Equation 9-10.

$$k_t = \dfrac{f_r}{\sigma_{t,\max}} \left[\alpha_t \left(\dfrac{\sigma_{t,\max}}{f_r} \right)^{b_t} - c_t \right] \tag{9-10}$$

In the Equation, $\sigma_{t,\max}$ is the maximum thermal curling stress which can be determined with the method in Chapter 6; f_r is the concrete bending strength which can be selected based on the traffic classification; α_t, b_t, and c_t are three regression coefficients which are dependent on the climatic zoning as listed in Table 9-19.

Table 9-19 Three regression coefficients of α_t, b_t, and c_t

Coefficients	Climatic Zoning					
	II	III	IV	V	VI	VII
α_t	0.825	0.855	0.841	0.871	0.837	0.834
b_t	1.323	1.355	1.323	1.287	1.382	1.270
c_t	0.041	0.041	0.058	0.071	0.038	0.052

Load-induced Fatigue Stress. In the national design specification[3], the fatigue stress at the concrete surface can be determined in Equation 9-11 even through the load-induced stress σ_{ps} may be different for different models:

$$\sigma_{pr} = k_r k_f k_c \sigma_{ps} \tag{9-11}$$

For the two-layer plate system on an elastic foundation model, the surface concrete fatigue stress is calculated in Equation 9-12 and the base layer fatigue stress should be calculated in Equation 9-8.

$$\sigma_{bpr} = k_f k_c \sigma_{bps} \tag{9-12}$$

For the composite plate system models, the fatigue stresses can be determined by Equation 9-11 and Equation 9-12, but the parameters should be those from the composite surface or base.

Load-induced Maximum Stress. In the national design specification[3], the maximum load-induced stress can be determined in Equation 9-13:

$$\sigma_{p,max} = k_r k_c \sigma_{pm} \tag{9-13}$$

Where $\sigma_{p,max}$ is the load-induced the maximum stress, which is determined through substituting the design axle load with the maximum axle load into the corresponding equations.

Thermal Fatigue Stress. In the national design specification, the maximum thermal curling stress has been determined in Chapter 6. The thermal fatigue stress is determined by the Equation below:

$$\sigma_{tr} = k_t \sigma_{t,max} \tag{9-14}$$

Where $\sigma_{t,max}$ is the load-induced the maximum stress, which is determined through substituting the design axle load with the maximum axle load into the corresponding equations.

9.5.3 Verification of Layer Thickness

After the reliability coefficient, the load-induced fatigue stress, and the thermal fatigue stress are determined, the concrete pavement thickness is verified according to the performance criteria of Equations 9-4, 9-5, and 9-6.

9.6 Concrete Pavement Design Examples

9.6.1 Single-layer Plate System on Elastic Foundation

[*Problem statement*] Design a JPCP for a class-II highway with four lanes located at national zone II. The subgrade soil is clay with a low liquid limit and the water table is 0.9m beneath the roadbed surface. Regional coarse aggregate is limestone. The annual average daily truck traffic of the first year is 200 standard axles(sa). The standard axle is 150kN. The traffic increasing rate is 6%.

Step 1: Traffic analysis: The annual average daily standard axles N_s = 200sa; Traffic increasing rate g_r = 6%; From Table 9-1, design life t = 20years; The transverse distribution of wheel track is 0.54 ~ 0.62 from Table 9-1, accumulative traffic N_e is computed:

$$N_e = \frac{N_s \times [(1 + g_r)^t - 1] \times 365}{g_r} \times \eta$$
$$= \frac{200 \times [(1 + 0.06)^2 - 1] \times 365}{0.06} \times 0.62$$
$$= 166.49 \times 10^4 (\text{times})$$

The traffic loading level is heavy according to Table 9-4.

Step 2: Combination Design: From Table 9-3, the construction quality variation level is moderate. Based on the known conditions including class-II highway, heavy traffic load grade and moderate variation level, one combination below is proposed, as shown in Table 9-20.

Table 9-20 Combination for the Single-layered Plate System on Elastic Foundation

Layers	Layer materials	Layer thickness
Surface	Plain concrete pavement with tie bars and without dowel bars	23cm
Base	Graded crushed stones	20cm
Subgrade		

Step 3: Mix Proportion Design and Layer Material Parameters: According to the national design specification[3] and section 9.5 of this textbook, the mix proportion and layer material properties are listed in the Table 9-21.

Table 9-21 Mix Proportion and Layer Material Properties for the Combination in Table 9-20

Materials	Proportion	Material parameters
Plain cement concrete	Details are not presented herein, but should be presented in the real project	Flexural tensile strength f = 5MPa; Young's modulus E_c = 31GPa; Possion's ratio v_c = 0.15; The coefficient of linear expansion of concrete with the coarse aggregate-granite α_c = 10×10^{-6}/℃
Graded crushed stones		The resilient modulus E_1 = 300MPa

Materials	Proportion	Material parameters
Subgrade soils	Clay with low liquid limit	The resilient modulus is 80MPa; humidity adjustment coefficient is 0.78 when the water table is 1.5m beneath the roadbed surface; the comprehensive resilient modulus on the top of roadbed: $E_0 = 80 \times 0.78 = 62.4$ MPa

continue

With the properties listed in the above table, Relative stiffness radius (r) is determined below:

(1) Determine Equivalent resilient modulus (E_t)

- $E_x = \sum_{i=1}^{n}(h_i^1 E_i) \Big/ \sum_{i=1}^{n} h_i^2 = \dfrac{h_i^2 E_i}{h_i^2} = 300 \text{(MPa)}$

- $h_x = \sum_{i=1}^{n} h_i = h_1 = 0.20 \text{(m)}$

- $\alpha = 0.26\ln(h_x) + 0.86 = 0.26 \times \ln(0.20) + 0.86 = 0.442$

- $E_i = \left(\dfrac{E_x}{E_o}\right)^{\alpha} E_0 = \left(\dfrac{300}{62.4}\right)^{0.442} \times 62.4 = 124.9 \text{(MPa)} \approx 120 \text{(MPa)}$

(2) Calculate bending stiffness of plain concrete surface (D_c)

- $D_c = \dfrac{E_c h_c^3}{12(1-v_c^2)} = \dfrac{31000 \times 0.23^3}{12(1-0.15^2)} = 32.3 \text{(MN·m)}$

(3) Relative stiffness radius (r)

- $r = 1.21\left(\dfrac{D_c}{E_t}\right)^{1/3} = 1.21 \times \left(\dfrac{32.3}{124.9}\right)^{1/3} = 0.770 \text{(m)}$

Step 4: Load Stress: The load stress caused by design axle load and maximum axle load on the critical loading position are determined by the following equations:

$$\sigma_{ps} = 1.47 \times 10^{-3} r^{0.70} h_c^{-2} p_s^{0.94}$$
$$= 1.47 \times 10^{-3} \times 0.770^{0.70} \times 0.23^{-2} \times 100^{0.94} = 1.756 \text{(MPa)}$$

$$\sigma_{ps} = 1.47 \times 10^{-3} r^{0.70} h_c^{-2} p_s^{0.94}$$
$$= 1.47 \times 10^{-3} \times 0.770^{0.70} \times 0.23^{-2} \times 150^{0.94} = 2.570 \text{(MPa)}$$

The load fatigue stress and maximum load stress are determined as follows:

$$\sigma_{pr} = k_r k_f k_c \sigma_{ps} = 0.87 \times 2.26 \times 1.05 \times 1.756 = 3.63 \text{(MPa)}$$

$$\sigma_{p,\max} = k_r k_c \sigma_{pm} = 0.87 \times 1.05 \times 2.570 = 2.35 \text{(MPa)}$$

Where the stress reduction factor considering the ability to transfer loads of joints $k_r = 0.87$, the comprehensive coefficient $k_c = 1.05$, fatigue stress factor $k_f = N_e^{\lambda} = (166.49 \times 10^4)^{0.057} = 2.26$.

Step 5: Thermal Stress: The maximum temperature gradient is 88℃/m. The temperature stress coefficient of comprehensive temperature curling stress and internal stress B_L should be calculated with the following equations:

$$t = \frac{L}{3r} = \frac{4.5}{3 \times 0.770} = 1.95$$

$$C_L = 1 - \frac{\sin(1.95)\cos(1.95) + \cosh(1.95)\sin(1.95)}{\cos(1.95)\sin(1.95) + \sinh(1.95)\cosh(1.95)}$$

$$= 1 - 0.171 = 0.829$$

$$B_L = 1.77e^{-4.48h_c} \times C_L - 0.131(1 - C_L)$$

$$= 1.77e^{-4.48 \times 0.23} \times 0.829 - 0.131 \times (1 - 0.829)$$

$$= 0.501$$

The maximum thermal stress is determined by equation as follows:

$$\sigma_{t,max} = \frac{\alpha_c E_c h_c T_g}{2} B_L = \frac{10^{-5} \times 31000 \times 0.23 \times 88}{2} \times 0.51 = 1.57(MPa)$$

The thermal fatigue stress coefficient K_t are determined by equation as follows:

$$K_t = \frac{f_r}{\sigma_{t,max}} \left[a_t \left(\frac{\sigma_{t,max}}{f_r} \right)^{b_t} - c_t \right]$$

$$= \frac{5.0}{1.572} \left[0.828 \times \left(\frac{1.572}{5} \right)^{1.323} - 0.041 \right] = 0.44$$

Thermal fatigue stress are determined by equations as follows:

$$\sigma_{tr} = K_t \sigma_{t,max} = 0.44 \times 1.57 = 0.69(MPa)$$

Step 6: Check the Limit State of the Structure: The reliability coefficient $\gamma_r = 1.13$ under the condition of class-II highway and moderate variation level. Check if the limit state of the pavement structure meets the requirements with equations as follows:

$$\gamma_r(\sigma_p + \sigma_{tr}) = 1.13 \times (3.63 + 0.69) = 4.88(MPa) \leqslant f_r = 5.0 MPa$$

$$\gamma_r(\sigma_{p,max} + \sigma_{t,max}) = 1.13 \times (2.35 + 1.57) = 4.43(MPa) \leqslant f_r = 5.0 MPa$$

Therefore, it meets the requirements of structure limit state. The selected thickness of the plain concrete surface layer (0.23m) can bear the fatigue loading and maximum loading.

9.6.2 Two-layered Plate System on Elastic Foundation

Problem Statement: Design a class-I highway with four lanes located at national zone IV. The subgrade soil is clay with a low liquid limit and the water table is 1.0m beneath the roadbed surface. Regional coarse aggregate is gravel. The pavement structure is plain concrete surface with cement-stabilized gravel base. The design axle load $P_s = 100kN$, and the maximum axle load $P_m = 180kN$. The daily number of passes of standard axle load is 3200. The traffic increasing rate is 5%.

Step 1: Traffic Analysis: The annual average daily standard axles $N_s = 3200\text{sa}$; Traffic increasing rate is 5%; From Table 9-1, design life $t = 30$ years; The transverse distribution of wheel track is 0.54 ~ 0.62 from Table 9-9, $\eta = 0.22$, Accumulative traffic N_e is computed:

$$N_e = \frac{N_s \times [(1+g_r)^t - 1] \times 365}{g_r} \times \eta$$

$$= \frac{3200 \times [(1+0.05)^{30} - 1] \times 365}{0.05} \times 0.22$$

$$= 1707 \times 10^4 (\text{times})$$

The traffic loading level is heavy according to Table 9-4.

Step 2: Combination Design: From Table 9-3, the construction quality variation level is low. Based on the known conditions including class- I highway, heavy traffic load grade and low variation level, one combination below is proposed, as shown in Table 9-22.

Table 9-22 Combination for the Two-layered Plate System on Elastic Foundation

Layers	Layer materials	Layer thickness
Surface	Plain concrete pavement with tie bars and without dowel bars	26cm
Base	Cement-stabilized gravels	20cm
Subbase	Graded Gravels	18cm
Subgrade		

Step 3: Mix Proportion Design and layer material parameters: According to the national design specification[3] and section 9.5 of this textbook, the mix proportion and layer material properties are listed in the Table 9-23.

Table 9-23 Mix Proportion and Layer Material Properties for the Combination in Table 9-22

Materials	Proportion	Material properties
Plain cement concrete	Details are not presented herein, but should be presented in the real project	flexural tensile strength $f = 5\text{MPa}$; Young's modulus $E_c = 31\text{GPa}$; Possion's ratio $v_c = 0.15$; The coefficient of linear expansion of concrete with the coarse aggregate-granite $\alpha_c = 11 \times 10^{-6}/\text{°C}$
Cement stabilized gravels		the resilient modulus of cement stabilization base layer is 2000MPa and the Possion' ratio is 0.20
Graded Gravels		resilient modulus of graded gravels is 250MPa and the Possion' ration is 0.35
Subgrade soils	Clay with low liquid limit	the resilient modulus of subgrade with low liquid limit clay is 100MPa; humidity adjustment coefficient is 0.8 when the water table is 1.0m beneath the roadbed surface; the comprehensive resilient modulus on the top of roadbed: $E_0 = 100 \times 0.8 = 80.0(\text{MPa})$

With the properties listed in the above table, bending stiffness (D_c, D_b) and relative stiffness radius (r_g) are determined below:

(1) Determine Equivalent resilient modulus (E_t)

- $E_x = \dfrac{\sum_{i=1}^{n}(h_i^2 E_i)}{\sum_{i=1}^{n} h_i^2} = \dfrac{h_i^2 E_i}{h_i^2} = 250 \text{(MPa)}$

- $h_x = \sum_{i=1}^{n} h_i = h_1 = 0.18 \text{(m)}$

- $\alpha = 0.26 \ln(h_x) + 0.86 = 0.26 \times \ln(0.18) + 0.8 = 0.414$

- $E_t = \left(\dfrac{E_x}{E_0}\right)^{\alpha} E_0 = \left(\dfrac{250}{80}\right)^{0.414} \times 80 = 128.2 \text{(MPa)} \approx 125 \text{(MPa)}$

(2) Calculate bending stiffness (D_c, D_b)

- $D_c = \dfrac{E_c h_c^3}{12(1 - v_c^2)} = \dfrac{31000 \times 0.23^3}{12(1 - 0.15^2)} = 32.2 \text{(MN} \cdot \text{m)}$

- $D_b = \dfrac{E_c h_c^3}{12(1 - v_c^2)} = \dfrac{2000 \times 0.20^3}{12(1 - 0.15^2)} = 1.39 \text{(MN} \cdot \text{m)}$

(3) Relative stiffness radius (r_g)

- $r_g = 1.21 \left(\dfrac{D_c + D_b}{E_t}\right)^{1/3} = 1.21 \times \left(\dfrac{46.4 + 1.39}{125}\right)^{1/3} = 0.878 \text{(m)}$

Step 4: Load-induced Stress: The load-induced stress caused by design axle load and maximum axle load on the critical loading position are determined by the following equations:

$$\sigma_{ps} = \dfrac{1.45 \times 10^{-3}}{1 + \dfrac{D_b}{D_c}} r_g^{0.65} h_c^{-2} p_s^{0.94}$$

$$= \dfrac{1.45 \times 10^{-3}}{1 + \dfrac{1.39}{46.4}} 0.878^{0.65} \times 0.26^{-2} \times 100^{0.94} = 1.452 \text{(MPa)}$$

$$\sigma_{pm} = \dfrac{1.45 \times 10^{-3}}{1 + \dfrac{D_b}{D_c}} r_g^{0.65} h_c^{-2} p_m^{0.94}$$

$$= \dfrac{1.45 \times 10^{-3}}{1 + \dfrac{1.39}{46.4}} 0.878^{0.65} \times 0.26^{-2} \times 180^{0.94} = 2.522 \text{(MPa)}$$

The load-induced fatigue stress and maximum load stress are determined as follows:

$$\sigma_{pr} = k_r k_{fc} \sigma_{ps} = 0.87 \times 2.584 \times 1.10 \times 1.452 = 3.59 \text{(MPa)}$$

$$\sigma_{p,\max} = k_r k_c \sigma_{pm} = 0.87 \times 1.10 \times 2.522 = 2.41 \text{(MPa)}$$

Where the stress reduction factor considering the ability to transfer loads of joints $k_r = 0.87$, comprehensive coefficient $k_c = 1.10$, fatigue stress factor $k_f = (1707 \times 10^4)^{0.057} = 2.584$.

Step 5: Thermal Stress: The maximum temperature gradient is 92℃/m. The thermal stress coefficient of comprehensive thermal curling stress and internal stress B_L should be calculated with the following equations:

$$k_n = \frac{1}{2}\left(\frac{h_c}{E_c} + \frac{h_b}{E_b}\right)^{-1} = \frac{1}{2}\left(\frac{0.26}{31000} + \frac{0.20}{2000}\right)^{-1} = 4613(\text{MPa/m})$$

$$r_\beta = \left[\frac{D_c D_b}{(D_c + D_b)k_n}\right]^{1/4} = \left[\frac{46.4 \times 1.39}{(46.4 + 1.39) \times 4613}\right]^{1/4} = 0.131(\text{m})$$

$$\xi = -\frac{(k_n r_g^4 - D_c)r_\beta^3}{(k_n r_\beta^4 - D_c)r_g^3} = \frac{(4613 \times 0.878^4 - 46.4) \times 0.131^3}{(4613 \times 0.131^4 - 46.4) \times 0.878^3}$$
$$= 0.199$$

$$t = \frac{L}{3r_g} = \frac{5.0}{3 \times 0.878} = 1.90$$

$$C_L = 1 - \left(\frac{1}{1+\xi}\right)\frac{\sinh(1.90)\cos(1.90) + \cos(1.90)\sin(1.90)}{\cos(1.90)\sin(1.90) + \sinh(1.90) + \sinh(1.90)\cosh(1.90)}$$
$$= 1 - \frac{0.200}{1 + 0.199} = 0.833$$

$$B_L = 1.77 e^{-4.48 h_c} \times C_L - 0.131(1 - C_L)$$
$$= 1.77 e^{-4.48 \times 0.26} \times 0.833 - 0.131 \times (1 - 0.833)$$
$$= 0.438$$

The maximum thermal stress are determined by equation as follows:

$$\sigma_{t,\max} = \frac{\alpha_c E_c h_c T_g}{2} B_L = \frac{11 \times 10^{-6} \times 31000 \times 0.26 \times 92}{2} \times 0.438 = 1.79(\text{MPa})$$

The thermal fatigue stress coefficient K_t is determined by equation as follows:

$$K_t = \frac{f_r}{\sigma_{t,\max}}\left[\alpha_t\left(\frac{\sigma_{t,\max}}{f_r}\right)^{b_t} - c_t\right]$$

$$= \frac{5.0}{1.79}\left[0.841 \times \left(\frac{1.79}{5}\right)^{1.323} - 0.058\right] = 0.442$$

Thermal fatigue stress is determined by equations follows:

$$\sigma_{tr} = K_t \sigma_{t,\max} = 0.442 \times 1.79 = 0.79(\text{MPa})$$

Step 6: Check the Limit State of the Structure: The reliability coefficient $\gamma_r = 1.14$ under the condition of class-I highway and moderate variation level. Check if the limit state of the pavement structure meets the requirements with equations as follows:

$$\gamma_r(\sigma_p + \sigma_{tr}) = 1.14 \times (3.59 + 0.79) = 4.99(\text{MPa}) \leq f_r = 5.0\text{MPa}$$

$\gamma_r(\sigma_{p,\max} + \sigma_{t,\max}) = 1.14 \times (2.24 + 1.79) = 4.79(\text{MPa}) \leqslant f_r = 5.0\text{MPa}$

So it meets the requirements of structure limit state. The selected thickness of the plain concrete surface layer (0.26m) can bear the comprehensive fatigue actions of design axle loads and temperature gradient during the design reference period and one-time ultimate action of maximum axle load under the maximum temperature gradient. Take 0.26m as the design thickness.

9.6.3 Composite Plate System on Elastic Foundation

Design a class-I highway with four lanes located at national zone II. The subgrade soil is clay with a low liquid limit and the water table is 0.9m beneath the roadbed surface. Local coarse aggregate is limestone. It is proposed to use the composite surface layer which is composed of the rubberized Portland cement concrete upper surface layer with low noise and the plain concrete lower surface layer. The base layer is built with cement stabilized gravels. The design axle load $P_s = 100\text{kN}$ and the maximum axle load $P_m = 180\text{kN}$. The daily number of passes of the standard axle load is 750. The traffic increasing rate is 5%.

Step 1: Traffic Analysis: The annual average daily standard axles $N_s = 750\text{sa}$; Traffic increasing rate is 5%; From Table 9-1, design life $t = 30$ years; The transverse distribution of wheel track is 0.54~0.62 from Table 9-1, Accumulative traffic N_e is computed:

$$N_e = \frac{N_s \times [(1 + g_r)^t - 1] \times 365}{g_r} \times \eta$$

$$= \frac{750 \times [(1 + 0.05)^{30} - 1] \times 365}{0.05} \times 0.22 = 400 \times 10^4 (\text{times})$$

The traffic loading level is heavy according to Table 9-4.

Step 2: Combination Design: According to Table 9-3, the construction quality variation level is low. Based on the known conditions including class-I highway, heavy traffic load grade and low variation level, one combination below is proposed, as shown in Table 9-24.

Table 9-24 Combination for the Composite Plate System on Elastic Foundation

Layers	Layer materials	Layer thickness
Composite Surface	Rubberized Portland cement concrete upper surface layer with low noise	8cm
	Plain concrete pavement with tie bars and without dowel bars	17cm
base	Graded crushed stones	20cm
Subbase	Graded Gravels	20cm
Subgrade		

The climension of cement concrete pavement slab is 5.0m × 3.75m. The longitudinal joints are the flat joints with tie bars, and the transverse joints are fake joints without dowel bars. The width of the hard shoulder is 3.0m. The surface layers of shoulders and the lanes that have the same thickness and are connected by tie bars.

Step 3: Mix Proportion Design and Layer Material Parameters: According to the national design specification[3] and section 9.5 of this textbook, the mix proportion and layer material properties are listed in the Table 9-25.

Table 9-25 Mix Proportion and Layer Material Properties for the Combination in Table 9-24

Materials	Proportion	Material properties
Rubberized Portland cement concrete	Details is not presented herein, but should be presented in the real project	flexural tensile strength f = 4.5 MPa; Young's modulus and passion' ratio are 27GPa and 0.15; The coefficient of linear expansion of concrete with the coarse aggregate-granite $\alpha_c = 10 \times 10^{-6}/℃$
Plain cement concrete		flexural tensile strength f = 5MPa; Young's modulus E_c = 31GPa; Possion' ratio v_c = 0.15; The coefficient of linear expansion of concrete with the coarse aggregate-granite $\alpha_c = 10 \times 10^{-6}/℃$
Cement stabilized crushed stones		the resilient modulus of cement stabilization base layer is 2000MPa and the Possion' ratio is 0.20
Graded Gravels		the resilient modulus of graded gravels is 250MPa and the Possion' ration is 0.35
subgrade soils	clay with low liquid limit	the resilient modulus of subgrade with low liquid limit clay is 80MPa; humidity adjustment coefficient is 0.75 when the water table is 0.90m beneath the roadbed surface; the comprehensive resilient modulus on the top of roadbed: E_0 = 80 × 0.75 = 60.0MPa

With the properties listed in the above table, bending stiffness ($\tilde{D}_c, D_b$), equivalent thickness ($\tilde{h}_c$), and relative stiffness radius(r_g) are determined below:

(1) Determine Equivalent resilient modulus (E_t)

- $E_x = \sum_{i=1}^{n}(h_i^2 E_i)/\sum_{i=1}^{n}h_i^2 = \dfrac{h_i^2 E_i}{h_i^2} = 250 \text{MPa}$

- $h_x = \sum_{i=1}^{n} h_i = h_1 = 0.20 \text{m}$

- $\alpha = 0.26\ln(h_x) + 0.86 = 0.26 \times \ln(0.20) + 0.86 = 0.442$

- $E_t = \left(\dfrac{E_x}{E_0}\right)^{\alpha} E_0 = \left(\dfrac{250}{60}\right)^{0.442} \times 60 = 112.7(\text{MPa}) \approx 110(\text{MPa})$

(2) Calculate bending stiffness($\tilde{D}_c, D_b$) and equivalent thickness ($\tilde{h}_c$)

- $\tilde{D}_c = \dfrac{E_{c1} + h_{c1}^3 + E_{c2}h_{c2}^3}{12(1-v_{c2}^2)} + \dfrac{(h_{c1}+h_{c2})^2}{4(1-v_{c2}^2)}\left(\dfrac{1}{E_{c1}h_{c1}} + \dfrac{1}{E_{c2}h_{c2}}\right)^{-1}$

$$= \frac{27000 \times 0.08^3 + 31000 \times 0.17^3}{12(1-0.15^2)} +$$
$$\frac{(0.08+0.17)^2}{4(1-0.15^2)} \left(\frac{1}{27000 \times 0.08} + \frac{1}{31000 \times 0.17} \right)^{-1}$$
$$= 38.7 (\text{MN} \cdot \text{m})$$

- $D_b = \dfrac{E_c h_c^3}{12(1-v_b^2)} = \dfrac{2000 \times 0.20^3}{12(1-0.20)^2} = 1.39 (\text{MN} \cdot \text{m})$

- $d_x = \dfrac{1}{2} \left[h_{c2} + \dfrac{E_{c1} h_{c1} (h_{c1} + h_{c2})}{E_{c1} h_{c1} E_{c2} h_{c2}} \right]$

$$= \frac{1}{2} \left[0.17 + \frac{27000 \times 0.08 \times (0.08 + 0.17)}{27000 \times 0.08 + 31000 \times 0.17} \right] = 0.121 (\text{m})$$

- $\tilde{h}_c = 2.42 \sqrt{\dfrac{\tilde{D}_c}{E_{c2} d_x}} = 0.246 (\text{m})$

(3) Relative stiffness radius (r_g)

- $r_g = 1.21 \left(\dfrac{\tilde{D}_c + D_b}{E_t} \right)^{1/3} = 1.21 \times \left(\dfrac{38.7 + 1.39}{110} \right)^{1/3} = 0.864 (\text{m})$

Step 4: Load-induced Stress: The load stress caused by design axle load and maximum axle load on the critical loading position are determined by the following equation:

$$\sigma_{ps} = \frac{1.45 \times 10^{-3}}{1 + \dfrac{D_b}{D_c}} r_g^{0.65} h_c^{-2} p_s^{0.94}$$

$$= \frac{1.45 \times 10^{-3}}{1 + \dfrac{1.39}{38.7}} 0.864^{0.65} \times 0.246^{-2} \times 100^{0.94} = 1.596 (\text{MPa})$$

$$\sigma_{pm} = \frac{1.45 \times 10^{-3}}{1 + \dfrac{D_b}{D_c}} r_g^{0.65} h_c^{-2} p_m^{0.94}$$

$$= \frac{1.45 \times 10^{-3}}{1 + \dfrac{1.39}{38.7}} 0.864^{0.65} \times 0.246^{-2} \times 180^{0.94} = 2.772 (\text{MPa})$$

The load fatigue stress and maximum load stress are determined as follows:
- $\sigma_{pr} = k_r k_f k_c \sigma_{ps} = 0.87 \times 2.379 \times 1.10 \times 1.596 = 3.63 (\text{MPa})$
- $\sigma_{p,\max} = k_r k_c \sigma_{pm} = 0.87 \times 1.10 \times 2.772 = 2.65 (\text{MPa})$

Where the stress reduction factor considering the ability to transfer loads of joints $k_r = 0.87$, comprehensive coefficient $k_c = 1.10$, fatigue stress factor $k_f = N_e^\lambda = (400 \times 10^4)^{0.057} = 2.379$.

Step 5: Thermal Stress: The maximum temperature gradient is 84℃/m. The temperature stress coefficient of comprehensive temperature curling stress and internal stress B_L should be calculated with the following equations:

$$k_n = \frac{1}{2}\left(\frac{\tilde{h}_c}{E_c} + \frac{h_b}{E_b}\right)^{-1} = \frac{1}{2}\left(\frac{0.245}{31000} + \frac{0.20}{2000}\right)^{-1} = 4634(\text{MPa/m})$$

- $r_\beta = \left[\dfrac{\tilde{D}_c D_b}{(\tilde{D}_c + D_b)k_n}\right]^{1/4} = \left[\dfrac{38.7 \times 1.39}{(38.7 + 1.39) \times 4634}\right]^{1/4} = 0.130(\text{m})$

- $\xi = -\dfrac{(k_n r_g^4 - \tilde{D}_c)r_\beta^3}{(k_n r_\beta^4 - \tilde{D}_c)r_g^3} = \dfrac{(4634 \times 0.864^4 - 38.7) \times 0.130^3}{(4634 \times 0.130^4 - 38.7) \times 0.864^3} = 0.232$

- $t = \dfrac{L}{3r_g} = \dfrac{5.0}{3 \times 0.864} = 1.93$

- $C_L = 1 - \left(\dfrac{1}{1+\xi}\right)\dfrac{\sinh(1.93)\cos(1.93) + \cos(1.93)\sin(1.93)}{\cos(1.93)\sin(1.93) + \sinh(1.93) + \sinh(1.93)\cosh(1.93)}$

$= 1 - \dfrac{0.183}{1 + 0.232} = 0.851$

- $B_L = 1.77 e^{-4.48 h_c} \times C_L - 0.131(1 - C_L)$

$= 1.77 e^{-4.48 \times 0.25} \times 0.851 - 0.131 \times (1 - 0.851) = 0.472$

The maximum thermal stress is determined by equation as follows:

- $\zeta = 1.77 - 0.27\ln\left(\dfrac{h_{c1}E_{c1}}{h_{c2}E_{c2}} + 18\dfrac{E_{c1}}{E_{c2}} - 2\dfrac{h_{c1}}{h_{c2}}\right)$

$= 1.77 - 0.27\ln\left(\dfrac{0.08 \times 27000}{0.17 \times 31000} + 18 \times \dfrac{27000}{31000} - 2 \times \dfrac{0.08}{0.17}\right) = 1.036$

- $\sigma_{t,\max} = \dfrac{\alpha_c T_g E_{c2}(h_{c1} + h_{c2})}{2} B_L \zeta = \dfrac{8 \times 10^{-6} \times 84 \times 31000 \times (0.08 + 0.17)}{2} \times$

$0.472 \times 1.036 = 1.27(\text{MPa})$

The thermal fatigue stress coefficient k_t is determined by equation as follows:

- $k_t = \dfrac{f_r}{\sigma_{t,\max}}\left[\alpha_t\left(\dfrac{\sigma_{t,\max}}{f_r}\right)^{b_t} - c_t\right] = \dfrac{5.0}{1.27}\left[0.828 \times \left(\dfrac{1.27}{5.0}\right)^{1.323} - 0.041\right] = 0.370$

Thermal fatigue stress is determined by equation as follows:

- $\sigma_{tr} = k_t \sigma_{t,\max} = 0.370 \times 1.27 \times 0.47(\text{MPa})$

Step 6: Check the Limit State of the Structure: The reliability coefficient γ_r = 1.2 under the condition of class- I highway and moderate variation level. Check if the limit state of the pavement structure meets the requirements with equations as follows:

$$\gamma_r(\sigma_p + \sigma_{tr}) = 1.20 \times (3.63 + 0.47) = 4.92(\text{MPa}) \leq f_r = 5.0\text{MPa}$$
$$\gamma_r(\sigma_{p,\max} + \sigma_{t,\max}) = 1.20 \times (2.65 + 1.27) = 4.70(\text{MPa}) \leq f_r = 5.0\text{MPa}$$

So it meets the requirements of structure limit state. The selected thickness of the composite surface layer composed of rubberized Portland cement concrete (0.08m) and ordinary concrete (0.17m) can bear the comprehensive fatigue actions of design axle loads and temperature gradient during the design reference period and one-time ultimate action of maximum axle load under the maximum temperature gradient.

9.7 Summary of Chapter 9

This chapter presents methodology, procedure, and examples of the concrete pavement design. Followed are key points:

1. The concrete pavement design is a mechanistic-empirical design method. Through mechanical analysis, the pavement stresses are computed and the empirical coefficients are used to transfer the mechanical results into the actual pavement responses. Then, with the criterion equations the pavement serviceability is evaluated to determine whether the proposed pavement configuration is acceptable or not.

2. The concrete pavement design consists of five steps, namely reliability determination, traffic and environmental analysis, concrete pavement configuration design, pavement responses and design criteria, and final design.

3. By following the five steps, examples of single-layered plate system on elastic foundation, the two-layered plate system on elastic foundation, and composite plate system on elastic foundation are presented.

Problems and Questions

1. Fig. P9-1 shows an alternative of jointed concrete pavement for expressways, answer the following questions:

(1) Determine the reliability coefficient if the variance level is medium;

(2) Identify the location of the dowel bar and tie bar;

(3) Compared with dowel bar and tie bar, which one is commonly round and smooth? Which one is mostly used to transfer vehicle loading? Whose diameter is normally larger?

2. There are five pavement structures as shown in the Table P9-1, could you identify the stress analysis models according to the national concrete pavement design specification?

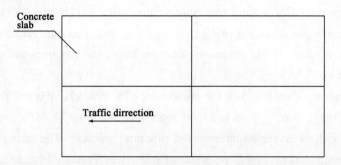

Fig. P9-1 an Alternative of Jointed Concrete Powement for Expressway

Table P9-1 Five Powement Structures for the Problem 2

Structure	1	2	3	4	5
Surface Layer	Concrete Slab 26cm	Concrete Slab 30cm	Asphalt Concrete 10cm	Concrete Slab 23cm	Rubber Modified Cement Concrete Slab 8cm
			Concrete Slab 26cm		Concrete Slab 17cm
Base Layer	Cement Stabilized Gravel 20cm	Rolled Concrete 18cm	Cement Stabilized Gravel 20cm	Graded Crushed Stone 20cm	Cement Stabilized Gravel 20cm
Subbase Layer	Graded Gravel 18cm	Graded Crushed Stone 20cm	—	—	Graded Gravel 20cm
Subgrade					

3. Given the linear expansion coefficient is $1 \times 10^{-5}/℃$; the concrete modulus is 29GPa; the concrete pavement thickness is 23cm; the maximum temperature gradient is 88℃/m; Coefficient $B_L = 0.5$; the concrete flexural strength is 4.5MPa; coefficient a_t, b_t, and c_t are 0.828, 1.323 and 0.041. Please calculate σ_{tr}.

4. For concrete pavement structure as shown in Table P9-2, please calculate the equivalent resilient modulus under the concrete pavement slab.

Table P9-2 Pavement Structures for the Problem 4

Concrete Slab
Granular Base Layer $E = 300$MPa, $h = 0.3$m
Granular Subbase Layer $E = 100$MPa, $h = 0.10$m
Subgrade $E = 55$MPa

5. Why an asphalt concrete interlayer is needed for concrete slab pavement with roller-compacted concrete base layer or lean concrete base layer?

6. Why a seal coat is needed for cement stabilized crushed stone base layer?

References

[1] Xuejun Deng. *Road Subgrade and Pavement Engineering*[M]3th. Beijing:China Communications Press,2000.

[2] Ministry of Transport of the People's Republic of China. *Specification for Design of Highway Asphalt Pavement*: JTG D50—2017 [S]. Beijing: China Communications Press CO. , Ltd. , 2017.

[3] Ministry of Transport of the People's Republic of China. *Specification for Design of Highway Cement Concrete Pavement*: JTG D40—2017 [S]. Beijing: China Communication Press, 2011.

[4] AASHTO. *AASHTO Guide for Design of Pavement Structures*[P]. American Association of State Highway and Transportation Officials (AASHTO), p. 594.

[5] HA (Highways Agency). *DMRB Part 3 Pavement Design (HD26/06) in Section 2 Pavement Design and Construction*[P]. 2006: Stationery Office, London, UK. p. 1-28.

[6] KBA (German Transport Ministry). *German Guideline for Pavement Design*[P], RstO 01 (in German). 2001, p. 1-150.

[7] Ministry of Transport of the People's Republic of China. *Technical Specification for Slipform Construction on Cement Concrete Pavement for Highway*: JTJ T037. 1—2000 [S]. Beijing: China Communications Press, 2000.

[8] Ministry of Transport of the People's Republic of China. *Technical Specification for Construction of Asphalt Pavement*: JTG F40—2004 [P]. Beijing: China Communications Press, 2004.

[9] Xiaoming Huang. *Road Subgrade and Pavement Engineering* [M]. 5th. Beijing: China Communications Press Co. ,Ltd.,2017.

[10] Aimin Sha. *Road Subgrade and Pavement Engineering*[M]. Beijing: Higher Eduction Press, 2011.

[11] Ministry of Transport of the People's Republic of China. *Specification for Lab Testing of Soils in Highway Engineering*: JTG E40—2007 [S]. Beijing:China Communications Press, 2007.

[12] Nicholas J, Garber and Lester, A. Hoel. *Traffic & Highway Engineering*[M]. 2009, 1120 Birchmount Road, Toronto ON M1K 5G4 Canada: Cengage Learning. p. 1-1249.

[13] Ministry of Transport of the People's Republic of China. *Specification for Design of Highway*

Subgrade:JTG D30—2015[S]. Beijing:China Communications Press Co. ,Ltd. ,2015.

[14] Ministry of Transport of the People's Republic of China. *Specification for Design of Highway Asphalt Pavement*:JTG D50—2006 [S]. Beijing:China Communications Press,2006.

[15] Dongguang Gao, Yaling Wang. *Hydrology and Hydraulics for Bridge Engineering*[M]. 5th. Beijing:China Communications Press Co.,Ltd.,2016.

[16] Ministry of Transport of the People's Republic of China. *Specification for Drainage Design of Highway*:JTG D33—2012 [S]. Beijing: China Communications Press,2012.

[17] John s. Miller , Y. Bellinger William. *Distress Identification Manual for the Long-term Pavement Performance Program*[M]. 2003: US Department of Transportation, Federal Highway Administration, p 1-164.

[18] Ministry of Transport of the People's Republic of China. *Specification for Lab Testing of Portland Cement and Cement Concrete in Highway Engineering*: JTG E30—2005 [S]. Beijing:China Communications Press, 2005.

[19] Boussinesq J. *Application des Potentiel a l' etude de l' equilibre et du Movment des Solides Elastiques*[M]. Paris:Gautier-Villard, 2015.

[20] Burmister DM. *The Theory of Stresses and Displacements in Layered Systems nd Applications to the Design of Airport Runways*[N]. Proceedings of the Highway Research Board, 1943 (23): p. 126-144.

[21] Burmister DM. *The General Theory of Stresses and Displacements in Layered Systems*[J]. Journal of Applied Physics, 1945. 16(2): p. 89-94.

[22] Yang H. Huang. *Stresses and Displacements in Viscoelastic Layered Systems under Circular Loaded Areas*[N]. Proceedings of the 2nd International Conference on the Structural Design of Asphalt Pavements. 1967. p. 225-244.

[23] Yang H. Huang. *Stresses and Displacements in Norlinear Soil Media*[J]. Journal of the Soil Mechanics and Foundation Division, 1968. 94: p. 1-19.

[24] A. T. Papagiannakis , Eyad Masad. *Pavement Design and Materials*[M]. John Wiley & Sons. Inc. 552. p. 1-552,2008.

[25] Yang H. Huang. *Pavement Analysis and Design*[M]. Pearson Education Ltd. ,2004.

[26] G. Pickett , G. K. Ray. *Influence Charts for Concrete Pavements*[J]. Transactions of the American Society of Civil Engineers, 1951. 116: p. 49-73.

[27] Ministry of Transport of the People's Republic of China. *Technical Guideline for Highway Pavement Base Construction*[P]. 2015, China Communication Press. p. 1-79.

[28] Ministry of Transport of the People's Republic of China. *Specification for Lab Testing of Hydraulically-bound Mixtures (HBM) in Highway Engineering (JTG E51—2009)* [M]. Beijing: China Communications Press,2009.

[29] Ministry of Transport of the People's Republic of China. *Specification for Lab Testing of Asphalt and Asphalt Mixtures in Highway Engineering*: JTG E20—2011 [S]. Beijing:

China Communications Press, 2011.
[30] Ministry of Transport of the People's Republic of China. *Standard of Climatic Zoning for Highway*:JTJ 003—86 [S]. Beijing:China Communications Press, 1987.